ESP in Life and Lab

ESP
IN LIFE
AND LAB

Tracing Hidden Channels

BY

LOUISA · E · RHINE

The Macmillan Company / NEW YORK

Collier-Macmillan Limited / LONDON

Copyright © 1967 by Louisa E. Rhine

All rights reserved. No part of this book may be reproduced or transmitted in any form or by any means,
electronic or mechanical, including photocopying, recording or by any information storage and retrieval system,
without permission in writing from the Publisher.

Printed in the United States of America

TO JBR

Whose urge to understand the uniqueness
of man's nature would not be satisfied by dogma
or speculation, but only by the results
of objective scientific investigation.

Contents

Everyone's philosophy of life depends directly upon what he thinks of his own basic nature, his place, his powers, and his destiny in the scheme of things. Yet of these matters we have only hypotheses or faiths. Assuredly then, we need not labor to justify the active exploration of an issue so fundamental to our way of life and code of valuation. More and more, those who are searching for a way of thinking by which life, individual and group, can be reliably and intelligently guided are coming back to the query: What is man with respect to the solid world of sense and mechanics? And today, in a scientific epoch, this issue leads inescapably to the inquiries of parapsychology, the psychology which has been overlooked.

J. B. RHINE, *Journal of Parapsychology*, 10, 18, 1946.

ESP in Life and Lab

CHAPTER 1

The Issue: Man or Machine?

WHAT is man? Is he a creature of "sense and mechanics" only, or something more?

The objective of this book is to call attention to the still almost unknown researches in the field of parapsychology because they bear on this ancient and important question. The answer is not to be found in the newest textbooks or the greatest universities. In fact, the question itself is in danger of being forgotten, of no longer being asked. In this proud and busy young space age, when the world's attention is so closely focused on the more obvious areas of exploration, the question of the total or unique nature of man is in danger of being passed up and the answer most in line with the mechanistic spirit of the age *assumed* to be correct without a test.

Increasingly, as the fields of physics, chemistry, and mechanics have developed, the impression has deepened that human beings are, to put it simply, just machines. Very complicated machines, of course, but still essentially mechanisms. Already many known laws of matter, body, and mind suggest it. The implication seems to be that given time enough, science will finally show man to be nothing but a glorified super-computer.

The great developments of which this age is proud, however, were not brought about by guesses, beliefs, or assumptions. They are the results of the careful, controlled methods of experimental science. Certainly the same reliable objective methods should be demanded for research on the elemental question of man's own nature. On this there will be no debate. The researches of parapsychology constitute such scientific experimentation, but the facts to support this are not yet general knowledge.

Parapsychology is a relatively new field of scientific investigation dealing with a rather obscure aspect of the human mind. It began as an experimental attempt to find out if information about the objective world ever gets into the mind without the use of the senses. Over the centuries, people had occasionally reported certain experiences which suggested that it did.

These experiences, though reported in innumerable different forms, can be sufficiently well illustrated here by three different examples. Each is an actual experience, as are all those to be given in later chapters, but each one typifies an individual point. For the moment they should be taken at face value, simply as illustrations, regardless of their verifiability.

The first happens to be a small domestic incident. It is told by a young New York mother.

"When my daughter was three and a half years old and busily playing in her own room, I had just finished reading a newspaper report of a weird happenstance in South Carolina. The paper reported that an old Negro cateress, who had served at weddings for some forty years in the town and as part of the town's tradition had always helped to dress the bride, had upon her sudden demise been discovered to be a man!

"As I thought of this oddity I realized that our own current family cook, Minnie, might almost be such a type. Just then my little one came running into the room, saying, 'Mommie, you know what Minnie is? She's a man-woman!'

"I can't believe it was just a coincidence."

The implication is, of course, that the child was actually affected by the mother's thought, and that it was not just a coincidence that her remark seemed to be a reflection of it. That possibility is the idea to keep in mind while considering the second example. This one too, as it happens, comes from a woman in New York.

"Several years ago I had a business trip through the New England states. It was most essential that I have my dresses, which were in a medium-sized wardrobe trunk. I arrived at my destination, but the trunk did not. I had checked it in New York City and had my check. The men searched and traced and no trunk. This went on until I would have to return to New York City as I had only what I had on.

"Then in a dream I saw my trunk covered with snow on an isolated part of a station platform, and there was no check on it. I telephoned the man who was conducting the search and told him of the dream. Oh, did he scoff!

" 'Well, young woman,' he laughed, 'we don't find trunks by dreams.' I answered, 'You don't find them anyway. Suit yourself, and the company can put up about $1,000 in cash.' I found out that he phoned all along the route, found the snow-covered, ticketless trunk, and I got it with apologies. So this was not a case of suddenly remembering where I had left it."

In that example it is necessary to suppose for the moment that in the dream the woman actually "found" her trunk; that it was more than a lucky guess. The next is still a different kind of experience. This one comes from a woman in Virginia.

"On the night of February 21, 1961, I had a dream that actually came true—twenty-four hours later. I dreamed that my husband's brother had died, and his wife called me long distance to tell me about it.

"In the dream she was crying and screaming, and I woke up terribly upset. I told my husband and later in the day, a neighbor. They both just laughed at me, and said that dreaming of a death meant a birth.

"However, the next day we got the phone call. I answered. It was my sister-in-law and she was crying and screaming just *exactly* as in the dream. She said her husband had been killed that morning. He had been topping a tree and fell. *It just can't be coincidence.* My husband has four brothers, so why should I dream about that particular one? It is so mystifying. I wish I knew what caused it."

In that case too, for the sake of argument, one may suppose that the dream was actually related to the fateful phone call, even though the dream preceded the reality. One must suppose that something more meaningful than coincidence was involved.

If the assumptions of these three experiences are added, the total is that in each, a person seemed to be affected by something with which his senses had no contact. The experiences were different in that the something in the first case was another person's thought; in the second, it was a thing; and in the third, an event that had not yet happened. Experiences like these are among the kinds that raised the question, Can the human mind escape the bounds of "sense and mechanics"? on which the researches of parapsychology are based.

Today, because of the strong drift of opinion toward a mechanistic concept of human nature, it is important to take seriously the suggestion made by such occurrences and see if anything more than coincidence could be involved in them. If it should be, and if they mean that at times the mind can be freed of its ordinary limitations, the fact would tell something very important about man's nature. It would mean that deep within his personality, at the center of all the regular processes that run according to the laws of chemistry and physics, is another *order* of operation, one which, whatever its ultimate secret may prove to be, means that the mechanistic model of human beings is incomplete.

This is where the researches in the field of parapsychology come in. Quietly, and largely overlooked by the scholarly world in general, this research has been going on for decades. It began with the basic idea of finding out if evidence could be obtained to show that people ever do know things hidden from their senses, as suggested by human experiences like these just mentioned.

It was not particularly difficult to stage properly controlled laboratory experiments to get an answer. Basically all that was necessary was to keep knowledge of a given fact, a "target," from an individual, a "subject," and see if he could guess that target correctly. Only it had to be done under conditions when the odds against doing so by pure coincidence could be computed. It was not difficult to manage this, and, as Chapter 2 will show, to find subjects who by mathematical measurement could guess so well that "chance" could not be the explanation. This meant that experiences like the three already given could indeed be more than mere coincidences. They could very well be evidence in life situations of a way of knowing about the world that is not dependent on the eyes and ears of ordinary sense perception. They could be evidence of another kind of perception, one that occurs without the senses, and which now has come to be called extrasensory perception, or ESP.

However, although it was comparatively easy to stage the experiment and to get the answer—yes, there is such a thing as ESP —it was not so easy to explain it or to convince a skeptical world that the answer was correct and that the results meant what they seemed to mean. After all, if the evidence was merely a mathematical value arrived at by a few obscure researchers, what of it? They had probably made a mistake, one way or another. For what could extrasensory perception mean? It did not make "sense."

The same question, What could extrasensory perception mean, was being asked in the laboratory, too, for the very results that showed ESP to be a reality raised the question from the start. What is the nature of this phenomenon? Where can it fit in? How can it make sense? Slowly, over the decades, an explanation, or part of one, has been worked out. It has come slowly because the research it has entailed is difficult in ways that one might not anticipate. And yet, who could expect that this research would be easy, for this is not a garden variety of experience. Had it been that, its secret would no doubt have been found out long ago. These experiments involve the human mind with all of its complexities and in one of its most subtle aspects. For one thing the mind of each person differs, for another, no person's mental content is ever twice the same. Like a river the mind flows forward. Like mercury it flits and changes, and gives no stable element for the test tube. But nevertheless progress has been made toward understanding the nature of ESP. The "sense" it makes is gradually becoming clear.

It is now known that ESP is not a single instantaneous—and extraneous—piece of magic, but a process which, like any other, can be traced as it begins, continues, and ends. Papers that describe this have been published regularly in scientific journals. But scientific journals are not generally available, and original research reports need background and interpretation to be meaningful. The various studies that show the kind of process ESP seems to be have not been put together and reported as a unified whole even for parapsychologists themselves. Of course they nevertheless have an idea of the nature of the process even if necessarily a rather disconnected one, but the wider audience has had no opportunity to know it even in bits and snatches.

And so in the following chapters, the objective is to show as much as possible of the nature of ESP by tracing the process that produces it from its beginning to its end and incidentally to indicate something of the kind of pioneer research that has been involved. To do so it is necessary to piece together the results of various experiments, each of which contributed its bit to understanding. In addition, the perspective achieved by a study of real-life experiences on the level of the three already given is used to help round out the picture. The total effort is to show that the process by which ESP is produced does make sense; that it is part of the mind's equipment, and therefore bears its testimony to the nature of man, just as much as his sense perception, his memory, reasoning ability, or any other of his mental characteristics do.

In the following presentation, certain researches have been selected for discussion, for this is not primarily a historical account, although much of the history of parapsychological experimentation is in it. But the experiments that established ESP, and the ones that give evidence of the kind of process it is, are far too many to be described within a readable length, and a complete historical account would show the acquisition of understanding of the kind of process this is only very slowly. Like a river running through a low-lying plain, researches in a new field proceed, recede, and circle around; they seldom travel a straight line to their objective. Their direction is finally visible in spite of, not because of, the meandering of their course. So it has been in parapsychology. The experimenters began where they could and made their discoveries as they could. But now the road they followed can be shortened. One can get a concept of the nature of the phenomenon without following in detail all the byways of its discovery, and without listing all the repetitions that have confirmed discovery.

For these reasons, one or a few representative research projects have been selected for illustration of each given point. The ones selected as examples were picked out more because they seemed to make describable units than because they were the "best." It would have been difficult to select on a criterion of excellence.

Since parapsychological research is still relatively new, scarcely any of the lines of research involved can be considered finished. As the narrative will show, the various stages to be detailed are in quite different degrees of development or discovery. Some problems are basic to others; some are more involved and more difficult than others. Some are impossible to solve now, and perhaps forever. After all, the techniques of laboratory procedure, though ingenuity can extend them to ever more fantastic lengths, do have limits, at least in any present time. Large interstices of ignorance remain among the small pinpoints of knowledge in this, as in any other developing scientific field.

One partial compensation for the breaks in experimentally established knowledge in this presentation is the fact that "life" as well as "lab" can be considered. The life side gives a much wider range of perspective than it has yet been possible to obtain in the laboratory. It can thus suggest or indicate what the truth may be in an area still unexplored experimentally. In addition it can help in the understanding and interpretation of some of the experimental results and give them deeper meaning.

While the life side gives perspective, the experimental side gives reliability. The two cannot be mixed because their bases of validity are too unequal. Case reports are only as good as human testimony, and even when a point is buttressed by the repeated testimony of many independent persons, its possible interpretation is still open to question. The answer still must be, this *could have been* an instance of ESP, not, this *was* an instance. Experiments, however, are not that way. In these the results are as reliable as the statistical value indicates. Taken in conjunction, evidence from life and laboratory can give a clearer, more meaningful concept than either side alone could give. After all, parapsychological research is carried on to find out how to interpret human nature. Therefore it should be eminently fitting to apply ideas arising from the human situation to results achieved by experimentation, and vice-versa.

The ideas and illustrations of the "life" side involved here are drawn from more than a dozen studies that have appeared from time to time in the *Journal of Parapsychology*. Those studies were based on a collection of more than ten thousand reports of life experiences and the illustrations were selected from that collection. Some of the people from whose letters quotations are taken may have made errors in their reporting; even so, no such error could be of major importance, for each illustration (with one exception noted in the text) is only a representative one. The point it illustrates could have been made by innumerable other experiences from other individuals. It has been repeated so often that it can be taken as a type of human experience rather than the isolated experience of one human being.

Each generation, as Tennyson said, is "the heir of all the ages," and as such has, or can get, all the answers mankind has yet figured out to all the questions that have been asked about the universe. Some of the answers are more complete and final than others, perhaps because only the easiest questions have been answered, or because they were asked first, or by the largest number of people. The question involving the total nature of man and his relation to the universe is certainly not the easiest, for although it has probably been asked the longest and by the greatest number of people, it is still unsettled.

Over the ages, answers to this question have been attempted in many different ways. But the particular angle of it embodied in parapsychology has not hitherto been attempted by the scientific method. The following pages cannot do full justice to the parapsychological research already done, but they can at least give a glimpse of the answer those researches are producing. They can also indicate some of the obstacles already surmounted, as well as those which still remain to be overcome before a complete understanding is achieved of the facet of personality comprehended by parapsychology.

CHAPTER 2

The Psi Process and Psi Research

WHAT is ESP? It is almost a household word today. Nearly everyone has heard of it and may use it upon occasion, but few could give a precise definition of it, and still fewer have any idea of the way it operates or of its deeper significance. Many people use the term "ESP" to cover a correct hunch or intuition or any inexplicable personal experience, such as those mentioned in Chapter 1. But they use it as a blanket term, and with only a vague idea of what it means. It is an expression whose popular usage has far outrun an understanding of its meaning.

This is not surprising because, like Columbus landing on a new continent, even the parapsychologists when they coined the term knew only that they had made a discovery. They did not know then, nor could they have known, just what it was; and even today they, better than anyone else, know how much about ESP is yet to be discovered.

The name was quickly appropriated by the general public, however, because it filled a need. It gave a title to an area of experience that had had no franchise for existence. Many people, many more than the world in general would suppose, had had puzzling personal experiences of a kind to which they could give no name, the common feature being only that these people seemed to know about something that was out of either direct or indirect reach of eye or ear. If they told others what had happened, the occurrence was likely to be relegated to "delusion," "imagination," or as a last resort, to "coincidence," even though the persons themselves were convinced beyond persuasion that none of these categories was adequate, that something else was involved. Better call it ESP, whether or not anyone knew just what that meant.

The name originated at the Parapsychology Laboratory at Duke

University in the early 1930s. Basic research had shown the existence of a mental ability to get information about the objective world directly, and at once a name for it was needed. This one was selected from a list of all those that had been from time to time proposed by those who suspected that a reality like ESP existed. Extrasensory perception, or ESP, seemed to be the most noncommittal of them all, and yet convenient. It meant merely getting information without the senses.

As soon as publicity was given this new research, people who had had experiences they thought would come under such a category began writing to the Parapsychology Laboratory at Duke University to tell about them. The letters, which came by the thousands, were testimony to the need people had to categorize experiences which did not fit any of the usual definitions. Although the experiences so reported are as varied in detail and setting, in type and form as the people who write them, still in effect they all ask the question, Is this ESP?, as does the inquirer in this example:

"I lived fourteen miles from Memphis, Tennessee. One day I went to town to see a movie. I had an uneasy feeling as I entered the movie that something was on fire at home. This feeling grew until I could endure it no longer. I left the movie with an overpowering pull that drew me homeward.

"Within a mile of home I saw the fields all black and smoking. A boy hunting rabbits had thrown a lighted match in a field and started a fire. It took the fire department and fifty volunteers to save my home.

"Was this ESP?"

One can scarcely suppose that the idea of fire at home would be one the person would have often. It is too specific to be counted as caused by a general worried state such as certain overanxious persons might habitually have. Therefore, and because presumably there was no reason for the person to expect this particular kind of calamity, the tentative answer can be yes, this could have been an instance of ESP.

A quite different kind of experience may raise the same question, whether explicitly asked or not:

"My husband, a building contractor, took our seventeen-year-old son with him to a town in Nevada where a building project was under way. One night I had a frightening dream in which my husband appeared dressed in a black suit. He looked at me with a tragic expression and said slowly, 'He isn't coming back.'

"I awoke feeling very ill and shaking like a leaf. I turned on the light, noted the hour—2 A.M.—and tried to convince myself that I had had a bad dream; but I was unable to return to sleep. I was quite sure that something terrible had happened.

"About 7 A.M., I arose as usual to prepare breakfast for my two other young sons, but felt a strange reluctance to send them off to school. Yet I did not know whether what had happened concerned my son in Nevada or my husband. I was certain it concerned either one or the other. When I related my dream to the boys, the older one said in disgust, 'Oh, Mother, just because you had a crazy dream you want us to stay home from school. Other times when I wanted to skip school, you have refused to give your consent. What a silly idea!'

"I halfheartedly agreed with him that perhaps I was just being foolishly apprehensive and told him to run along to school. The younger one said, 'Mother, you look awfully sick. I will stay home with you.'

"Later in the day I asked my young son if he would care to drive with me to the post office to see if there might be a letter from Nevada. We set out—we lived at that time about two miles from the post office. Halfway there my son suddenly said, 'Mother! There is Dad parked at the side of the road. I think he is crying!'

"Instantly I applied the brakes and stopped. My husband sprang out of his car and came toward me saying heartbrokenly, 'Darling, how I hate to have to tell you this horrible news on the street. We have lost Jack!'

"Uncomprehendingly I asked, 'What do you mean? Where did you lose him? Don't cry, dear, we'll find him.'

" 'No, he's in the lake, Lake Walker in Nevada. He built himself a raft and went out on the lake to test it. A sudden storm came up, and he disappeared. The Marines have been out all night and all day looking for him. Not a trace of either Jack or the raft have been found!'

"A month later—to the day—his body was found miles up the lake.

"Of course, we have continued to live with our sorrow. Time does soften such awful blows, as you know; but at the time I just wanted to die myself. I tried to cling to the strange feeling that possessed me as the truth of what my husband was telling me sank in. It was as if I were suddenly enveloped in a mystical caress of great tenderness and love, and a voice seemed to say, 'Don't grieve, please don't grieve. Jack is quite all right now!' I could not begin to explain it. On the few occasions when I have related this story exactly as it happened to me, I have been confronted with expressions of unbelief—kind, yes, but obviously amused.

"My husband and two sons will bear me out, however. This is a true story."

While that person did not get a specific "message," still she knew there had been a calamity. It seemed more than just a bad dream. The effects of bad dreams wear off. This seemed to go deeper. This was different. It could have been a case of ESP.

Even when the information the person receives concerns someone else's thought, as in the case of the little girl in Chapter 1, or his mental imagery, if no ordinary kind of communication can explain it, one can tentatively consider it the result of ESP. In the following report, apparently the information transferred was that of mental imagery.

"I have had accurate premonitions of danger. Sometimes it is a dream, at other times a dead certainty I should or should not do a particular thing. But the experience that sticks in my memory and actually sends chills down my spine happened one night when I was eleven or twelve.

"I awoke suddenly and sat bolt upright in bed. There above me and suspended in the darkness was a face, normal size, surrounded by a white cloud or haze. The face was looking down at me, and of course I was terrified. I blinked my eyes and felt at the bed to make sure I wasn't dreaming. The face then moved. It just floated down at me slowly, and I seemed to be hypnotized, staring into the eyes of it.

"And those eyes! I don't know how to describe them without sounding melodramatic. They were the most wicked I ever hope to see. The mouth was thin and cruel and curled in a grin. It was truly the most horrible thing I ever saw—this face.

"As it got near me, I pulled back away from it and was gasping for a breath when it stopped coming forward, and still grinning at me dissolved, just disappeared. I was badly frightened and got back under the covers.

"I didn't say anything about it to my parents and would not be telling you now either if afterwards I hadn't heard my father in a hushed voice telling Mother of his experience the night before.

"It was the *same* experience as mine! I listened to him describe the face just as I had seen it. Then I burst into the room and gushed out my own story.

"We've never been able to explain it, of course, but don't try to convince Father or me that there was no face at all—although neither of us has ever seen it since. This may not be in the realm of your research, but at least I've told it to someone 'official.' "

In this particular case, it seems unlikely that by coincidence alone two people would have had the identical nightmare the same night. The suggestion, therefore, is strong that some sort of mental "leakage" or "contagion" occurred. But which one had the real nightmare, which one merely copied the other's imagery, nothing in the circumstances tells.

In each of these cases the person seemed to "know" something not told him in any sensory way. Each one, therefore, could well have been a case of ESP. Of course, in these cases and all the rest used as illustrations later, the judgment that ESP could have been involved is based on the information given, and on the fact that the account is typical of many others in import though different in specific detail.

The research on which the name ESP was based goes back to a day in 1930 at Duke University in North Carolina. It can be said to have begun then, although of course, like all scientific investigations, it had its roots in the past.

On this day the young instructor of a psychology class, J. B. Rhine, gave each of his students a well-sealed, opaque envelope and told the class he wanted to try a new but simple and easy kind of test.[1] Each envelope, he explained, contained a card on which was stamped a number. It might be any one from zero to nine. He wanted each student to guess the digit in his own envelope and write his guess on the outside.

The reason for the test, the instructor told the students, was that some experiments in such guessing had been carried on at Harvard and elsewhere, and it seemed that once in a while a particular individual showed up who could guess the numbers better than the one hit in ten to be expected by pure chance. He wanted to see if he could find such a person in his class.

The reason given the class that day was quite sufficient for the students, but it was only a superficial outline of the real reason the instructor had for conducting such an experiment. After all he was not trying to make an easy experiment on guessing patterns. He had in mind the larger objective of finding out something about the far reaches of the human mind. Could the mind get information about the objective world not supplied by the senses? A few earlier tests made by others and reported in the literature of psychical research had seemed to show that sometimes it could[2] just as did many odd experiences people had sometimes reported over the years. A few good guessers had also been reported under fairly adequate test conditions.

Nothing, however, had been proven conclusively. The question was still open, and it needed to be settled. The positive results that others had reported needed to be confirmed if, after systematic examination, confirmation was the truth; discarded, if it was not. The instructor knew the "laws of chance" (which of course are not really laws, but measures of the inherent probability of an occurrence), and that ordinarily and in the long run, they

[1] Rhine, J. B. *Extra-sensory Perception*. Boston: Bruce Humphries, 1934, chap. 5.

[2] Estabrooks, G. H. A contribution to experimental telepathy. *Journal of Parapsychology*, **25** (1961) 190–213. Rhine, J. B. *Op. cit.*, chap. 2.

hold. He knew that students in a class like his would get scores in a test like the one he would administer that would average one hit in ten—unless he should be lucky enough to discover one of those good guessers he had heard of. If he could find one of those, and then experiment with him, it should be possible to find out if his good guessing were simply a short, lucky series, soon canceled by average scores, or something more.

And so on five different days the envelopes were passed out to the class. At the end of the test the instructor had 495 marked envelopes. But the checkup showed nothing startling. There were only sixty hits, when chance alone should give one hit in ten, or 49.5. Thus, the general results, although slightly encouraging, did not seem spectacular. One student, however, had guessed three of his five envelopes correctly.

On the possibility that these correct guesses might have been more than lucky hits, the student, Adam J. Linzmayer, was called in and given some further tests. As it developed, he proved to be just what the instructor was looking for: he had an uncanny ability to guess correctly much oftener than the average student. It appeared uncanny then because it was so unusual.

Linzmayer was a student at Duke for several semesters after that, and he continued to come in and take tests until eventually he had made a total of 32,247 guesses. After the initial class tests, the cards used as the "targets" for the guesses were changed from the original number cards, in which by chance alone one in ten would be expected, to specially designed "ESP cards" which had geometric symbols instead of digits printed on their faces. There were only five symbols, so that the chance of a hit per trial now became one in five. The symbols—cross, star, circle, square, and wavy lines—had been selected to be as simple and as distinct as possible. Five cards with each symbol made a deck of twenty-five, and this deck soon became a standard tool in the research, not only with this student, but with many others.

Linzmayer's guesses, of course, were always made when the symbols or targets were entirely concealed from view. In the course of his experiments, which extended from 1931 through 1933, a number of different conditions were tried, some when he was in a good mood, some when he was not. But by the end of

1931 six hundred tests, made under conditions which were similar so the results could be added, gave 118 hits more than would have been expected by chance. That made it an average of 9.9 instead of 5 per run of twenty-five trials, a rate very much higher than chance should give. As time went on, a decline gradually set in, and by 1933, for two thousand similar trials, he averaged only 5.9 per run. Even such a rate is much more than chance alone should give, though definitely showing a "wear-and-tear" effect that parapsychologists would be long accounting for.

But decline or no, these results were definite indication that something besides coincidence was operating. And because of the results, Linzmayer's performance alone can be used to illustrate the establishment of ESP. It is hardly fair to single him out to the exclusion of others who were involved later—including another unusual "high scorer," Hubert J. Pearce—but one can concentrate on Linzmayer because he was the first high scorer discovered, and his results alone are so far from explicable in terms of chance or any sensory kind of perception that they could, if need be, carry the full weight of the discovery.

Since Linzmayer's results show that many of his guesses were correct, one can say that somehow he *knew* in those cases what the card symbols were. One can also say that the woman in the movie *knew* of the fire at home; that the mother *knew* something had happened to either her son or her husband. And curiously, too, somehow in the third case, one or the other, son or father, *knew* about the horrible face in the other's nightmare. Of course the knowing in these cases was not on a fully conscious level, as when one knows the amount of his salary check. Nevertheless these people can all be said to have had some information on their respective topics; and therefore one can say they *knew,* until our English language is expanded to cover fine points of difference such as these.

But how could they know? In each instance the knowledge the person seemed to get was hidden from his senses. He did not see or hear or otherwise "sense" it. In these days, over thirty years after Linzmayer established his record at Duke University, and after all the countless guesses made by other students, it is easy to give the phenomenon a name, and to say they could have done it by extrasensory perception, or ESP. But a name is not an explanation, although this one has a descriptive fact tied into it: the fact that information was secured without the senses. This fact was established by years of research in which it was checked and studied and proved to be a reality. What wonder that the questions it posed, What is the process back of it? and How does it fit in with other mental processes? have been subjects of inquiry in the field of parapsychology ever since.

These questions about ESP have not been the only line of inquiry in the field, however. Another one has gone on more or less concurrently, which in popular terminology would be known as the question of "mind over matter," or whether matter can be affected by mind alone, an effect which has been named psychokinesis or PK.[3] Research on it had two reasons for being initiated —first, certain experiences people occasionally reported suggested that such an effect had occurred. The second reason was a more or less theoretical one. The experiences involve a physical occurrence of some kind, one which occurs in such a fashion that it seems to be a "sign" or a message of a kind. Although such experiences are deeply tinged by the aura of superstition—even more in fact than those that seem to involve ESP—they are occasionally reported in circumstances that raise the question, Could an unknown force have been involved here?

Take for instance a few examples, first the following occurrence reported by a man in Ohio:

"One Sunday afternoon I was sitting at my desk reading. Suddenly I felt a surge of blood racing through my veins; and at the same instant a picture of a close friend, hanging on the wall above my desk, dashed to the floor, breaking the glass but not injuring the photograph. Even before picking up the picture, I sat down at my typewriter and wrote to the friend. He lived about seven hundred miles away.

"In due time I received a reply giving the address of a hospital. It seems that at the precise instant when the picture fell and I felt the sudden increase in blood pressure, my friend was driving

[3] Rhine, J. B. *The Reach of the Mind*. New York: William Sloane Associates, Inc., 1947, chap. 6.

in his car across a railroad track and was struck by a locomotive.

"I was living in Cincinnati, and he in New York State. He was recuperating from the accident when he replied to my letter.

"The picture had been hanging there for six or eight months, and it was the string that broke. The picture was in an 8 x 10 wooden frame, and there was no heavy traffic or other jarring or vibration that could have caused it to fall. It fell without warning."

In this instance the significance of the episode depends on the fact that the picture fell at the time the person it represented was in a serious accident.

Sometimes the kind of event itself may be the factor that seems most important, as for instance in the next case:

"My father had a younger brother, Ben, who fought in the Second World War. On their farm in Missouri they had an old grandfather's clock that had not run for many, many years. One day the old clock began to run as though nothing had ever been wrong with it. At the same time Ben's devoted shepherd dog began to howl. This howling continued all day.

"A few days later the family received a telegram from the War Department. Ben had been killed in action at Aachen, Germany, November 29, 1944. This was the day the clock started and Ben's dog howled. These strange phenomena still puzzle me to this day."

Of the two unusual events reported there, the inexplicable starting of the old clock is the one of interest here. Traditionally, clocks that stop at times of death are more familiar than those that start. But presumably both occurrences can be put in the same category.

The second reason for initiating research in psychokinesis at the Parapsychology Laboratory was, as already indicated, a theoretical one. By 1934, after four years of research on ESP, J. B. Rhine was asking himself, If the mind can know without ordinary means of knowing, can it perhaps also move objects without the ordinary means of moving? In other words, can mind move matter directly?

The question was sparked into actual research one day by a young gambler who said that upon occasion when he was properly keyed up he could make dice fall as he willed. Dice controlled by mind? "Mind over matter?"

The suggestion was not only possible but even easy to try out. Soon the ESP subjects at Duke were also trying to make dice obey their wills, and they had considerable success. Other influences being equal, a six-sided cube, a die, should have one chance in six of falling on any given face. The dice that the subjects in these tests threw averaged considerably more than that for the desired face. It was the objective of the experimenters in this research, then, to see that all counter influences, like imperfect dice or tricky throwing, were ruled out by the conditions of the experiment. Accordingly, they imposed controls which were built into the plan of the experiment. On the matter of imperfect dice, it was soon decided that no dice, or cubes of any kind made of any material—plastic, wood, or whatever—could be trusted not to have imperfections. But if in each experiment no one single face of the die was allowed to be the only target, and if all six were used equally, the imperfections would cancel each other. If a score was secured that varied sufficiently from the one in six allowed for by chance, then it could not be charged to imperfections of the dice.

Tricky throwing, if any of the subjects had been adept at it (which never seemed to be the case), was controlled by using a container with a corrugated lining in which the dice were shaken and from which they were thrown onto a padded tabletop. In some of the later investigations, rotating cages were used so that the subjects never touched the dice. But even before the introduction of this automatic method, the point had been reasonably well proven that somehow the dice fell as the subject wished too often to be explained other than by a kind of mind-over-matter force.

The early association of the PK research with dice and gambling, although purely an incidental one, troubled some of the subjects, particularly one young man, a divinity student named William Gatling. He saw in the PK research tremendous implications for the relation of mind and matter. He was not going to let those implications be lowered by a base association, for he thought the principle behind PK might be similar even to that of prayer. And so he reasoned that PK was not especially for gamblers, that they were not a specially gifted group, and he thought he could prove it.

He organized a PK contest.[4] For it he recruited two teams, one made up of four divinity students, volunteers to whom he explained the situation. He believed and they believed that this is a God-given ability, and it is not just gamblers who have it. The other team was made up of the four best "crapshooters" on campus. In selecting them he had only hearsay evidence, and the fact that they said they had a lot of luck throwing dice. Since they agreed to try, it seemed to show that they really believed they were good.

History does not record the atmosphere or the intensity with which each side worked. Only the mathematical outcome is on record. But presumably the young divinity students were just as determined to beat the crapshooters as the latter were not to be outdone by fledgling preachers.

Both sides, of course, worked under the same standard conditions. They threw six dice at a time from a cardboard cup with roughened rubber lining onto a table with padded top and sidewalls. They used each face of the die as target the same number of times around the die, to correct for any bias the dice might have. The basis of evaluation was the run, which consisted of four throws of the six dice, or twenty-four individual die falls.

The result was that both sides won—against chance, but not against each other. Their scores were so nearly the same, in fact, that the difference between them was insignificant, and neither group could be called the winner. A total of 540 runs was thrown by the gamblers with a positive deviation of 282, or an average run score of 4.52 per run instead of the 4.00 to be expected by pure chance. The ministerial students threw 702 runs and got a deviation above expectation of 359, which was an average of 4.51. In

___

[4] Gatling, William, and J. B. Rhine. Two groups of PK subjects compared. *Journal of Parapsychology*, **10** (1946) 120–125.

fact, the mathematical evaluation of their total results (critical ratio 9.97) was four times as high as is necessary in general science to be considered significant of something more than chance coincidence. That something more here was just the effect for which both groups were striving, and it was good enough that they felt they had demonstrated something greater than their own superiority.

This contest between the divinity students and the gamblers was only one episode in a long series of experiments to find out if the human mind can affect inanimate matter directly. Although in some experiments the results were at chance, in others again and again the statistical outcome was such that it was significantly above it. The only reasonable interpretation was that the mental action of the subject had caused it. In personal experiences like those when pictures fall or clocks stop or start at times of human crises, the suggestion is that a physical effect has occurred which has a human meaning and therefore, presumably, a mental cause. Now in these experiments a physical effect occurred, which, it seemed, could only have had a mental cause, the one named psychokinesis, or PK.

After ESP and PK had been brought into the limelight by the early researches at Duke University, a psychologist then at Cambridge University, Dr. Robert H. Thouless, felt the necessity of a single name to apply to both of them. It needed to be a short, convenient one that would make no assumptions about the nature of the phenomenon. Its nature was, of course, something still to be discovered.

In an article by Dr. Thouless the Greek letter *psi* which had been suggested by his collaborator, Dr. B. P. Wiesner, was proposed, just because, like the algebraic *x,* it was noncommittal.[5] The process (or processes) by which the effects are produced was thus characterized as an unknown. If at some future date its nature were discovered, a more descriptive name could then be given it. The suggestion was accepted, and now for decades the term *psi* has been used in parapsychology whenever it is de-

[5] Thouless, Robert H. The present position of experimental research into telepathy and related phenomena. *Journal of Parapsychology,* **7** (1943) 158–171.

sirable to speak of the phenomena of the entire field. It is thus a more general term than either ESP or PK alone.

Once the occurrence of ESP was established, research in parapsychology can be said to have entered a new stage. Even though no sharp division can be traced, still it then became no longer necessary to perform experiments which would simply show that ESP occurred. Researchers began to try to frame their experiments to tell something about the nature of the phenomenon. Over the years considerable progress toward this end has been made, in spite of difficulties which could not have been foreseen, but which form an integral part of the development of parapsychological research in its early stages.

The difficulties which beset the newly developing field of parapsychology arose both from the research itself and from the kind of reception which reports of it received from much of the scientific public.

Fairly rapid progress toward the understanding of psi might have seemed likely in the early days of research, because the evidence for ESP had been fairly easily and quickly acquired, and also because other experimenters in other places were soon able to confirm it.[6] From a start like this no one could have anticipated the amount of effort it would take even to begin to untangle the complexities by which the nature of ESP was obscured.

One of the first signs that progress toward understanding would not be made quickly was in evidence even at the beginning, though hardly recognized then for the stumbling block it was. This was the fact that experimental results fluctuated from test to test. A good experiment in chemistry or physics yields the same result on Monday it yielded on Friday. But ESP tests were variable and a given experimenter using the same subject and conditions he thought were identical could not be certain of getting results the second time which would be comparable to those he got the first.

Now it is easy to see why the difficulty arose. In an ideal experimental situation, as for instance in an experiment in chemistry, all the factors involved are named and numbered beforehand, and only one is varied at a time. The results achieved can then be

6 Rhine, J. B. *New Frontiers of the Mind*. New York: Farrar & Rinehart, 1937, chap. 9.

ascribed to this single variable. But the situation in the parapsychological experimentation was not so simple. This was a case in which contributing factors were almost all unknown, some even, as one can see now, unsuspected. Working with human beings—and with obscure aspects of their mental processes at that—every new experiment was unavoidably different from the others in innumerable subtle ways.

The inability of experimenters to get comparable results from experiment to experiment meant for one thing that it would be difficult to make comparisons and thus to find out reliably whether a given procedure, technique, or condition was better than another. Even worse, experiments frequently turned out to show no sign of ESP at all. The results were quite at the "chance" level, and because one cannot test something unless he has it to test, the entire project was a failure.

All of this meant, of course, that the experimenter must first succeed in getting evidence of psi in his experiment before he could say anything about his results. This requirement makes, and always will make, experimentation in parapsychology different from that in all the fields in which the thing to be tested is stable or already existent, whether it be a chemical in chemistry, or an ability like sense perception in psychology. It means that experiments in this field must begin with the creation of circumstances that will first enable the phenomenon to occur. Then and only then can the experimenter actually "experiment with psi." The situation is a little like that of a bird watcher stalking a rare and elusive specimen. He must first find the bird before he can learn anything about it. If he does not find it, he cannot conclude, as some unsuccessful would-be experimenters in parapsychology have concluded, that this phenomenon does not exist because he has failed to get evidence of it.

Difficulties in connection with the reception of reports of ESP research by other scientists arose primarily because the idea of ESP as a way of knowing about events was revolutionary. It ran counter to the idea which for centuries the scholarly world had assumed to be the truth. That assumption was based on an old Greek dictum: "Nothing enters the mind except by way of the senses." This assumption meant that no one, neither the experimenters nor those in the outside world, would be easily convinced that the contrary was true. Consequently, in this research, even the parapsychologists themselves needed much more evidence than researchers usually do before they trusted their results. Of course, this was true ten times over for scientists outside the ranks.

Considering this, it is not too surprising that when results like those of Linzmayer and the rest of the ESP subjects were published, they were received in general with anything but acclaim. They had about as much chance of being taken seriously as if they had meant the earth is flat. Few of those in the outside professional world even looked at the results, or gave them a hearing on their merits.

This professional resistance to the idea of ESP would probably have crumbled fairly quickly if psi had been found to have a reliable practical application. If Linzmayer's ability had had a market value, the theoretical basis on which it rested would not have been questioned long. But this ability was not easily put to work. The fact that it was undependable, that no one knew for sure when evidence of it could or could not be obtained, only tended to undercut the use of it by some of those who professed to have "psychic ability." Mediums, clairvoyants, and prophets over the ages had claimed to be able to know things hidden from the senses. Now the actual ability on which their claims were based was shown to be far from reliable. Like an insufficiently tested drug, it was a commodity not yet ready for the market.

Another reason, too, why those in other professions were slow to take the claims of parapsychology seriously was the result of the very thing that made the research difficult: the fact that results were not predictable, that a subject who scored significantly above the chance level one day might give no extra chance scores the next. The saying became current in critical circles that experiments in ESP were not "repeatable," and were therefore beneath consideration. It took a long time for parapsychologists to counter this criticism, and to make the point that the degree of "repeatability" in the strict sense of a chemical or physical experiment is a measure of the complexity of the situation and the stage of understanding a project has reached. As a matter of fact, each time an experiment in ESP achieved a firm statistically *significant* level, the repeatability of an ESP test was affirmed. Failures were of course only indications that some necessary constituent of an ESP test was lacking. The objective of this, like that of any pioneer investigation, was to discover what the essential ingredients were.

The unreceptive attitude of the scientific and professional world (not so much of ordinary laymen, some of whom almost too easily accepted the idea of psychic ability as a reality) continued therefore and, at least indirectly, prevented any large or immediate growth of resources and research personnel for the further investigation of psi. Consequently, in academic psychology departments particularly, students were not encouraged to take parapsychological problems for research, or even to consider them seriously. As a result of this, comparatively few of them did so.

However, a fortunate combination of circumstances at Duke University, where Rhine had led in the application of the more modern research methods in parapsychology, made it possible for work to continue. The University had a tradition of freedom of thought and investigation. Its president, Dr. William Preston Few, had a degree of personal interest in the unusual research. Also, he had chosen for the head of his newly formed psychology department a psychologist who did not follow the beaten path and who opposed the mechanistic trend of psychology toward behaviorism. This was Dr. William McDougall, earlier from Oxford, then from Harvard University. In contrast to most psychologists, Dr. McDougall was interested in psychical research. This was in part at least because in his psychological system he needed to know the nature of man with relation to the physical order. He felt that psychical research promised to give evidence that no other source had yielded.

It was because of Dr. McDougall's special outlook and because he was backed by President Few that he encouraged his young instructor, Rhine, to begin his experiments in the first place. With Dr. McDougall's support and sponsorship (until his death in 1938) the research on the psi effect continued in spite of its lack of a favorable scientific reception.

In the mid-thirties the Duke Parapsychology Laboratory, at first as part of the Psychology Department and later as an independent laboratory, was formed with Rhine as director. With the aid of voluntary gifts, mostly from a few interested private individuals, and with space, secretarial help, and Rhine's own salary coming from the University, the laboratory was able to exist modestly from year to year. A small staff of workers, mostly graduate students but including a few full-time researchers, was maintained, and a fairly steady succession of research papers resulted.

The Parapsychology Laboratory, small as it was throughout most of its history, nevertheless was the one parapsychological research center in which full-time researchers were employed. It was there in 1937 that the *Journal of Parapsychology* was established as a vehicle for reports of experimental research in the field. In 1957 a scientific society, the Parapsychological Association, originated at the laboratory. It now has a membership of over a hundred and fifty members. In the work of the Parapsychology Laboratory, basic methods for research and standards for conditions and evaluation of results were established that not only withstood the years of criticism directed at parapsychological investigations, but that have now become routine in most of the research carried on elsewhere.

In 1965 J. B. Rhine reached the mandatory age of retirement from the University and the natural consequence was the dissolution of the Parapsychology Laboratory. Although still small in number of workers, the laboratory had become something of a world center to which isolated individuals interested in the field often turned for advice, encouragement, and help in their research projects. In order that the continuance of that function as well as its research program might be assured, Rhine and his colleagues established an independent organization to sponsor both. The organization, called the Foundation for Research on the Nature of Man (FRNM), was organized in 1962 with the broad objective of encouraging research appropriate to the study of the unique nature of man wherever it might be going on, in or out of the specific field of parapsychology. However, when the organization began to function, all sponsored research was within the parapsychological field.

In 1965 the FRNM was strong enough to begin active operation. With the Institute for Parapsychology as heir to the Parapsychology Laboratory, it moved, in the spring of 1966, to quarters of its own adjacent to the University campus. At this new and independent location, parapsychological research and the sponsorship of it elsewhere is being maintained and expanded as the resources of the Foundation make it possible.

While the fortunate circumstances at Duke University had permitted the Parapsychology Laboratory to exist there, this was by no means the only place at which research was or is being done. Long before the tests for ESP began at Duke University, societies for the investigation of psychic phenomena were formed in various countries. From them came nearly all the reports of studies that made up the background against which the work at Duke began. Those studies served to focus the problem which led to the question of whether the human being has the ability to get information without the use of the senses.

This direction was given because the primary if not exclusive question that motivated the societies was one concerning the destiny of man; specifically, whether the human spirit survives death. This was true, for instance, of The Society for Psychical Research, founded in London in 1882, and in the American society of the same name, founded in New York a few years later.

As a result, numerous studies were made in which mediums were so controlled that the possibility of fraud or deception of any kind was ruled out. Still, in many cases the mediums who were investigated gave correct information. This information was usually given as if from someone deceased. The question was, did it actually come from a "surviving" personality or did the medium herself have an ability to obtain information without use of the senses.

The study of mediums thus led to heightened interest in discovering what psychic powers the medium herself, as a living human being, might have. These older studies thus led quite directly to inquiries like those at Duke and made it important to discover whether a faculty like that of ESP exists.

The answer to this question of the source of the medium's information was made no easier by the discovery, in the early thirties, of the reality of ESP. In 1934 the question was focused particularly at the Duke Laboratory, when a study was made there of one of the most famous mediums of the time.[7] This was Mrs. Eileen J. Garrett, who in the desire to understand her own powers better offered to come to Duke and be tested.

Under stricter conditions than any ever before used for similar tests she gave communications in the trance state that contained information peculiar beyond chance coincidence to a series of individuals. These, one at a time, were seated in an adjoining closed-off room, so that she never saw any of them, or knew their identity.

During the same period the medium was also given a series of ESP tests using the same card technique that had been used with Linzmayer, Pearce, and the other students, whose results had proven the occurrence of ESP. Her results on these tests were highly significant too, and showed that she possessed a high level of ESP ability. While the ESP tests of course did not prove that her mediumistic communications were not from a "surviving" spirit, they made it impossible to conclude that they did come from that source.

Thus it was that as a consequence of the discovery of the psi ability, the hope of a direct answer to the question of spirit survival was practically extinguished. It may well be that the best approach to it will be a more indirect one than the mediumistic studies promised. It may turn out that this question will find its eventual answer in the understanding of psi ability in the living. At any rate the study of mediums has now practically ceased, and has been replaced to a large extent by experiments on ESP and PK.

Other areas of active research in parapsychology have developed from the support of a few psychologists besides Dr. McDougall. Of those who have been interested in the field from its beginning, several are outstanding. One of these is Dr. Gardner Murphy, Director of Research at the Menninger Foundation at

[7] Birge, William R., and J. B. Rhine. Unusual types of persons tested for ESP. I. A professional medium. *Journal of Parapsychology,* 6 (1942) 85–94.

Topeka, Kansas. He has written many articles and a book on the subject, has encouraged students, and has guided research projects at the American Society for Psychical Research in New York.[8] One of his students who has been most productive and in turn has encouraged students of her own is the psychologist Dr. Gertrude R. Schmeidler, of City College, New York. Some of her work will be discussed in a later chapter.

Another prominent psychologist who has contributed research of his own and considerable writing, including a book on experimental parapsychology, is Dr. Robert H. Thouless.[9] He was mentioned previously as one of the proponents of the expression "psi" for parapsychical.

Several small one-man centers in colleges or universities have existed and some still exist. In these usually a college teacher with the help of an assistant or two does some parapsychological research. Also, in this and many other countries there are many individuals sufficiently involved in the scientific aspect of the field to deserve to be called parapsychologists. They can be found in Sweden, Denmark, Holland, France, Germany, Czechoslovakia, Russia, South Africa, India, Japan, Argentina, and Chile. From this geographical distribution it is evident that interest in the problems involved has no national boundaries. Largely because of this universal interest, which in most cases has developed spontaneously and without financial backing or organization, the idea of a foundation to encourage such efforts arose.

The FRNM, if it can be adequately financed, should in time not only help support interested researchers wherever they are, but also make it easier for them to integrate their efforts. In the past, because workers were isolated and entirely on their own, many research projects were necessarily chosen in what would seem to have been at least semi-impromptu fashion, instead of as the result of leads suggested by work already done. But since it was a pioneer field, for which there was in the beginning neither chart nor guide nor compass, the wonder is that substantial progress has

8 Murphy, Gardner. *The Challenge of Psychical Research.* New York: Harper & Brothers, 1961.

9 Thouless, Robert H. *Experimental Psychical Research.* London: Pelican Books, 1963.

been made, and that the early results have been confirmed, the basis for scientific development laid, and a sufficient understanding of the process achieved, so that it is now possible to trace it at least in outline from its beginning to its end.

CHAPTER 3

ESP in the Unconscious

ESP begins in mystery. In the slow-motion study it is necessary to make to understand the psi process, it is clear that ESP begins below the level of consciousness, in an area of mind still so ill-defined that even the name of it is tentative. It will be spoken of here loosely as the unconscious, using the term to cover all of mind that is not conscious. But it is also necessary to speak of levels of it and to refer to the *deep* unconscious, because ESP can be traced there, to a mental region still sealed to parapsychologist and nonparapsychologist alike. No person can know directly what goes on there. Only by indirection, by inference and supposition, can the deep unconscious be known, its secrets be pried into. Because ESP begins there, it begins in mystery.

This much is clear—by inference: When ESP occurs, and a person gets information about some distant or hidden event, that information, or message as it can be called, was somehow *available* at this unconscious level. A direct contact must have occurred between the objective world and some central, unconscious part of the mind difficult to define or specify. Perhaps the name "psyche" is as good as any. Webster calls it "the vital principle which constitutes the inner spring of action and development."

One can say that this contact occurred at a deep unconscious level. But the unconscious is not a place; it is neither deep nor shallow, nor does it actually have levels like a lake or river. It is simply part of the sum total, mind. Yet for convenience, psychologists tend to use spatial terms for mental processes. One can therefore speak of the deep unconscious with something of the same understandable imprecision of such expressions as, the sun goes *down*, the moon comes *up*.

The point is that this contact does occur but in some way probably forever out of consciousness. For it is not like forgotten items that can reappear or be remembered later when some circumstance of attention or suggestion brings them back. Even under hypnosis nothing of this contact between reality and the "inner spring" of mind can be recovered. Someday when all is known, it is possible that the area of the mind at which ESP begins will prove to be the very deepest, most elemental level from which any sign ever thrusts up to consciousness.

This unconscious origin of ESP has led to much frustration in the field of parapsychology. It means, of course, that whether in life situations or in tests, the person has no idea that ESP is taking place, until the message or some part of it makes its way across the conscious threshold. And when the message does appear *it gives no hint of whence it came*. From this combination of unconscious origin and unannounced arrival spring many of the difficulties of parapsychological research. However, although the origin is secret and mysterious, the message, when it gets to consciousness, is no secret. It is known then, and usually accepted by the person just like information he might get from sight or hearing. All the examples so far given show this, and they show too that the recipient does not know where the new idea came from. Many times the message fits in so smoothly that the person does not realize that it came incognito and was different from a sense perception. A woman from Connecticut tells of such an experience.

"For a long time I have had dreams that come true. However, often I do not remember I had the dream until it happens. Then every detail is as though I had lived it before except that I know I dreamed it.

"A minor example was one Sunday last fall in church. The minister started to read the Bible selection (Isaiah 55). I thought to myself, he read that passage last week, but then I remembered I had dreamed it."

In fact experiences like that one are almost the same as some of those classed by psychologists as déjà vu. The difference here is only that the person did recall her dream. In some of the instances of déjà vu, very likely a dream preceded, too, but was not recalled. Unnoticed for what they are, this is the way some of the messages from lower mental levels slip into consciousness.

In some instances, the meaning may be startling and may suddenly become clear, stark, and undisguised—and with no indication whatever as to whence it came, or how the person knew it, as was true for a woman who writes:

"My first experience happened in 1918, when a very close friend who was then fighting in France wrote me to please contact his mother, as he felt if anything should happen to him I might be of great comfort to her.

"I had not met her, but called and asked her to come and have dinner with my family and me the following Sunday.

"On that day, my mother and I and two friends who were also visiting were taken desperately ill with flu. I was delirious off and on.

"Although the phone was ringing constantly, I was so ill I could not have been less concerned. However, on the fourth day about 6 P.M. I heard the phone ring, sat up in bed, and insisted that the nurse go downstairs and answer. She replied that my father was there and would answer, but because I was so unhappy and insistent, she did go down. When she returned, she said nothing. I again inquired who had called. She answered, 'Oh, just another friend inquiring about you and the family.'

"I sat up in bed and said, 'No, it was word of Leslie. He has been killed in action!'

"As it proved later, it was a telegram saying Leslie had been killed in action."

Where did that knowledge come from? Even though the person herself had no inkling how she knew, it somehow crossed the threshold of consciousness without showing a trace of its origin.

At times, too, the person may simply *act* as if he knew something, and only later realize he did not know, and had no rational reason for his action. A man in Connecticut tells of such an experience.

"The following personal experience is one I shall always remember. It was in the Second World War and concerned the 'Battle of the Bulge.' I was on Salisbury Plain, near Tidworth.

"While dug in one night there seemed to be a larger number of night flares than usual. The enemy's phosphorous flares were of various mechanical types, and they brilliantly illuminated a sizable area. All were arched up by a mortar-type device. Some would streak unlighted to a zenith point, open a parachute, flash on, hang suspended, go out briefly, only to again burst most unexpectedly into another bath of intense light. Some would come on as many as three times. Others were only the Roman-candle type that simply streaked through a vivid arc and sputteringly thudded into the earth.

"And then, alone in my foxhole, I knew I had to get out. Leaving the security of a hole could be dangerous. Reason and orders dictated that I stay in my hole. But *I knew I must get out.* I didn't know why, but get out I had to!

"I had crawled out only a few yards and a Roman candle flare shot up, burning vividly and—whamo! It smashed into my foxhole dead center.

"I shook all over.

"Why I got out of that hole, I'll never explain. I only knew I had to get out. The knowledge was strong, clear, undeniable.

"Before and afterward I was in foxholes in similar situations, but I had no such compulsion then. Why did I have it the one time my foxhole was hit? I decided that the good Lord wanted me for something better. Before the war ended, I occasionally wondered if maybe the devil wasn't saving me for something worse."

It was not knowledge. But it was a compulsion to action from the unconscious. It had no other signal in consciousness.

Each of these experiences shows in its separate way that the message slipped into consciousness unobtrusively and with nothing except the meaning itself to tell that any such information had been received. But this is just what should be expected. Items from unconscious mental levels constantly come into consciousness unannounced, a fact which since the time of Freud and the development of psychiatry has been more widely and more popularly recognized than earlier. Those items may concern almost anything that enters the mind of man. They can include information obtained by ESP, and this will rise to consciousness just like any other item. Even though direct inspection of this unconscious process is not possible, still something of the methods or "paths" by which the ESP information reaches consciousness can be deduced. In later chapters these paths will be traced in some detail. Here we need only note that ESP messages come into consciousness like any other kind, unannounced.

When Linzmayer or any of the other students correctly guessed the hidden symbols on the cards, their guesses of course came from deeply unconscious levels. The subject in the test simply named the symbol that came to mind, and when the average number of correct hits was more than would occur by chance, then one could say that the surplus of correct answers was supplied from information coming from an unconscious level of that student's mind.

But even in the original classroom test, when Linzmayer called correctly three of the five digits in his envelopes, and even if one knew for sure that the three calls were the result of ESP and not just random hits (which, of course, no one does know), he also guessed, but incorrectly, the digits in the remaining two envelopes. His task was to name the digit he thought was in each envelope and that he did. He probably felt no differently about the two incorrect guesses than he did about the correct ones. We can say this now because the unconscious origin of the information secured by ESP is recognized. But in the early experimental work, the fact had not yet been fully appreciated. It still seemed strange to the experimenters that even subjects whose scores were high usually did not seem able to tell correct from incorrect guesses, but had to wait for the checkup to be certain how well they had succeeded.

A classic example of a case in which the subject could not judge her own success was reported in 1937 by Dr. Bernard F. Riess, then an assistant professor at Hunter College of the City of New York.[1] This professor did not believe in ESP. It happened that a student in his class knew a girl who was supposed to have high ESP ability.

A test was arranged and was carried out in the respective homes of professor and subject. The professor, with a shuffled pack of ESP cards, at a specified time on a specified evening, picked up the top card, looked at it, wrote the symbol on his record sheet, and then put the card to one side. At the same time, in her own house about a quarter of a mile away, the subject made her guess about that card. A minute later the professor repeated the performance and the subject timed her second guess to match. Thus they continued through fifty guesses a session. Sessions continued at stated times from late December until April of the following year, when 1,850 trials had been made. In these trials, the checkup showed the most spectacular series of hits that has ever been reported over as long a series. The average number of hits per run of twenty-five calls, instead of the five expected by pure chance, was over eighteen. One entire run of twenty-five hits appeared and several of twenty-four.

Then something happened. The girl got sick for about three months and the tests had to be suspended. After that they were again resumed briefly and 250 more calls were made. On these the average score was only 5.3 per twenty-five. It was quite clear that the situation was different now. The strange ability she had shown before was no longer working. But the young lady thought her scores this last time would be just the same as they had been before.

She did not know the difference.

Here again the situation is what might be expected of an ability which is not under conscious control. The point is easy to see now, but its full import was only gradually recognized by parapsychological researchers. However, that recognition occurred to Rhine one day in the 1930s when he was discussing ESP with another professor in the Psychology Department.

The other man made a suggestion, one which has occurred to

[1] Riess, Bernard F. A case of high scores in card guessing at a distance. *Journal of Parapsychology*, **1** (1937) 260–263.

various people but which springs from a misunderstanding of the way the mind works in such a situation. He said, "Give your subjects a series of tests in some of which you use a deck of ESP cards in the regular way. In others use blank cards but do not tell your subjects. If the subject is able to know by ESP as you think, then he will not make any guesses if there are no targets."

"Oh, yes he will!" the answer was. "He will, because he is set to call symbols, and he *doesn't know how* he does it. He doesn't know when he's wrong or right. *It's unconscious!*"

And that said it. The unconscious origin of ESP was emphasized then in the mind of at least one parapsychologist and one who would continue to think about it, to apply the idea in the interpretation of experimental results, and to pass this knowledge along to students.

When the ESP process was considered as involving the expressing of information that comes from unconscious areas of mind, some of the difficulties of testing for ESP became more understandable. The extreme delicacy of a process of transfer of meaning from lower mental levels into consciousness was now appreciated. It could be seen as the possible explanation for some of the early failures.

For one thing subjects had varied greatly in what one could call their "durability." Many scored well above chance at first, but if sessions of testing were continued over weeks or months, most of them eventually ceased to be able to score significantly. Linzmayer and several others were exceptions in that they lasted for a longer time, but even they could not continue indefinitely to score significantly. Before long it was taken by experimenters as a mark of ESP, that it was a subtle and fleeting ability. A "decline" in scoring rate over a period of time was almost a sign of genuineness. In one way this fact was reassuring. It showed that the subjects were not *learning,* as they might presumably have done if they were somehow cheating and getting cues from the cards the experimenters thought were hidden. But on the other hand, it was exasperating to an experimenter to be unable to reproduce the good scores a subject gave at first when the test was repeated later.

But now, if the process was quite unconscious, it seemed clear that somehow the repetition, the continued carrying out of a somewhat monotonous task, tended to interfere with it. Another thing fitted in. It had been noted almost from the first that even a good reliable subject like Hubert Pearce, who worked even longer than Linzmayer and scored just as well or better, usually was adversely affected if a visitor came into the experimental room.[2]

At first, reports of the high scoring of the special subjects brought visitors who wanted to watch. But spectators practically always interfered with success. On the face of it that looked bad. Skeptics, and they were plentiful, were quick to say that subjects could not score when watched because their tricks would be detected. But fortunately or unfortunately, the answer was not so simple as that.

Strangers, mere observers, seemed to produce a degree of self-consciousness in the subject, just as posing for a picture, let us say, does for almost everyone. This self-consciousness was obviously inimical to the state of mind necessary for the information secured by ESP to break through into consciousness. Once it was realized that the tenuous path from deep unconscious levels into consciousness was involved, it was easy to see why observers did not belong in the experimental room. Trial and error showed, however, that when the observation of a second person was desirable, it could be obtained in a different way. The observer could be given a reason for being there. For instance, he could act as a coexperimenter and have a job to do. The subject would then accept him and forget about him, and the scoring would be uninterrupted.

Today it is certain that unconscious mental processes are involved. In experimenting, the fact is taken for granted, and the problem is to arrange conditions so as to interfere with those processes as little as possible, a job which in itself is a fairly tall order considering the complexities involved. Much remains to tell of this in later chapters. But first must come some "rules of thumb" by which ESP can at least tentatively be recognized.

[2] Rhine, J. B. *Extra-sensory Perception.* Boston: Bruce Humphries, 1934, p. 102.

CHAPTER 4

Recognizing ESP

AN old recipe for possum stew begins, "First get your possum." The study of ESP begins similarly. First, get your ESP. Try to recognize it. But to do so means to overcome one of the worst perplexities arising from the unconscious origin of psi.

The difficulty begins because of the secret nature of the deep unconscious, and because the messages of ESP slip unobtrusively into consciousness along with all kinds of other thoughts. Even the person himself is generally unaware of any difference, so how can others tell? Usually they cannot. Only by rules and definitions is it possible to find criteria for discriminating and tentatively identifying those messages that involve ESP.

The unconscious has been called a storehouse because memories, hopes, anxieties, all the countless remnants of past experience are stored there. As everyone knows these days, the practiced eye can trace many aspects of human behavior back to the unconscious. But ESP makes it more than just a storehouse. ESP brings in fresh information new to the individual. It is not concerned with materials already stored, although it may be affected by them. But the ESP information is mixed with all the rest, and only careful sorting can distinguish it from certain borderline experiences sometimes reported, which can easily be misjudged. They may be taken as the result of ESP when it is not necessarily involved. In experiments too, borderline results may or may not involve ESP, and a criterion for discriminating is most essential.

The criterion for judging whether an experience probably involves ESP is simple. It must be one that brings information new to the person and that brings it without sensory mediation. But the distinction between new information and the secondary derivatives of past experience may not always be a clear one. Because of this, the kind of misjudging just mentioned can occur, as for instance in a case like this one:

"For three years I have kept this experience to myself except for a friend and minister who I knew would not try to put me in a straitjacket.

"In July, 1958, I was in the hospital—attending physician, Dr. A. I had almost lost two sons earlier due to ruptured placenta, and had lost a little girl for the same reason in 1957. This one according to medical facts should have been lost too, and if she lived would have total brain destruction because at 6:10 A.M. the placenta had ruptured. There was no heartbeat, no oxygen supply to the baby. I was under oxygen and transfusion, but no drugs. I had had no pain, no contractions. My pulse was gone. The nurse at my head kept slapping my face and saying, 'Breathe, Mrs. M., breathe.'

"Dr. A. made hurried arrangements for an emergency sectional. He went out and told my people, 'The baby is lost. We are trying to save Mrs. M. Don't give up.'

"They ran down the hall with me, tanks and jars attached. I was placed on the table, the nurse still slapping my face.

"Right here I want to stress the fact that I was conscious and I was praying so very, very hard that the baby would be given life instead of myself and that my husband and mother would be able to raise it well and correctly. I guess it was the first time I had ever *really* prayed. Because I had always had a little bit of doubt that God was real, that Christ lived, I had probed into the old psychology books my father had studied at college in 1920, into yoga, the Rosicrucians, etc.

"But that day all of a sudden in the midst of feeling the incision being made and of having my face slapped, somewhere I saw Christ and my father who had died in 1957 standing guard. They weren't smiling. They were watching me with an intense expression. But they were with me, and they knew I saw them. Then they were gone.

"Then Dr. A., said, 'It's a girl.' The nurse said, 'Oh, Dr. A., you cut off her hand,' which was of course said to get a response out of me. But I didn't respond. I deliberately went to sleep. I knew everything was all right.

"When I awoke my bed was surrounded with friends all looking at me as if I were a corpse. They all wanted to be the first to tell me it was a girl. I had been married eleven years and always wanted one so much. But I already knew. I hated to disappoint them so I pretended to fall asleep again for I wasn't half as thrilled over having a daughter as I was over knowing Christ does live and that my father is with him. I kept repeating to myself, 'Now, I know.'

"Dr. Rhine, the proof that this wasn't a dream is definite because the baby lives. Another proof is that if I had been dreaming, Christ would have looked like the picture I have had in my house every day of my life and the way I have seen the world since then. The difference is more than a three-dimensional movie compared to a snapshot!

"As for me, I don't need any proof. Nothing could make me doubt it was a real miracle made possible by 'mind.' That is concentration in prayer, sincere and humble, and that, of course, *has* to come from the mind."

Was it new information? The question is, of course, did that person's vision of Christ and her deceased father have anything of an objective cause? Certainly she had a very convincing experience, overwhelmingly meaningful to her. But was "seeing" in that situation comparable to experiences bringing new information of extended reality? Today questions of that kind cannot be settled either way. Certainly items of memory, hopes, anxieties, early training, could have entered in, thus making a decision for present purposes impossible. And so, in this and every tentative case of ESP in which a question comes up as to whether the information is new or not, the old formula "when in doubt, say no," applies. Cases thus excluded as not necessarily involving ESP may have other values, but they could be misleading if included in the list of those to be used in the attempt to get a better understanding of the ESP process.

Sometimes peculiar mental states may momentarily be confused with ESP. One such is a phenomenon that is often called "out-of-the-body," a kind of experience fairly commonly reported. It evidently may occur under a range of physiological conditions wide enough to include what appear to be ordinary normal mental states as well as those which may be caused by severe physical or emotional crises. The state itself is not an ESP effect, even though ESP may occur in it. In the example below, the mental state was the result of injury:

"I was hurrying to finish a commercial painting to send to New York that night. I was alone in my upstairs studio except for our little fox terrier, who was evidently tormented with the summer fleas. Noting the hour, I judged I might give her a quick bath and still be able to finish the painting on time.

"After a quick tubbing she ran down the stairs, and I followed to open the screen door.

"Suddenly I found myself standing in my neighbor's front hall, and she was asking, 'What happened, Mrs. A.?' I was completely mystified.

" 'I don't know,' I said.

" 'But look at your smock!'

"I looked down. It was bloodstained. They called my husband from his office. A local doctor, too. Bleeding from mouth and ear and other symptoms indicated a 'melon' fracture of the skull. I had, it seemed, fallen the full length of the stairs.

"I remembered starting down, then only one other thing. I seemed to be standing upright at the foot of the stairs. But in absolute darkness. *At my feet* was something moaning, something lying on the floor.

" 'This means more trouble for Louis.' (My husband was near nervous collapse because of a disastrous financial loss.) 'Perhaps Mrs. T. (my neighbor) can help.' Between that thought and my awakening in her hall, everything is blank.

"I must have gone down our front steps (no handrail) along the street to the next house, up her steps (equally unsupported) and along her piazza, where I rang her bell and asked politely if Mrs. T. was in, *all* while I was unconscious and in a condition which made it impossible for me to stand without support after I did become conscious.

"The strangest part of this experience was the very clear sense of standing upright in the dark *above* the body that lay moaning on the floor."

The actual viewpoint from which the person seemed to view her own body "moaning on the floor" was the unusual aspect in that experience, which is of interest here. To see things, sense things, from a viewpoint outside one's self is, of course, no very unusual feat. In itself it does not necessarily mean the separation of mind and body which, naïvely, might seem to be implied. The agility of the mind is much too great for such an interpretation to be reliable.

Another kind of case occurs which poses the difficulty that for long confronted experimental work in ESP, and no doubt delayed its establishment until the present century. This is the problem the research itself was designed to solve, the difficulty of being certain that more than chance coincidence is involved. An experience described by a woman in California raises this question.

"Shortly after the end of the Second World War my husband was sent from his base in Italy to become a part of the Army of Occupation in Japan. It had been more than two years since we had seen each other, and our only communication was by letters.

"About the middle of January, 1946, I learned from a doctor that our young boy needed some drastic rectal surgery. The date set for the operation was January 31. About January 15 I wrote an airmail letter to my husband, begging him to telephone me the night of January 30, to hitchhike to Tokyo if necessary to make the right transoceanic telephone connections. But telephone me, he must! I had to be reassured by his voice, not by a letter which would be small comfort for me in this crisis.

"His most recent letter had stated definitely that the soonest he could possibly get home would be November, 1946, as the fellows were going home on a rotation basis, and he was quite far down the list.

"My neighbors, on the other side of my duplex living-room wall, remained awake the night of January 30, as I had told them my husband would call me at 11 P.M. (Why I believed that so intensely, I'll never know.) Suddenly at 11:05, the telephone rang; I flew to a wonderful connection to Tokyo, and then almost fainted as he told me he had never received any letter asking him to telephone, that he knew nothing about our son's scheduled surgery, but that he was calling from a booth on the pier at San Francisco and was to be discharged within three days.

"Several days later we compared stories and laughed at the chain of 'coincidences' which had almost a supernatural air about them.

"On January 15, the day I wrote the letter mentioning the surgery and setting January 30 as the date to place the telephone call, my husband was writing to me from his quonset hut near Yokohama. Suddenly a corporal dashed in and said, 'Sarge, the captain says you're going home—get packed, you're leaving in twenty minutes from the docks.' Thinking it was a joke, my husband checked, but found it was true. His captain said there was no explanation of how or why he had been picked, just that of the five hundred men in the area, his name had suddenly come up to go home. Of all the men in his company he was the only one to go home on that particular ship. To quote him: 'I didn't ask questions; I just hightailed it out of there.'

"My neighbors vouched for the fact that I had told them quite definitely my husband would telephone me the night of January 30 at 11 P.M., and they were also listening through the thin walls when I answered at the first ring. They rejoiced with me that I could hear his voice so clearly, and they were even happier when, eavesdropping, they learned he was already in the States. Proof enough of precognition?"

Precognition? It is a topic for a later chapter. Possibly it could explain the setting of the date when her husband would telephone. But the rest—her husband's orders to return and the actual timing of his call—must be relegated to coincidence. Even if more might have been involved, it is better in studying ESP to decide conservatively.

The phrase, "Just a coincidence," however, is one that has long been overworked where ESP is concerned. Until the discovery of

ESP, the easiest way to dispose of any puzzling experience now recognizable as involving it was to say it was only a coincidence. It is a way sometimes used even yet when skepticism and ignorance of the evidence for ESP are combined. According to this, all of the experiences so far given would be explained by the one blanket formula, coincidence, if their validity were accepted long enough for any explanation to be required.

Against this formula no one attempting to sort out presumptive instances of ESP from other kinds of experiences also coming from unconscious sources had a decisive argument until the actual existence of the ESP ability had been proven in the laboratory. Only then could a defense for them be made.

Now, knowing ESP does occur, one can claim for it with a much higher degree of assurance than before those experiences that fulfill the definition. Now one can say in defense of cases like those of the illustrations in this book, this is the way ESP would be expected to occur in life situations. New information would be received when the senses would not be involved. But the above case was different. ESP could hardly have brought the husband home just when he was needed; therefore his arrival can logically be called a chance coincidence, although a rare one.

The definite establishment of ESP by controlled research thus shows up as a solid foundation on which other explorations can be based. But the discovery of ESP as a definite human ability could not be made until a way was found to deal with this matter of coincidence, or as it has been called, the Hypothesis of Chance. And this in turn awaited the development of the field of statistics. Before that, attempts to find out experimentally whether such an ability as ESP existed were as difficult as were attempts to prove it in life experiences.

For instance, in 1882, in Derbyshire, England, lived a clergyman, the Reverend Mr. Creery.[1] He had five daughters, then between the ages of ten and seventeen. All but the youngest, as the father reported to the then newly founded Society for Psychical Research, in London, could frequently guess correctly cards or other objects hidden from them.

[1] Barrett, W. F. First report on thought reading. *Proceedings of the Society for Psychical Research, 1882–1883*, vol. 1, pp. 13–34.

A committee of eminent scholars went to the Creery home and made a number of tests with the girls. Although eventually suspicion was raised that the conditions of some of the experiments did not preclude the possibility of sensory cues, the question whether all of the results were obtained honestly does not change the fact that the investigating committee faced an insuperable difficulty in deciding the value of the results, even granting they were valid. The results were "good," but how good? Were they really beyond chance? How could the investigators be sure?

For instance, a few items from the first group of tests reported were:

OBJECT	RESULT
A white penknife	Correct
Box of almonds	Correct
Box of chocolate	Buttonbox
Threepenny piece	Failed
Penknife hidden	Failed to name place

Then, among other things, a series of tests with playing cards was tried and the report of results starts off like this:

CARD	GUESS
Two of Clubs	Right
Queen of Diamonds	Right
Four of Spades	Failed

The report goes on to say that out of fourteen successive trials nine were guessed correctly the first time, etc.

It is easy to see that even in the case of the card guesses, the chance, or probability of getting a hit, would be only one in fifty-two. But although the girl guessed nine out of fourteen correctly, what of it? It was not like finding an arrowhead or a diamond, or anything objective whose existence was a tangible fact. This was a case of judging the probability that a person could make that many hits just by chance; and though it seemed unlikely, still how unlikely was it? In the case of the penknife or the threepenny piece, not even a criterion like one in fifty-two could be cited to say whether the hit was a probable or improbable one.

A few years earlier, in France, Professor Charles Richet of Paris used the mathematics of probability in card experiments with his subject Leonie B., with whom he was making experiments in hypnosis and who in the hypnotic state had given suggestions of the extrasensory ability which is known as clairvoyance. To test it he enclosed playing cards in envelopes and asked the subject to identify them. In 1889, in one instance, comparable to that of the Creery result, she got twelve hits in fifteen trials.[2] Professor Richet gave the odds against chance of such a result on the basis of a chance expectation of one in fifty-two as "one quintillion to one." Thus it was that even before the end of the nineteenth century, statistical principles were beginning to be applied in parapsychology in cases in which it would be necessary to judge how probable a given outcome would be.

The necessary statistical principles for the evaluation of results in ESP card tests are based on an estimate of what coincidence by chance alone would produce under the given circumstances. Chance in such a context is, of course, the value which would result from entirely haphazard causes. With that value as the standard, the statistical procedure is to determine how much above or below it the actual results prove to be.

The values that chance alone would give in situations in general like these in card-calling tests had long before been worked out, first of all because gambling establishments needed to know them. At some early date in history it had been established, no doubt by trial and error, that if a guess were made at one of a known number of targets, arranged without any system or order, and so a purely random one, a hit would be made by chance, on the average, once in that number of trials—if the guesser knew the number of targets and did not know the targets themselves; that is, if the try were a "pure guess." For instance, if two decks of the twenty-five ESP cards were adequately shuffled and their orders compared, both decks would be randomly arranged; the hits would be chance and would average approximately five.

But if the person guessing the order of a pack of cards had some way of knowing what some of the cards are, say he could see the

[2] Rhine, J. B. *Extra-sensory Perception*. Boston: Bruce Humphries, 1934, p. 33.

top or bottom one or could recognize some of them by the backs as he tried to make one deck match the other, then his score should be higher than five per run. But if he could not see any of the cards or get any other kind of "sensory cue" from them and if then his score averaged higher than five, he must have known some of the symbols by ESP. But his excess over the chance average for the number of runs he made would have to reach a certain level or norm on which scientists have agreed before it could be considered acceptably significant of something more than chance.

In most sciences an experimental result is considered to be significant if it would not be expected to occur by chance more than once in twenty such tests. But ESP was something whose occurrence was, according to the expectations of the day, very unlikely to be a fact. On this account proof of it had to be stronger than ordinary. To be doubly sure, the criterion for significance in this field was set at one in fifty.

The first necessity in planning experiments that could be evaluated statistically, like the card-calling tests of ESP, had been that the number of targets be specified. From the beginning of the tests made at Duke University it was arranged that way—there were, for example, ten digits, or five symbols—instead of using free material like penknives and boxes of almonds for targets. In this the example of Richet was being followed.

More than that, statistical formulas had by that time been worked out so that, as with the playing-card deck of fifty-two cards, a numerical value could be given to show *how* good a result was, and how often it could be expected to occur by chance alone. Since it is easier to work with fives and tens in mathematical formulas than with fifty-two's, the simpler decks were preferable. But not only for this reason. Subjects seemed better able to keep in mind and respond to a small as well as to a limited number of choices.

The formula (based on the "laws of chance") would tell the result to be expected by chance alone, in the given number of trials with a given set of choices or targets. If the results were better than this "mean chance expectation" (MCE), the experimenter could tell how much better. A standard basis for comparison existed. Different conditions could be compared, their relative values studied. Thus, as these statistical methods were applied to ESP experiments, the guesswork went out and the new science, parapsychology, began.

Today, with the statistical tools available, multitudes of problems of everyday living as well as the relatively simple ones in this field can be solved. Fortunately it is not necessary for everyone to be a statistician in order to get the benefits of statistics. In fact, probably few people realize the extent to which statistical procedures affect their lives, from medicine to income taxes, because the end product, if not the process by which it is achieved, is painless. In the same way in parapsychology statisticians examine the results and judge their validity, and nonstatisticians take their word for it when they say the results are such that they are "mathematically significant." And because one can rely on the statisticians, it is possible in this presentation to minimize the statistical aspect. Interested mathematicians can always go to the original reports to find out what the exact values were.

However, the meaning of a few statistical terms which will be used in the presentation of some of the experimental results should be explained for the benefit of nonmathematicians. Since the result to be expected by chance alone in a given test depends on the number of trials, and with twenty-five trials in a standard ESP run, the expected chance average (MCE) is, of course, five. (The subjects in such runs are not told whether their individual calls are correct until the end of the run.) Thus in twenty-five runs, the number to be expected by chance, the MCE, would be $5 \times 25 = 125$.

These scores secured by chance alone, however, only *average* five, but individually they fluctuate around it. However the greater the number of runs, the nearer the total number of hits produced just by chance will approximate the average of five. The range of deviation from the five average was worked out long ago, and a "yardstick" called the standard deviation or SD was agreed upon to measure it. The SD thus is a measure of how far chance alone would be expected to vary in the number of scores to which it is applied. An SD for each number of runs is now available in appropriate tables in standard statistical manuals, and those likely to be needed in ESP experiments are given in some of the parapsychological books.[3] For runs up to ten and a few assorted higher numbers, the table says:

RUNS	SD
4	4.00
5	4.47
6	4.90
7	5.29
8	5.66
9	6.00
10	6.32
25	10.00
100	20.00

The number of hits in the given number of test runs is measured against the standard deviation. For instance if in twenty-five runs of ESP tests the total number of hits should be 150 when the mean chance expectation is only 125, then the experimental deviation is +25, or if the total test score should be only 100, it would be −25. The table says the standard deviation for 25 runs is ten, and so the experimental deviation thus is 25 ÷ 10 = 2.5 or two and a half times as great as chance alone should give. This value is called the critical ratio, or CR, the measure most frequently used in the following presentation.

The CR of course takes account not only of the rate of deviation but also of the number of runs that produced it. One could get a CR of 2.5 as in the example above in four test runs if the total score was 30. In four runs the chance average is 4 × 5 = 20, and so the score of 30 would mean an experimental deviation of +10. The standard deviation for four runs as shown in the table is 4, and therefore the CR = 10 ÷ 4 = 2.5. Carrying the comparison a little farther, 100 runs which yielded 550 hits, or a deviation of +50, would also yield a CR of 2.5, since the SD for 100 runs is 20. But the average score there would be only 5.5 while in the four-run example it would be 7.5.

While a CR of 2.5 usually represents a probability of about one

[3] Rhine, J. B., and J. G. Pratt. *Parapsychology, Frontier Science of the Mind.* Springfield: Charles C. Thomas, 1957, chap. 9.

hundred to one, in parapsychology it is taken as one in fifty. This is because a negative (below MCE) deviation can also be produced (by certain special psychological conditions, as will be seen later). The same statistics apply to a negative as to a positive deviation.

Although other values and other statistical procedures beside that of the CR are used in some of the evaluations of experimental data especially in more recent research, this is the most generally useful one, and the only one necessary to consider in the experimental work presented in these pages. Since the theory back of the CR is essentially simple, and with it as the basis of a vast amount of statistical analysis outside of parapsychology, the experimental research in the field has never been open to the charge sometimes made against it, that "the statistics are wrong." The statistics are reliable, when the conditions they demand for their application are met. It has been the aim of parapsychologists to meet those conditions by guarding against errors of recording, of sensory cues, of selection of data, etc., by requiring a high standard for significance, and by repetition of experiments and the confirmation of results by other workers. It is by the combination of all these rules and safeguards that the possum in this stew is to be recognized.

CHAPTER 5

Belief in the Truth of ESP

"I SAW it myself! I heard it myself. It must be true."

One might hear statements like that any day of the week; what is seen or heard is likely to be taken for the truth. In actual vision, or other modes of sense perception, doubts have little place. Sometimes the person can be argued out of his belief, but initially he believes his senses.

But what about ESP? Does he believe that too? Its secret origin shrouds all aspects of its inception in mystery. Yet it would seem that here too the information would be believed. Obviously in ESP a contact with the objective world is made, for tests do succeed. Equally obviously it would seem that the reality so encountered would be recognized for what it is, and so believed. But often the end result in consciousness does not bear this out. As Chapters 3 and 4 suggest and as later ones will show, the messages may or may not be recognized as true. Certainly they do not always, maybe not even often, stand out distinct from all the other items of the unconscious. They seem not to carry the assurance of "I saw" or "I heard." Either doubt was present from the start or else the conviction, "This is true," got lost along the way.

The question is important; more so than might at first appear, because the explanation of all the experiences that bring less than complete messages, and all the experimental results that are less than perfect; in fact all the mistakes and imperfections of ESP must be explained. Either the initial contact of the psyche with the external world is faulty so that the person never gets a perfect impression and doubts the truth of his message from the beginning, or else he gets it truly enough at the inception but then secondary influences come in before the message gets to consciousness, and because of them, the mistakes and imperfections are introduced. The latter seems to be the case rather than the former because, for one thing, in some of the experiences people have, there is evidence to show that initially the message was believed, that it was taken for the truth.[1] From these experiences and from others that show uncertainty, it is possible to reconstruct what really seems to have happened and to see how initial belief can be destroyed as secondary influences come in along the way.

An instance in which belief persists, and even seems to get stronger, comes from a woman in New York.

"My very young daughter was working with the United Nations in Korea before the Korean War. At that time people hardly knew where Korea was on the map. She was the only woman traveling around on trains with a group of men setting up election booths getting ready for the free election. The details of their time there are long since forgotten. But she was there and very far away.

"One morning I woke up with a slight feeling, 'Alice might call me today,' although I knew that this was a very long telephone call. This feeling persisted through the day and I did a lot of things and ran around being made very restless by it. Late in the afternoon I stopped in at the house of her grandmother who was ill and blue and begged me to stay to dinner with her and help her pass the evening. 'No, Mother, I can't. I have the idea that Alice will call me tonight.' And Mother, although she was very stiff about most things, said, 'If you feel so, then she will call!' I went home. Well, when I got inside my front door, the knowledge of her call hit me like a thunderbolt. It was not guesswork, or hoping, or wishful thinking; it was pure, direct knowledge. I was unable to eat and for some reason was exhausted. I went to bed, and finally thinking I might go to sleep I left the light on near me. I fell heavily asleep. At 11 P.M. the telephone rang (I knew, of course, what it was) and it took twenty minutes for the various centrals to connect up with one another and then came the little voice so clear 'Hello, Mother—are you surprised?'

"The point about this sure knowledge is the greater because Alice herself did not know that she was going to call me that

[1] Rhine, Louisa E. Conviction and associated conditions in spontaneous cases. *Journal of Parapsychology*, 15 (1951) 164–191.

evening. It turned out that someone else who was going to call America couldn't do so for some reason and Alice at the last minute substituted her call. In short I knew long before she did that she would call."

In experiences such as that, and they are by no means infrequent, the message is not only a complete one, but it is obviously taken with conviction. As this person says, it was "pure direct knowledge," and she knew it was.

Even when the message is incomplete, when some essential part of it is missing, it often happens that an emotion appropriate to it is felt anyway. In such instances the emotion itself is evidence that in the deep unconscious an impression about reality is being taken seriously.

The girl in the following case might not know the nature of the threat but she believed one existed nonetheless.

"I loved my father very specially, and we were close in sympathy. I was a child of his first wife who died when I was born. My father idealized her, and I guess I idealized Father as I grew up. I disliked my stepmother. She caused unhappiness to my father. I was always deeply sensitive to his moods and feelings. I believe the closeness of feeling and mental contact made possible the experience I will speak of. I do not think it would have happened in my case except with someone I am deeply concerned about.

"I was a young girl around twenty years old. It was Sunday. I was worried about Dad's not being happy over the home situation. After dinner he disappeared. We lived on a small farm. It was not unusual for him to take a stroll over the grounds to observe crops, etc. Even so, all at once a terrible sense of fear took hold of me, so great it had a physical effect like a terrible weight on my heart. I felt frantic. I felt I must find Dad. I thought something was happening to him. I never felt such terror and extreme worry. I had no way of knowing which way he had gone. I ran over the farm. I asked neighbors a quarter of a mile away if he had been seen. No one knew. My stepmother did not know. I told no one of my fright as I tried not to believe it. But I was as if desperate. I finally felt helpless. I went to a favorite tree and there alone I knelt and prayed for father to be protected. I never prayed like that before. All at once my nerves quieted and I felt at ease as if something were lifted from me. I went back to the house. Quite a while later Dad came back.

"But later on, of his own accord, he told me of his experience. He had gone into the woods adjoining our farm. He came across an old deserted barn and had gone into it. He was looking at some things in it when all at once he heard a sound. He turned and saw a huge rattlesnake coiled to spring a few feet away. He was stunned, but found a stone and an iron bar and succeeded in killing it just in time and saved himself. He said it was a huge snake and very dangerous. The time coincided with the time when I felt that fear. It was unmistakable."

The fear and its specific cessation in that case was the substance of the ESP impression. It and the action she took because of it is testimony that she believed her father was in danger and did not question her own certainty.

Sometimes the actual idea and the emotion too may be lacking, but the person does something, takes some action appropriate to the situation, anyway. Of course no direct preventive action was possible in the preceding case. The girl could not control the snake. She could only hope and pray, but in cases like the following one, something quite specific could be done.

"I am forty-four years old, the wife of a trial attorney and the mother of a teenage daughter and an eleven-year-old son.

"Ten years ago when my daughter, D., was only six years old, we lived high on a hill—from which we could see over the entire valley. My daughter had to walk down our hill to the corner, then turn and go down another block to the corner where she caught the school bus.

"Usually there were a few other children who went down and came back at the same time, and as I had a baby boy about a year old and as there were eighty-eight steps down our front yard, I sat in our breakfast nook and watched her both coming and going. She was well trained to look for cars and had only one street to cross, which was not a busy one.

"On this particular day, as was my custom, I sat in the breakfast nook about two o'clock waiting for the bus to bring D. home. But this day both my baby and I were recovering from a siege of flu and I was still in my robe while he was taking a nap.

"As I sat smoking a cigarette and drinking a cup of tea, an uneasy feeling came over me. I tried to dismiss it, but it would not go away. I tried to pinpoint the cause of it but could not.

"All of a sudden it came to me that D. was going to be in danger and so strong was the feeling that I flew into my bedroom, put on some clothes, woke up the baby, bundled him into warm things, put him in the stroller, and got us down the steps and to the bus stop.

"In a few minutes the bus came and D. got off, but for some reason no other children got off with her. She seemed fine—nothing was amiss—and I was disgusted with myself. Scarcely waiting for her, I wheeled the stroller around and started up the hill, D. some forty or fifty feet behind me.

"Suddenly I heard a man's voice say, 'Little girl, come here. I want to show you something.' Turning around I saw the most vile looking man on a dilapidated bicycle that looked as if it had come off a junk heap. He was clothed in a filthy black leather jacket and torn, dirty pants. He had several days' growth of beard, shoes so worn they had slits in them.

"One hand inside his jacket low, he said he had a puppy he wanted to show her. I put the brake on the stroller, told D. in firm tones to come to me and ordered him to leave. D., in her hurry, dropped her pencil box and papers and stopped to pick them up. He kept on trying to persuade D. and even started up the hill after us.

"I told him I would call the police if he did not leave, so with a vile remark he pedalled off into traffic. I called the police, and a very nice officer came out and heard my story. He said since the man had neither threatened D. nor touched her they could do nothing, but that they would be on the lookout for him.

"This experience shook me to the core and I have never forgotten it."

Action as in that instance, taken sometimes against inclination, almost against common sense, speaks for a basic conviction that it was necessary. One can say that had the persons in such situations actually seen the dangers with their eyes, their responses would have been the same. The same emotion would have been elicited, the same action taken, and so in these cases when the message comes from the deep unconscious, a basic conviction that the impression is true is shown.

In the ESP process, then, there is reason to think that believing may be primary, too. But here doubts may come easier, or perhaps the conviction that the impression is true is more easily lost. At any rate, in ESP experiences doubts about the truth of the message often do come when the person begins to think about the situation, and those doubts dull the first sure edge of certainty. Often it is possible to see the reason why. For one thing conscious reflection can conjure up a multitude of reasons why the message cannot be true. Sometimes it may be simply because the information is too unwelcome to be admitted. Such may have been the reason the woman in the following letter did not act on the intuition when she had it.

"A year ago the 25th of last January my husband had been in ill health and to some degree despondent, over a period of several weeks, although he continued to work. Not realizing the seriousness of his illness, I too continued to work (as I had throughout the twenty-four year period of our married life with the exception of the times I had given up to bring our children—four girls and one boy—into the world).

"On Monday morning, January 25, 1954, I arrived at work and things went on as usual until 10:02 A.M. (I am certain of the time as I checked my watch), when I was suddenly aware of a very peculiar sensation that something was wrong and the two words 'Howard's dead' went through my mind. For just a moment I was terribly befuddled, but after assuring myself that such could not possibly be the case I became quite calm and serene. I never gave it another thought for the balance of the day, until 4 P.M., when my phone rang and a neighbor at home informed me that there had been an accident and I was wanted home immediately.

"The thought never occurred to me that it might be one of the children; my first question being, 'Is it Howard?' Yes, it was—my husband had shot himself that morning and the doctor and medical examiner placed the time at 10 A.M., stating that he had died instantly. The 'instant' part of it evidently could well have been the cause of the peaceful sensation I experienced after I heard those two terrible words in my mind that morning."

One can almost see there too that in the first instant there was belief. But the message with all its emotion-stirring potential was at once rejected by the rational conscious mind, which would not entertain a thought so unacceptable.

There are also cases when the thought, whether or not acceptable, is a very unlikely one:

"Five years after [another experience] I was [actually] being strangled. I won't take up space with the details but it was very close to the end for me. I was fourteen hundred miles away from my mother, estranged from her, hadn't written her in many weeks. In fact she had said she wanted never to see or hear from me again.

"However, I did go home and was welcomed about four months later. One day, in a confiding mood, she told me that she'd had a terrifying experience about four months before about midmorning (10:30 A.M.). She was working at the kitchen table when suddenly she saw my face before her, and it was hideous—swollen and purple with my eyes popping out. She was very upset, but the family convinced her it was just another of her 'imaginings.'

"Though I was sure her vision had happened as it actually did to me and at the same time, I never let on to her. I wanted to keep her from further upset and probing."

Surely just because the impression was a gruesome and unwelcome one, it might have been rejected. But even without that, doubtless the person could have been argued out of belief in it because it was unexpected and unlikely. The conscious mind builds heavily on the rationality of its beliefs. It anticipates that new experience will conform, to an extent, with old, and is always reluctant before the unexpected. "I could scarcely believe my eyes," is another any-day-of-the-week kind of expression.

In other cases it seems that just a bit of self-doubt may break conviction down to uncertainty. This evidently was true in the case of the college girl who told of the following experience:

"I was in college. I led a rather simple life on the whole while there, as I was not very strong. My studying was done mainly at 6 A.M. rather than at night. (I could thus accomplish much more in a shorter period of time.) Nine P.M. found me getting into bed on a week night.

"It was late January. Suddenly the college was thrown into a state of consternation by the fact that the wife of one of the faculty members was missing. I did not know her, had never even seen her. I knew her husband only by sight. Local papers worked on the theme that she had last been seen walking along the main highway when it was snowing. For no obvious reason, I *dis*believed this. Shortly I began having an inner picture every night upon retiring as to where the woman was. This went on for a number of weeks. In this inner picture I saw her lying in a wooded swampy area in which the region abounded. I saw her hat and coat, the coat trimmed with a fur collar. She was partially in a puddle of water. At the same time, I was having to repress on numerous occasions when out for a country drive an impulse to tell the driver, when we reached a certain crossroad, to turn *left*. All I would say was that I felt the woman to be out that way and not anywhere near the high road. My fear of being ridiculous kept me from saying, 'Turn left and go very slowly.' I felt I well might lose the scent many times before actually finding the woman. (Later, my friends remarked that I had made the comment more than once when we struck the crossroad that I believed the lost woman to be out there.)

"Then finally, in March, her body was discovered by a woodsman in the very spot and area that I had inwardly seen and felt it to be, and in the very position. When the news broke of the find, I said to my friends, 'Before you read me the account of the find, I want to tell you something.' I related my experience. They were trembling violently when I finished my account. 'How did you know?' they asked. 'That is exactly as the account is given in the newspaper.' To this of course I had no answer. They were also concerned because I had not told them to turn left on the road all those weeks when we drove out that way. 'You would have considered me out of my mind; also, we might have had to do it a number of times; I might very well have not hit it the first time.' "

In such a case, one can see the effect of the perfectly rational conscious thought, "I could be wrong. How can I possibly know for sure?"

In these and other ways it is quite evident that rational mental processes can come to overshadow the initial feeling of certainty, of conviction that the message was true. But still, it appears that the impression was at first taken for the truth.

Of course the subject matter is not always so important. It may simply be a casual occurrence and as such not raise a question of whether it is or is not true. It may even be forgotten until fulfillment brings it back to memory. For instance, take an episode like this one:

"One night I dreamed that I walked to a nearby butcher shop. When I got up the street I had to walk around a moving van that was drawn up over the sidewalk. As I got to the other side of the van, there were two old friends who had married years ago, and in all those years I had never heard of them.

"The next morning I had forgotten the dream but decided to go get some meat. Then a block from home I had to walk around a van and there were my friends, just as I had dreamed."

It is easy to see that in a case like that, not particularly significant or outstanding in any way, the dream was just as innocuous as the reality, and so for that reason did not stand out, nor did the question of its truth come up.

Thus it is that from accounts of life experiences, the conviction aspect seems to be a real and integral part of them. Received unconsciously and believed unconsciously as the message is, it is only later that the implicit belief in the truth of it may be impaired, and usually when the message, often because of the emotional impact it makes, comes in conflict with rational considerations.

In the laboratory, the picture at first sight seems different. There, for instance, when a subject makes a series of guesses, say at the symbols in a deck of ESP cards, he identifies some of them correctly (when total scores are well above the number chance coincidence would give) and misses others. He does not know from guess to guess the correct ones from the incorrect ones. Occasionally he may have a definite feeling that a given call is correct, but about most of them he only hopes, and does not feel convinced.

Various experimenters have asked their subjects to make "confidence checks" beside the calls they think are surely correct.[2] Then the checked calls are tallied separately. But usually they prove to be only a very little better than the others. Even a little has a degree of significance, of course, if it occurs with sufficient regularity; but certainly the fact that almost as many of these calls as of the unchecked ones are incorrect shows that in general the feeling of conviction in tests is not a very reliable one.

But if in experiments the person has no reliable feeling of conviction about the correctness of his calls, what about the assumption just made in connection with life experiences, that initially the information is believed to be true? Does the psyche in this situation not believe that its impressions of the targets were correct even when they were? Is the situation in tests different from that in a real-life ESP experience? It is a point that needs to be looked into carefully—particularly to see if here too, as in the life experiences, there could have been initial certainty that might have been lost because secondary influences undermined it.

Of course one can remark here, incidentally, that if the situation in experiments had been such that the person had a reliable feeling of conviction about his responses, the questions raised by ESP would have been solved long ago—at the same time, let us say, that the questions about sense perception began to be under-

[2] Schmeidler, Gertrude. An experiment on precognitive clairvoyance. Part V. Precognition scores related to feelings of success. *Journal of Parapsychology,* **28** (1964) 109–125.

stood. Extrasensory perception, in that event, would have been as obvious as seeing and hearing. But the situations are different in many ways. The question is, Why are the calls in tests not believed to be the truth when they are in fact correct? Why should this lack of confidence be shown in test calls, instead of the conviction of truth expressed in many of the life experiences?

In the first place it can be taken for a certainty that reported cases are necessarily selected to some extent by the people who report them. Certainly an experience that carried with it strong conviction from the start would be noticed and remembered, and therefore have a much greater chance of being reported than if it had made a lesser impression. For this reason the high number of cases that show the person convinced of the truth of his impression may in reality represent something like the small excess of correct calls of those which in experiments are given confidence checks. In other words, it may not really be true that confidence or conviction is shown in life incidents more often than in tests.

It is certainly true that strong conviction is often absent in experiences too. As the examples show, it is lacking for various causes ranging from the doubts raised for emotional reasons, to those of conscious reasoning and even by simple inattention, whether that inattention is above or below the conscious level. But it is clear in life experiences that most of the reasons for lack of, or loss of, confidence are secondary. Those discussed earlier in this chapter are only a few of the factors that can be seen to destroy the person's confidence that his ESP impression was correct. In later chapters others will appear, but all of them seem to be secondary. They do not preclude the possibility that the information may have been received initially with belief.

It seems logical then to look for secondary reasons why conviction is lacking in experimental calls, just as it is destroyed by secondary reasons in life experiences. It is logical, but a logic bolstered by facts, to assume that in this situation too, the pertinent information—say about the order of the symbols in the deck—if known at all is known as the truth. The facts that support the logic result from a number of so-called empirical checks.

In the early days of experimentation at Duke, and after the first results had been published showing that subjects like Linzmayer had identified targets very much more frequently than chance co-incidence could account for, the question was raised whether the basis for estimating the chance expectancy was sound. Rather than trust to the well-established rule that in a situation like that of the ESP card deck, in which the statistical assumption was that the likelihood of coincidence by chance alone was on the average one in five, or five per deck, certain critics thought the subject's calls should be checked against an actual series of cards *for which they were not intended*. The supposition was that somehow there might be peculiarities in these guesses made by a human being, so that they would match other decks as well as those intended.

And so a number of empirical checks were made by various experimenters. One of these checks (by Carpenter and Phalen) involved 10,000 matchings of calls against shuffled decks for which they were not intended,[3] another (Martin) involved 25,000.[4] But the empirical check to top all empirical checks was made by a young mathematician then at Duke, and, at the time, a consultant of the Parapsychology Laboratory, Dr. J. A. Greenwood.[5] His check included 500,000 matchings. It was made, he said, "with all known factors but chance ruled out as far as possible." For it he used the calls of the first twenty runs of each of the five best Duke subjects. The calls were copied from the actual records. Then by a complicated ritual of randomizing decks of new cards, these call runs were checked against the order of the cards in the new decks.

The result of all the empirical checks just proved the foregone conclusion that the "laws of chance" operate, even when ESP cards and actual calls are used, if ESP is excluded by the conditions.

In at least a negative way these empirical checks have a bearing on the question of whether in tests information is admitted in the unconscious with the unquestioned assumption that it is true.

[3] Carpenter, R. C., and Harold R. Phalen. An experiment in card guessing. *Journal of Parapsychology*, 1 (1937) 331–343.

[4] Martin, Dorothy R., and Frances P. Stribic. Studies in extra-sensory perception. I. An analysis of 25,000 trials. *Journal of Parapsychology*, 2 (1938) 23–30.

[5] Greenwood, J. A. Analysis of a large chance control series of ESP data. *Journal of Parapsychology*, 2 (1938) 138–146.

They show at least that when tests are made using specified decks of cards, if significant results are obtained, then these decks and no others were accepted as the target decks. It seems safe to assume then that the incorrect calls, and also the lack of conviction about which calls were correct, would have to be ascribed to secondary causes. Even at this stage of the discussion it is not too difficult to find at least one secondary factor that might have been involved, the factor of intensity of the subject's interest. For the most obvious difference between the case and the experimental situation is that of the motives and interests involved. In life the subject matter is of direct, often vital, concern to the person; even if it is not a crisis, still it is a real event in real life. As such the individual is personally involved and implicitly interested.

In the laboratory the subject's interest is at best "contrived." Even the most interested, enthusiastic, and devoted subject cannot care deeply whether the next symbol he is to guess is a cross or a star or a wave. Usually he would like to please the experimenter and acquit himself well, earn approbation both from himself and from others by making a high score. But even so, his actual attitude is probably nearer that of the woman in the little episode that occurred on her way to the butcher shop than that of the woman who pushed the stroller down and up the hill to protect her little daughter from the suspected pervert.

Another inherent difference between life and laboratory situations comes in when the laboratory situation involves a series of individual trials. For instance the calling of symbols of an ESP card deck is a "25 in 1" kind of trial. It has *duration,* and repetition of effort, which calls for an appreciable interval of sustained and unwavering attention and concentration. If any one of these factors changes even temporarily, the likelihood of a miss is increased. But all this is in contrast to the life situation, which usually is more like getting a momentary if not instantaneous glimpse of something, or, of snapping a camera for a single scene rather than having it run on as when a series is taken.

All of this suggests that in the laboratory the need is to provide special and enduring motivation if the subject is to keep the task in focus long enough to succeed.

Only a few occasions are on record when it seems that such

especially strong motivation was induced in the laboratory situation, a motivation that approached that of real life. One such occasion arose in connection with a little girl named Lillian.[6] It was in the spring of 1936, and Lillian was then nine years old. She came of a large and broken family and was in a children's home, the Wright Refuge in Durham, N.C., until the family situation could be straightened out. One does not know for sure, of course, just what a child's state of mind may be in such a situation, but it seems safe to suppose that Lillian's little world was considerably shaken. A new star in her firmament might have quickly come to be important.

At this particular time a young woman at the Duke Parapsychology Laboratory, then Miss Margaret Pegram, had undertaken an ESP experiment with some of the children at the Refuge. The object of it was to try out a number of different techniques in testing ESP in children to find out which one was best.

The tests were carried out like a little game, on a low table at the edge of the playground, experimenter and subject usually sitting on the ground on either side of it. In all, twelve girls and nine boys from six to thirteen years of age took the tests, using five different techniques. The results, although statistically significant, were not published in detail because the conditions were not as stringent as the laboratory standards demanded. The flaw was mainly that only one experimenter handled the test. In fully approved ESP experiments then, and even today, a two-experimenter arrangement is required. This requirement goes beyond the demands made upon researchers in other sciences, but parapsychology then, and in some quarters even today, was very low on the totem pole. The accuracy and even the simple honesty of experimenters were not taken for granted by the scientific world.

The test that Lillian was taking is the one called "open matching." The experimenter would place one card of each symbol, making five key cards, in a row face up on the table between herself and the child. Then she gave the child a well-shuffled, inverted deck of ESP cards and asked him to lay each one oppo-

[6] Reeves, Margaret Pegram, and J. B. Rhine. Exceptional scores in ESP tests and the conditions. I. The case of Lillian. *Journal of Parapsychology,* **6** (1942) 164–173.

site the key card he thought it matched. When all had been placed, the experimenter turned each pile over, counted and recorded the number of hits.

Each child was given a candy reward for "trying," no matter how poorly he did, but a bigger piece if he scored a seven (five, of course, being "chance"), or two pieces for a twelve; and, if anyone could get all twenty-five cards right, fifty cents!

Lillian had become, through successive test periods, one of the four best subjects. She had an average of nearly six per run over one hundred runs of twenty-five.

Nothing in the record indicates whether or not it was her winnings thus far that motivated her, but one can well suspect a stronger motive in the making. One day she got a twenty-three. No other child had made a score approaching that, but Lillian seemed to be bothered by the two she missed almost more than pleased about the twenty-three she hit.

It seems clear it was not the fifty-cent prize she had just missed that troubled her as much as something else which comes out in the letter she wrote and gave to Miss Pegram before the next session. It ran like this:

May 11, 1936

Dear Margaret,

I enjoy you coming. I am very glad you can come. We like to play cards with you. I hope you enjoy playing too. I am glad I got 23 of the cards right. But I want to get all of them right. —I like you very much. I don't want to go home, for I will miss you very much. I am going to try to come to Duke [to Lillian, Margaret of course was "at Duke"] when I go home so I won't be so lonesome.

With much love,
Lillian

At the next session, with a deck of cards she had not seen before, Lillian scored first only a three, then an eight. But then, saying that this time she would get twenty-five, she turned first slightly away from the table with a serious, "Don't say anything. I am going to try something."

She closed her eyes for a few seconds, then, moving her lips as if speaking to herself, she slowly dealt out the cards. After she finished and before the cards were checked, she remarked, "I was wishing all the time that I would get twenty-five!"

She did. Every card was in the correct pile opposite its own key card.

In the scientific report of this little drama the situations are carefully analyzed for evidence to show that this small girl could have been cheating and that somehow she outwitted the experimenter and the several child observers, none of whom saw anything suspicious in Lillian's performance. But nothing could be found to suggest that she could have peeked.

Now that ESP has been firmly established, the episode can be taken to be one of the rare occurrences when in a formal test special motivation was so aroused that it became after all practically a real-life situation. It could scarcely have been otherwise to a lonely, affection-starved youngster, who by a perfect score could win the approbation of the new bright star in her heaven.

A case like this seems to say not only that the psyche can make contact with reality even in test situations, but that even when the item is a whole deck of cards, the message about them can include the correct identification of them all. But such instances are fairly rare. The circumstances are difficult to stage, and do not often come about naturally.

In most experimental situations no such real-life pressure exists. Even the strongest motivation that a given experimenter and subject combination can produce as a test series is undertaken is likely to be a somewhat flickering and wavering thing. In the course of twenty-five responses, let us say, many mental crosscurrents can affect the subject's scoring. And these add up to interfering secondary effects, different from those in the life examples, but still analogous to them. Considering all this, it is a lucky feature of ESP that it does operate in test situations to a sufficient degree that statistical evaluation proves it. The difference between real-life and laboratory situations is something like that in mining: sometimes a real vein is struck, but at other times the miner must be content to screen out fine particles of ore from the sand of the riverbed. If he is in the latter situation, he is glad to get even a small residue. He knows he well might have failed even to find that much.

The situation in the laboratory, then, is one of sifting out the particles of ore and being thankful that it is possible to find a residue. In this case the residue may be considerably dulled by impurities, so that the bright, true color of the ore (the conviction) seems absent. But there is reason to think that, after all, it is just the same underneath. After all, it is reality that has been tapped. It would appear that the initial impression must have been taken seriously, no matter what crosscurrents later led to doubt and uncertainty.

CHAPTER 6

The Types of Subject Matter

ESP, like seeing and hearing, brings the person information. Like seeing and hearing, it brings direct information about reality, about the extended world: a fire at home, danger or death in the family, and, in tests, things like the symbols on hidden cards. But here no sense organs intervene. The route of this information traces back to the deep unconscious where, somehow, it was *available*. There, in some still mysterious way, a direct contact of mind and external reality must have occurred which as yet no man-conceived law explains.

Unable yet to answer how, the next logical question is what. What part or kind of reality is thus available? The answer comes from the experiments and experiences that involve ESP. The range of availability of material can be measured by the spread of information these embrace. That spread, however, can be viewed in different ways. One can see it objectively, as it involves the world of space and time, or subjectively, as it concerns the personal values and relationships of the individual. The first one, the range of accessibility over the outside world, concerns us here. The psychological range is another question; one for a chapter of its own.

History had a hand in revealing the areas of reality that are available to ESP, a fact which has both fortunate and unfortunate aspects. History says they are of three different types: human thoughts, impersonal objects or events, and also occurrences of the future. The fortunate aspect is that at least the job of their discovery is done. Today we can take it from there. But unfortunately the illogic of history has considerably tangled up and slowed the understanding of psi ability from what it might have been.

Had pure logic been involved, instead of the quirks of history, the first question which would have been asked when human experiences suggested that information could come in without the senses, would probably have been the one asked here: What is this range of information? What types of psi can be distinguished? Although that was not the way it started, the answer to these questions might have been hinted at by the experiences themselves. For example the topic might have been an inanimate object, as in this instance from California:

"Once I was accused of taking a watch from a bathroom in the house where I roomed and boarded. Everyone thought I was guilty and shunned me. I was very upset—to move out would convince them all I was the guilty one, so I prayed and repeated over and over, 'Where is that watch?' After a week I had this dream about the bathroom. There wedged between the tub, its leg and the wall, was the watch, suspended (old type bathtub). As I awoke and the dream cleared up, I said, 'That's where it is.'

"I went to the bathroom, and sure enough there it was—what to do now. I was in a worse spot. I didn't take it, but I knew where it was so I lay awake thinking. To clear myself the watch must be found. If I told I dreamed it, I would be laughed at. So I went to work and while there I gathered letters from pieces of paper, etc., to make up the words, 'Look between leg and wall of bathtub for the watch.'

"Placing the same lettering on the envelope, I sent it to the owner of the house. The day the letter was received the watch was found. And, when I returned, they asked me if I knew they had found the watch. I said, 'No,' and asked who found it. Then they showed me the letter. I acted amazed, of course. They apologized. They connected it with some visitor in the house because of no name on the envelope, and I was cleared—through a dream."

From all experiences such as this, in which the impression received in the unconscious concerned an inanimate thing or event, the type of ESP now referred to as clairvoyance would have been recognized.

Then there would have been the experiences that involved only someone's thought, as in this example from the same woman in

California who dreamed about the watch, and who incidentally is typical of many people whose experiences come in various types and forms.

"When I was about twenty I was employed in a department store in Milwaukee, Wisconsin. One day as I was busily waiting on a customer I heard my mother call loud and clear, 'Violette.' And to the amazement of my customer, I turned and answered, 'Yes, Mother,' in a loud voice. All standing near turned to me. I felt very embarrassed; I told the lady whom I had been waiting on that I had distinctly heard my mother call. She calmed me by saying, 'I wouldn't believe otherwise, for you answered as if she were across the store.' No need to say more of that except I wrote my mother who lived four hundred miles from there about my uncanny experience, and she wrote back that on that very day she was in the garden and wanted the hoe, and had momentarily forgotten I wasn't home and turned toward the house and called me—fully expecting an answer. Then she realized I was gone and felt funny about it all—but wasn't it strange that I heard and answered her?"

From experiences such as these, the suggestion is that thoughts as well as things can be available to ESP. The type of occurrences now known as telepathy would have been isolated long ago had such reasoning prevailed.

Anyone analyzing reports of human experiences and making classifications of them such as these of clairvoyance and telepathy would soon have noticed that the information, were it thing or thought, was apparently available regardless of where it was located, whether near or far from the person. It does not take many cases to show in this kind of process, that space apparently loses its character, for it does not appear to separate or limit information as it does in sense perception. In examples already mentioned, for instance, the girl dreamed about a watch in the bathroom of the house in which she lived, and also heard her mother's call when they were four hundred miles apart.

With distances obviously immaterial, pure logic alone might then have asked, "Without distance, what is time?" and the third kind of case, that involving the future, would hardly have been surprising. It might rather have been expected, or even looked for. However, it would not have been necessary to hunt for instances in which the subject matter available in the unconscious was something that had not yet happened. A category of perception of "future events," the one parapsychologists now call precognition (a term similar to the old-fashioned word prophecy), would have built up probably even more rapidly than those of clairvoyance and telepathy, for experiences are reported very frequently in which the subject matter is some future situation or event, for instance as in the experience of a man who now lives in Brooklyn:

"I am a U.S. Customs official. In the closing months of 1948 I had a dream that concerned a visit by me to Germany, which happens to be the land of my father's birth. I often had ideas, however remote, of someday visiting the place, but the probability of such a venture seemed very slight, especially in view of the unsettled conditions that existed in Germany for some years after the war.

"Back to the dream. I dreamt that I had surely visited Germany and one of the things that stood out was the fact that I was in a railroad district and observed several men in very sombre attire with lamps strapped across their chest. The surrounding country was a shambles and a general atmosphere of poverty prevailed. In the dream I ventured into a restaurant and after ordering my meal the waiter asked me how I intended to pay for it. I explained by opening my wallet and displaying a liberal amount of paper currency. The waiter appeared to be satisfied and explained that they had been having considerable difficulty with military personnel who had been presenting bogus currency or other currency not acceptable at that time. As I opened my wallet and displayed the money, I suddenly realized that I had been indiscreet. There I was in a strange country—hostile a short time before. After that the dream became a bit vague and disconnected.

"It was during the week following the dream that I was called into my superior's office and asked whether I would have any objection to going abroad for several months. I asked where, and was told that the mission would take me to Germany. I would like to point out here that the nature of my position did not at this time include trips outside the U.S. Arrangements were made that afternoon for my plane trip to Washington, clearance through the State Department, and orientation for the mission. I left Washington, D.C., the following Tuesday by Army transport plane for Germany, and arrived in Rhein-Main Airport, Frankfurt, Germany, in the early hours of the morning. On the plane trip I related the strange dream to the chap I was to work with for several months.

"We checked in at the Hotel Carlton in Frankfurt and made arrangements to proceed to Berlin via the military train, the only train leaving Frankfurt for Berlin at that time. The departure time was 6 P.M.

"It was during this trip that the dream began to crystalize. It being my first trip abroad, I remained awake most of the night, peering out of the windows at the countryside. There was not much to be seen because of the darkness, added to the fact that there was an almost continuous downpour. When we arrived at Kassel, Germany, just before crossing over into the Soviet Zone, I was especially curious and was quite amazed to see two men in shabby clothes which appeared to be dyed army uniforms with fatigue caps. *Strapped to their chests were the lamps that I had seen in my dream.* They were evidently employees of the railroad.

"It was during the conduct of our official business in Berlin that my partner and I, upon the recommendation of a chap we had met at the Harnick House (hotel), decided to visit the Intourist Nightclub in the Soviet Sector of Berlin. Accompanied by two friends, Germans, we made the trip by automobile and arrived at the nightclub about 11 P.M. During the meal, which was served by German waiters, though the establishment was under Russian management, my friend had left the table for a few minutes and it was at this time that the German waiter approached me and asked *how we intended to pay for the meal. I automatically opened my wallet and showed him the American currency.* It so happened that I had in addition to other bills, fifty new American one dollar bills and it made quite a wad. *I had done unthinkingly exactly what I had done in my dream.* Needless to say I experienced the same feeling that I had in the dream, that is, that I had been indiscreet in displaying the currency in a public place of doubtful reputation.

"P.S. I neglected to relate that the waiter upon viewing the currency stated that it was the policy of the restaurant to accept only American currency or Swiss francs."

If the dividing of cases were to have gone on like this, after all those had been classified that definitely concerned the three types, of things, thoughts, and the future, a great many would have remained that did not fit into a single category, but had elements of more than one of them, or whose elements could not be totally disentangled. For instance the dream of the woman in an early example that involved her husband and their son's death by drowning, could have been based on the drowning. If so, then it was of the clairvoyant type. But the dreamer could have been getting her information by telepathy from her husband's thought. As the dream imagery was given, one can only guess which was the situation, for no signpost indicated which the actual source was.

Or take a still more confusing experience like this one told by a woman in Illinois.

"This does not concern a dream which forecast an event, but instead, the undeniable certainty that I went through a harrowing experience *at the time it happened—with the person it happened to,* and physically I was fifty miles away from the scene at the time.

"I had been living away from home for some time, but usually drove the fifty miles home to see Mom on weekends. On a particular Wednesday evening, I found myself restless—to the extent of pacing the floor. I tried to read, but could not concentrate on the written pages. I never minded being alone, I loved to read, and I was not nervous by nature. As the evening wore on to ten o'clock —eleven—the feeling of uneasiness increased until I was asking myself, 'What's the matter with me?'

"The household where I roomed was quiet—all had gone to bed. By midnight I had caught myself several times just standing in the middle of the room with my hands clasped and feeling chilled. My landlady tapped on the door separating our living quarters and asked if I was all right. I admitted her and we talked a short time during which I told her of my unaccountable feeling of fear and apprehension.

"After she left, I prepared for bed, thinking if I could just get to sleep and relax I'd laugh about the whole thing in the morning. It was around a quarter of one when I turned out my light, dozed. Then it happened.

"I awoke—stark staring wide awake with a roaring and rumbling noise filling my ears. I sat up in bed trying to see through the blackness of my room. Over and over I asked myself, 'What is it? What is it?' Then I could see it! Black oblong shapes passed my view with glimpses of gray light in between. The rumble and clatter increased and I cried aloud, 'A train—a train—it's a train!' Then I heard a scream—my mother's voice calling me by my nickname, 'Betsy!' It was a terrified scream for help. I went from my sitting position to a praying position in the middle of my bed and over and over I prayed, 'No, God, no—no, God, no!' I must have repeated the words dozens of times, not even knowing why I did so. Then I lay back on the bed and cried.

"My landlady tapped at the door and came in, and turned on the light. She had heard me talking and crying and was alarmed for me. I told her of the experience I had passed through and debated with her about calling home. I decided to follow her advice and wait until morning to phone. My exhaustion brought sleep quickly and I slept until my usual waking time.

"My waking thoughts brought everything back vividly, but I could not, in the morning sunshine, bring myself to call home with my story. The rest of the week passed uneventfully with no word from home. Saturday came and I drove home as usual. At the house I greeted Mom with a hug and kiss, unpacked my few things and we sat down in the living room to talk.

"I hesitated to bring up the subject—but I had to know. I asked, 'Mom, where were you Wednesday night a little after one o'clock, and were you anywhere near a train?'

"Her answer was in annoyance. 'You've been talking to Emily! I told her not to tell you or anyone about it!'

"I answered that I had driven straight home to her house and not talked with anyone, but that a little after one o'clock on Wednesday night I awoke from sleep, saw and heard a train, and heard her scream my name. She turned quite pale and it was some time before she said anything. Then she explained that she and a friend had been on their way home from the local dance club, and when they drove up the incline to the railroad crossing at the edge of town, there was the train practically on them. She had wheeled the car sharply into a ditch alongside the track to avoid the crossing! Also, she said she could have sworn afterwards that she hadn't said a word during it all, but her friend told her she had screamed, 'Betsy!'

"Through the chill that came over me as I talked, I told her how I had seen the train, heard it, and heard her cry to me—and prayed.

"Now—what was it? I'll never sit at a railroad crossing at night and watch a freight train go by—the light of the sky showing between the cars as they flash by—hearing their clatter on the rails— any more vividly than I did that night. Come to think of it, I have never sat and watched a train at a crossing in the dead of night— except the one I saw that night—fifty miles away."

In that instance several different areas of reality seem to have been combined in one experience. The hearing of the call suggests a telepathic element, but the person also had some knowledge of the "black oblong shapes," the train, which would have been clairvoyant. And, in addition, she had an emotional disturbance long before the danger to her mother developed. This could have been a precognitive aspect. If so, obviously such a case would be a blend of all three types. To classify this kind, then, it would be necessary to make a fourth group, which would include all those with general or indistinguishable types of ESP. For brevity one might label it general ESP, or GESP.

With this fourth group, as a blend of the other three, all the experiences would be classified except a few which feature a physical effect instead of just a mental one. These would be similar to two cases mentioned in Chapter 2, in one of which a man's picture fell from the wall at the time of his accident, and in the other a clock acted strangely at the time the son of the household was killed in the war. Such accounts would belong to a fifth group —not ESP, but tentative instances of PK. But these, if assessed in terms of the kind of information they supplied, would not have introduced a new area of information, for they too refer to human crises, whether of thoughts, things, or future events.

Thus if the discovery of the types of ESP had proceeded logically, the experiences of people in life situations would have suggested that availability of information in the unconscious involved the three types of reality—thoughts, things, and future events, —with PK an enigma to be kept in reserve until some insight into its meaning and origin could be gained.

Logically then, experiments would have been performed to see if these three types could be demarked under the controlled conditions of the laboratory. And thus, presumably, the broad range of availability of reality to ESP would have been demonstrated. The line of reasoning and of consequent discovery would have been direct and probably could have been completed in a comparatively short time, and without controversy or countercharge.

But of course the advance of science in every field is one of progress against odds of many kinds. In this instance, the line of discovery began with a deeply ingrained prejudice, particularly in England, where many of the earlier investigations were made by people interested in combatting the rise of materialistic thought. It *seemed* acceptable and therefore more logical to them to suppose that thoughts rather than inanimate objects were accessible. Not only experiences like those of the child who reflected her mother's thought about the "man-woman" were taken as instances of the transfer of thought, but practically all other kinds too were packed into the same mold. For instance, a case like that of the fire, the first case in Chapter 2, would not have been classed as an instance of clairvoyance; it would have been supposed that the woman at the movie got her impression because of the thoughts of someone at home who knew there was a fire. It too would therefore have been considered a telepathy case. The train sensed by the girl in the last example above would have been supposed to be a reflection of the mother's awareness of it. Even the dream of the lost watch would have been laid to the thought of the unknown person who put the watch behind the tub, if someone did put it there. If it got there by accident and no one knew its location, then the dream would have located it "just by coincidence."

In this atmosphere the first experiments made, beginning about the latter quarter of the nineteenth century, were supposed to be tests for telepathy. Usually an experimenter looked at an object, tried to "send" the idea of it to a subject (sometimes under hypnosis), and the subject tried to name the object. Tests like those with the Creery sisters, for instance, were made in this way —an object and the experimenter's thought of it, both serving as the target. The idea that the object itself could be a target was so remote a possibility in the prevailing mental climate that investigators entirely overlooked the fact that tests made this way did not discriminate between telepathy and clairvoyance.

When Rhine began his research at Duke University in the early 1930s, a few preliminary tests were made using this same method; but by the time Linzmayer was discovered, the inadequacy of the method to show whether a thought had been transferred had been recognized. The object itself as much as the thought of it could have been the necessary "target" feature. Also, by this time the quest was to find out whether, as some early French investigators thought, inanimate things as well as human thoughts could be available to ESP. It was recognized that if the experimenter had an object to look at as he tried to send the thought of it, then the test could not show whether a thought had been transferred, or instead, the idea of a thing. To make a telepathy test there should be no object, only the thought of one; to make a clairvoyance test, no thought but only an object.

The tests with Linzmayer, which were discussed in Chapter 2, were clairvoyance tests. No one knew the order of the cards he guessed. A number of other subjects were also tested for clairvoyance during the period when Linzmayer was piling up his evidence for it. Then, in addition, the special subject Hubert Pearce took part in an even greater number of clairvoyance tests than Linzmayer, and he generally scored even higher.[1]

Sometime in this period the clairvoyance procedure was varied,

[1] Rhine, J. B. *Extra-sensory Perception*. Boston: Bruce Humphries, 1934, chap. 7.

and a different technique of handling the cards was introduced and frequently used successfully by Pearce. In this the cards were not removed one by one from the deck, as before; instead Pearce simply called the symbols in the order he thought they were down through a shuffled deck—with no one touching the cards until he finished. Then the cards were checked against the record of the calls.

When Pearce first tried this "down-through," or DT method, he started off with scores of 8, 8, 12, and 6 per 25 when 5 was the number to be expected by chance. The first 275 trials, or 11 runs, yielded 87 hits, a gain of 32, or an average of 7.9 per run through the deck instead of 5 per 25. (The SD for 11 runs is 6.63 and so the CR for this series was nearly 5.) Later another even longer series of tests was made using this same method. Pearce called 1,000 cards at an average only slightly lower, 7.5. The total value of results like these is a figure so high as to give certain evidence that these calls were not the result of chance and that somehow the symbols on those cards were available to the unconscious of this young man. Added to the results of the Linzmayer tests, Pearce's tests provided strong proof of clairvoyance. However, these are only the results of two unusual early subjects at the Parapsychology Laboratory. Proof of clairvoyance only begins— not ends—with them.

When the idea of testing for telepathy, too, was injected into experiments with Pearce, the experimenter or one of his assistants, in an attempt to change methods gradually, went back temporarily to the early method of looking at the cards as they were removed one by one from the shuffled deck. But in 175 trials, or seven runs, Pearce averaged only 6 hits per run. Although even at this rate he was probably showing a trace of ESP, it was a sharp drop from his previous scoring rate. Obviously something had happened which affected him; and because the main change was the introduction of the telepathic possibility, the lowered scoring rate could have been taken to mean that the telepathic addition was responsible.

However, Pearce was the same subject who had been adversely affected by visitors. The experimenters had noticed early that he was sensitive to any change in his habitual way of procedure, although he usually readjusted after a little time. It was not that he consciously resisted change. The reason was a deeper one, a clearly unconscious effect that he could not consciously control. So the experimenters did not conclude that it was the telepathic condition per se which was bad for Pearce but simply that he must be given more time for readjustment. This turned out to be the correct interpretation. After the initial seven runs, when he averaged only six, suddenly the scores increased; and for fourteen more runs, or 350 trials, he got an average of fourteen hits per run, which, of course was a lot higher even than his usual level. (SD for 14 runs $= 7.48 =$ CR, 16.8.)

But now, of course the old question inherent in this method came up again. What did these high scores mean? This was a general ESP condition, like that of the girl who "saw" the train and "heard" her mother scream. Different types of ESP were inextricably mixed up in it. The high scores could have been secured because of any one of several different causes. The thought aspect may have been especially effective, or the combination of thought and thing as target may have been the secret. But there was another possibility too. Pearce, as well as the experimenter, was very much interested in the outcome of all this. It could have been that the excitement and attention stirred up by this novel attempt had given him extra motivation to succeed. The very atmosphere of expectation then, not the method of procedure, just possibly may have done it.

Even if the result could not be interpreted, it served as a transition link to a telepathy experiment. It showed that Pearce could work with the telepathy condition, so that now some tests could be made using no cards at all, with the experimenter merely thinking of the card symbols. But, at least at first, it would be better if Pearce did not know when the telepathy method was being substituted for the clairvoyance method. This need necessitated some changes.

In most of this early work at Duke, both the experimenter and the subjects felt they were pioneering, trying to find out truths almost wholly for the pure joy of discovery. Later, refinements of technique and nicety of conditions were introduced. But to begin with, for instance, experimenter and subject merely sat at the opposite sides of a table, with the cards face down between them, or behind the experimenter's book or some other handy concealing object, but with the two in sight of each other.

Now a large screen was set up on the table between them, so the experimenter could shift from one procedure to the other, without the subject's knowing which was used. With the clairvoyant procedure the technique was as usual, the experimenter removing card after card from the shuffled, inverted deck and, without looking at any of them, placing them in order in a second stack. Now, since the subject could not see the experimenter, a telegraph key to signal ready was added.

The other procedure, the one for telepathy, was very simple at first, although later it had to be much refined.[2] In this first method the experimenter "held in consciousness" one of the symbols in a sequence planned ahead for each five trials, and tapped the signal key, just as for clairvoyance. Here, however, he made a record of his target choice after each of the subject's calls.

In the light of later improvements, many details of this procedure now sound a little unguarded. But actually the tentative conclusions arrived at by these first eager, almost spontaneously performed test methods, were entirely confirmed later when the most stringent precautions against alternative hypotheses ever used in psychological testing had been applied.

Now again with the novelty of the screen and the variety of conditions Pearce knew the experimenter would use, he needed a period of adjustment. His first ten runs averaged only 6.4, very low for him. Eventually, however, his scores rose; and in forty-nine runs of pure telepathy (SD = 14) he averaged 7.2 per run against an average of 7.1 for clairvoyance on seventy-one runs.

Since these scores were so much the same in this period when the two conditions were used at comparable times, the experimenters felt that they not only had strong indication of telepathy, but also that Pearce's ability in telepathy was about the same as in clairvoyance. Both suggestions coming from Pearce's work were later made over and over again in the results of other subjects and by other experimenters, until the point was established that both

[2] Rhine, J. B. *New Frontiers of the Mind.* New York: Farrar & Rinehart, 1937, chap. 10.

clairvoyance and telepathy occur, in spite of occasional individual variations, to about the same extent under the same general conditions. Thus in the laboratory at this stage it could be said that both thoughts and things were about equally accessible.

At the time these tests with Pearce were going on, the question of the effect of distance came up. Other students were also being tested. One of the girl experimenters, Miss Sarah Ownbey, working with another student, George Zirkle (to whom she had recently become engaged—one of the first recorded ESP romances), decided to vary their usual procedure of being in the same room, and tried some tests farther apart. They worked in adjoining rooms, using a telegraph key for signaling. Zirkle's scores did not decrease with the distance, but were even a little higher, as if possibly he was less distracted from the test, when by himself, than when in the same room with his fiancée.

After this encouragement about the possibility of success even at a distance, it happened that Miss Ownbey's roommate, Miss Frances Turner, who had also scored well in tests the two had made together (an average of over seven hits per run), was going to spend a week of vacation at a summer camp some 250 miles away, at Lake Junaluska in western North Carolina. The two girls worked out a schedule, and at stated times carried out their tests, making in all two hundred trials.[3] These were telepathy tests, in which Miss Ownbey at Duke "held in consciousness" her selected symbol, and Miss Turner, in Junaluska, wrote down her successive calls.

As Rhine records it, "Miss Turner was a particularly good subject for this since she has never shown the usual drop with new conditions—but her previous work had not prepared me for the shock of the first results of this 250-mile test. The first score was 19 hits in 25!"

In succeeding days the scores fell off somewhat, even ending with an inglorious two. But even so the total series averaged 10.1, much higher than Miss Turner's scores had been when the girls were in the same room. Distance obviously did not prevent ESP. It had gone on just the same.

[3] *Ibid.*, p. 168.

The saying is that big ideas change the world. Big or little, the idea that ESP is not prohibited by long distances changed parapsychology. The idea took a decade or so to incubate, but parapsychological thought was broadened by it ever after, for until then it might have been said only that both thoughts and things are available in the unconscious. But when the fact was inescapable that space does not inhibit that availability, the next question was inevitable. What about time? Does time inhibit ESP?

The question was momentous. So far as is known, up to then (December, 1933), no one had attempted a scientific answer. The general belief was that prophecies had been made—in ancient times at least—by prophets, soothsayers, etc., but the unspoken assumption about them was that those prophecies were miracles made by especially inspired individuals who transcended the natural order. Neither they nor their inspired words, therefore, had any connotation for the race in general. This assumption probably accounts for the fact that no record of any controlled test for precognitive ability has ever been found. Of course, one would not expect it in prescientific ages, but in the recent centuries during which man's old assumptions have so largely been rechecked, no one, it seems, had considered a general ability to prophesy sufficiently likely to bother about.

At Duke the test for precognition was made as soon as the question crystallized. The answer was a quick one, really, though no one could quite believe it then. The test was simple—so easy a child could do it. It consisted only of asking a subject, in this case Pearce, to make his calls to match the cards, not as the deck was then, but as it would be later after it was shuffled and cut.

The result was that Pearce's rate of hitting was quite comparable to that in his other tests. In one series of 212 runs, he averaged 6.3 hits per run; in another of 223 runs, his score was 7.1 per run.[4] Scores like these over so many trials, of course, yield fabulously high CR's and cannot be discounted as meaningless by any stretch of the imagination. The scores seemed to mean, in fact, that it mattered little in ESP like Pearce's if the target card order

[4] Rhine, J. B. Experiments bearing on the precognition hypothesis: I. Preshuffling card calling. *Journal of Parapsychology,* **2** (1938) 45.

was a present or a future one. Such scores seemed to indicate an affirmative answer to the question of whether the future is accessible to ESP.

If precognition had been a run-of-the-mill unknown, results like these might easily have been taken at face value and considered proof of the point. But precognition is an *extra*-ordinary concept. It is one that runs directly counter to the established idea of causality. Of course, clairvoyance and telepathy also are unexplainable by ordinary rules, but the fact is less obvious, apparently, for it has turned out that to the majority of informed and thoughtful people, the idea of precognition as an actual human ability comes hardest of all. On that account its discovery has called for an unprecedented weight of evidence. It is small wonder that in the laboratory even the experimenters scarcely believed their own results, and between themselves and others outside a host of possible counterhypotheses were proposed that have taken years of work involving many people and even other discoveries to rule out. Yet one can go back now to these initial tests with Pearce and see that the answer was there even then.

While only a sample of the later research and of the counterhypotheses which had to be dealt with can be given here, the turning point toward realization in the laboratory that in these tests precognition must be occurring can be traced back to a major experiment made in June, 1939, and reported in 1941 by Rhine and his assistant, Mr. Paul Gibson.[5] But many experiments both in and out of the direct line of progress were made in the six years after the initial precognition tests with Pearce and before this one was performed.

After Pearce's encouraging scores, other experimenters with other subjects naturally tried the same kind of test. The technique they used and which came to be called the "pre-shuffle cardcalling test," was exactly that. The shuffling at first was done by hand, using a specified number of dovetailed shuffles and a final cut at the end. Over the six-year period, different projects were carried out involving eleven different experimenters working with a total of forty-nine assorted subjects.

[5] Rhine, J. B. Experiments bearing on the precognition hypothesis: III. Mechanically selected cards. *Journal of Parapsychology,* 5 (1941) 1–57.

These projects gave varying results; some were unsuccessful, some successful in that they yielded positive deviations from the chance average of 5 per run. The spread of average run scores obtained in different trials ranged from a low of 4.9 to a high of 5.9. When this entire block of experiments was taken together, it was found that a total of 113,075 trials or 4,563 runs had been made. They gave a positive deviation of 614, a significant CR of 4.5; even though the average score per run was very little more than MCE. It still was strong evidence that something more than chance was operating within this collection of tests as a whole.

Was it precognition? In tests in which the average score per run was only slightly over five, a very few additional hits would do it. With this technique was there any conceivable way by which such extra hits might be made other than by precognition? If so, it would have to be by some unfortunate combination of factors, some artifact, introduced in the method of getting the target list, which meant in the shuffling of the cards, for the matter of targets and their selection in precognition tests presented a problem different from that encountered in earlier tests like those of clairvoyance. In those, one great danger and possible weak spot was that the subject might get sensory cues of the target. But that danger was not present here, where no target was in existence when the subject made his calls. In this, and in all precognition tests, the critical point of procedure therefore shifted to the manner in which the targets are selected, for they must be entirely random and not in any way related to the subject's calls. For instance they would not be random in relation to the call order if the person who arranged the targets had any idea of the call order and tried to make his targets match it. Even if he were to do so by ESP, the results, if successful, would only show a clairvoyance test "in reverse," because then the actual subject would be the person who selected the targets, and the actual targets would have been the subject's calls; no precognition would have been involved.

Trying to think of a way by which an error, a nonrandom factor, could be introduced by the shuffling, someone made a suggestion that sounded so unlikely it seemed scarcely worth taking seriously. It was that possibly in hand shuffling or in cutting the deck, the person could be guided *by ESP* to arrange at least a card or two advantageously and so to obtain scores a bit above those that chance alone would give. Several laboratory members did take it seriously enough to try it out, with results that were about as unbelievable at the time as precognition itself. They designed experiments to test this "psychic shuffle" and to find out if a subject could shuffle a deck blindly to make it match another in any appreciable degree, simply by wanting or wishing his shuffling to result in more hits between the two when he finished than the average five to be expected by chance.

They began half-unbelievingly by giving the possibility that this could be done every chance. The experimenter shuffled a deck of cards, the target deck, and placed it before the subject, although being careful that none of the cards were visible. The subject was then given a second deck and asked to shuffle it until he felt it was arranged like the first. Eventually 5,451 runs were made this way by 9 different experimenters using 129 subjects in all. A positive deviation of 1,405 was secured, which gave the very significant CR of 9.3. Following this, a more guarded method was used. The target deck was shuffled and cut behind a screen so the subjects never saw it. But a positive deviation was secured nevertheless. In 2,720 runs the deviation was 494, which still gave a significant CR of 4.63.

Various restrictions on the number of shuffles were then imposed and some decrease in the rate of deviation resulted accordingly. But still, the fact that such a phenomenon as the psychic shuffle could occur showed clearly that it was possible, to some extent, at least when trying, to shuffle or to cut one card deck to match another. And therefore if the targets were selected by hand shuffling, significant scores could not be attributed reliably to precognition even though in the test cases the experimenters had had no conscious intention of trying to make their target decks match the subjects' call orders.

As a result, mechanical shuffling was introduced and various other changes tried out in an attempt to escape the possible effects of the psychic shuffle. A matching technique replaced the card calling in many tests, including the one to be described next. In this technique five blank spaces on a table were designated on which later five "key" cards would be placed. The subject would lay out face down, one by one, the cards of an inverted shuffled deck in piles by the key spaces, trying to sort them so they would match the key cards which would later be put in place. The random element in this technique lay in the order of these key cards, which was determined by the mechanical shuffler after the subject had placed all his cards.

In June, 1939, Rhine planned an experiment incorporating all the safeguards against all the possibilities counter to precognition which had been advanced, to see whether evidence of it could still be obtained. But in framing the plan for this experiment, he took advantage of the results that had been obtained in two introductory experiments. In these preliminary experiments, the subjects had given low scores—so low they yielded negative deviations.

At that period in parapsychological research, the late thirties, the problem of negative deviations was only beginning to be taken with seriousness. It was recognized, of course, that statistically a deviation below the mean (a negative deviation) is just as much an indication of extra-chance results as one above (a positive deviation), and that scores significantly below would represent a phenomenon as real as those significantly above. But to an experimenter trying to get positive results, it was a frustrating outcome to get negative ones instead. However, if the negative trend were anticipated, it would be a different thing. Then it would be a desired result and an experiment yielding it would be a successful one.

Because of all this, the experiment planned that June was based on the expectation that the subjects would score negatively; the subjects, that is, who had given the negative scores in the preliminary tests. These were all adults, some of them laboratory members. Most of them had doubts, if not about precognition itself, at least about their own ability to predict card orders.

After his years of experience and of watching the results of other experimenters as well as his own, Rhine had a fairly strong impression that negative scoring tended to occur when something in the situation bothered or upset the subject. He thought the reason the subjects had scored negatively in the precognition tests might be related to their attitudes toward those tests. Therefore, he planned the new test with them, expecting negative scores.

On the other hand, it seemed that subjects without inner conflict about the test should score positively. In earlier tests using children, positive scoring (often enhanced by rewards of candy) had been obtained, and since children would not be disturbed by the theory behind the test, it was expected that they would make good subjects from whom to expect positive results. Two types of subjects, adults and children, each played a part in the ensuing experiment. Although they were not matched in numbers so that the results could be treated together statistically, the hope was that the two kinds of subjects would afford an interesting contrast.

The method used was tightly controlled against all kinds of error. The details are hardly necessary here, although they cover more than four pages of description in the report made in the *Journal of Parapsychology*. In general, the subjects worked in groups of eight, four on each side of a table, a tray for key cards in the middle of the table between each pair. After all subjects had placed their cards before their respective key card spaces, a signal was sent by an electric system to a room entirely shut off from the experimental one where the assistant, Gibson, had been shuffling cards in a shuffling machine. At the signal he shut it off, collected the cards, and in routine manner took the top card as the key for space number one at the west end of the experimental table, the next different one for key number two, and so on for the series of shallow trays in which they were placed and taken to the experimental room, one tray of key cards for each pair of subjects. In the meantime, Rhine had taken the card record before the key cards came in, and to be entirely sure of accuracy, a separate independent record of the card order was then made, the double set of records compared, and any discrepancies resolved by reference to the piles of cards themselves. The number of hits was then counted in the presence of Rhine, Gibson, and the subjects.

While a number of secondary conditions were itemized in the report, some involving series in which rewards were given and some series in which they were not, and in which sometimes a dice throwing machine was used for the randomizing instead of a shuffling one, those details are not necessary here. The over-all results were the ones that gave the verdict on precognition.

As expected, the adults scored rather consistently below chance. In 1,108 runs, their totals were 239 below the mean. This was, as expected, a negative score. It averaged per run only 4.784. The CR was a significant 3.59. As expected, too, the children scored positively. In 500 runs they had an average per run of 5.246, a CR of 2.75. The results of each group were thus statistically significant, the adults' negative, the children's positive. In fact, their average deviations per run from the mean were nearly the same, the adults' being .216, the children's .246.

The conclusion drawn from all this after pages of discussion of the extent to which alternatives had been excluded, was, in the words of the report, that "ESP is not limited to present events but is precognitive as well." But the caution still felt is reflected in the next sentence: "However, considerable restraint is needed in offering and accepting this conclusion, and more evidence is needed to give the hypothesis full and final establishment. The legitimate assumption at this point is that the evidence has reached a stage at which some new alternative hypotheses are needed if precognitive ESP is not to become an established phenomenon."

The story, which could be called "The Trials and Tribulations of the Precognition Hypothesis," of course, did not end in 1939. One after another, various criticisms of the methods of getting the target lists came in. After each, a new attempt was made to circumvent the possibility, whether it was an actual weakness or only a supposed one. For a while, among other innovations, the experimenters used a so-called "weather cut," which seemed above criticism. It meant that the final cut on a machine-shuffled target deck would be made on the prescribed future date according to a systematic code based on the prediction of the weather as given in a specified daily newspaper by the U.S. Weather Bureau. But even the "weather cut" was eventually discontinued when the criticism was seriously advanced by some few that possibly the parapsychologists were influencing the government's weather readings.

Eventually a complicated ritual was worked out by which dice were thrown, their faces used in complex calculations, and the results used to enter random number tables to get the target series from which the target deck was arranged accordingly.[6]

For a decade or so now, this involved procedure of getting targets has been followed routinely, and with it, as with each of the earlier methods in the evolution of this research, results have been obtained that seem to say the same thing which Pearce's original results said—that precognition, like clairvoyance and telepathy, is a fact. Even though the way to this conclusion was longer and more tortuous than either that of clairvoyance or telepathy —longer, indeed, than the outline given here can indicate—now, fortunately, it is history. Now the precognition technique is used routinely in much of the parapsychological research on other questions because it is the easiest of all to administer and to control. It is particularly useful when subjects are working alone or at a distance. They write their calls on record sheets at their own convenience, and later the experimenter gets the targets by the routine method. He thus has his defense ready made against any possible mistake or lack of honesty on the part of subjects working without surveillance, and in confirmatory tests the experimenter's honesty and carefulness is supported by the two-experimenter method, which means that it does not depend on one person's testimony only. The second experimenter can observe the first from the time he receives the records, then as he secures the targets, and in the final checking of the records against the targets. While such an added safeguard is not usually called for or used in scientific work, in parapsychology the tendency of the scientific world to charge that fraud or incompetence explains the results has been so widely made that extra safeguards of this and other kinds have had to be adopted. This is a healthy development, however, because it tends to insure the validity of the results not only for the outside world but for the experimenters themselves, who usually have few illusions about the human tendency for error. No other technique so easily permits this method.

With the establishment of ESP and its three types, the job of research this far has been completed; the areas of reality that can become available to ESP have been discovered. Other persons'

[6] Rhine, J. B., and J. G. Pratt. *Parapsychology, Frontier Science of the Mind.* Springfield: Charles C. Thomas, 1957, chap. 3.

thoughts, inanimate things, and events both present and in the future can be accessible in the deep unconscious.

How much of reality is included in this range? Or rather, is any of reality excluded from this list? The past is not in it, someone may say. For past events, just as those in the future can affect the present. But for ESP, or at least for the detection of it, the situation regarding the two is very different. The future has no objective traces to confuse the issue. But the past leaves records, memories, and objective remnants of many kinds. In fact, it is only because of these that human beings know the past at all, and it is only by these that any direct ESP of a past event could be checked for correctness. But if the evidence exists against which the ESP impression can be checked, then that evidence just as well as the past event could have been the source of the impression, and the ESP would then be of the ordinary clairvoyant type. No way to distinguish between the two possible sources would exist; the situation would be uninterpretable. The question whether the past is available to ESP, then, is not a real one, for the past in this context is only an abstraction, and ESP of the *present* encompasses it.

The range of availability of information as it concerns the world of reality is thus spread out as practically unlimited. Yet, it takes no proving that, after all, availability is limited, too. At least, persons are limited in the ESP of which they are conscious, and subjects in tests are limited in the number of targets they identify. The range of availability thus is obviously affected by the person, and somehow limited by him. Personal values and relations and their effect on the availability of reality, obviously integral factors in the ESP process, must also be considered.

CHAPTER 7

Topics of ESP (Life)

THE unconscious is the storehouse of man's past experiences, but it is not just a dusty old attic full of memories. It is a workshop where many of life's significant mental processes go on. With ESP apparently it even has a "door," a rather secret one, which somehow, in effect, opens directly on the objective world.

By this door, information can be secured about events outside. But even though the range of those events can be as wide as the horizon, still, in actuality, only a few of the world's myriad activities are thus known. In the light of examples already given, no answers to the great puzzles of the universe appear, but mainly news of the personal affairs of individuals. This suggests that the "door" in the unconscious is guarded, or perhaps one should say that it is a selection point. It means at any rate, that here at this beginning stage of ESP is an initial point of judgment or selectivity where a decision is made about the topic which will be admitted. Somehow, here, the psyche sometimes decides, "This one I will take. This item is of concern to me."

The question is, On what basis are items so selected? What sort of interest guides the choice of items from the world outside? Even the person's own affairs, it seems, are monitored, because experiences like those already given are obviously just isolated episodes; now this, now that, selections from the uncounted items of any one person's total number of life experiences.

Logically, one might suppose, since the contact of mind and world in ESP is direct and does not wait for the time and place of sense perception, the items of information chosen would be those of the greatest degree of importance and urgency. One might think that the material first to be admitted would be that which needs to be known at once, as in the case of the soldier in the foxhole. He seemed to be commanded, "Get out! Get out now!" without even time for the reason why.

And then, too, when some overwhelming crisis or tragedy is at hand, a shattering fact which soon must be faced, the idea might be, "Be prepared, face it now." Such a supposition might explain a dream like that of the woman whose son was drowned. Soon she would have to know it. The idea could have been to prepare her for the worst.

These reasons, however, would not explain such simple little telepathic flashes as that of the girl clerk in the store who heard her mother's call, when all the mother wanted was the hoe she had forgotten to take with her to the garden. Neither would they explain the case of the man who previewed in a dream a scene he would actually see in Germany, a scene certainly not more significant than a hundred others he did not preview. Such reasons would not bear at all on a trivial little dream of a scene on the way to the butcher shop or any other which was of only slight importance to the person.

On these less important levels, none of the obvious rules are explanatory. However, no one who knows much about unconscious mental operations would ever suspect them of being guided by the rationality of consciousness. Instead, unconscious mental processes can almost be depended upon to operate with seeming illogic. That is the reason, of course, that psychiatry is a profession. If unconscious mental processes could be accounted for the same as conscious ones, no one would need an interpreter in order to understand himself.

All of this means that the rules of admission for information secured by ESP cannot be deduced by ordinary logic. But at least it can be done by inspection, and, as in Chapter 6, the list of topics of actual experiences can be scanned to see how widely they range. From such observation something of the rule, or lack of rule, by which the topics must have been selected should be discernible.

In order to give an approximation of the range of topics covered in ESP experiences, the topics of a large group of them were tabulated.[1] For this tabulation only one kind of experience was

[1] Rhine, Louisa E. Factors influencing the range of information in ESP experiences. *Journal of Parapsychology*, **28** (1964) 176–213.

used, however, in order to avoid ambiguous cases. The kind used was that of dreams that came true, dreams which seemed to picture an event in correct detail. Numerous examples of such dreams have already been given. Because the details of the dreams and of the reality check, it is easy to judge that ESP probably did occur in them. Realistic dreams that seem to involve ESP are so frequently reported that over 2,500, a number large enough to be fairly representative, were on hand for this study.

In all these experiences, the dreamer himself in the background, whether actually a character in the dream or not, was of first importance; the question always was, In what manner did the subject matter of his dream concern him? If one knew that, presumably the rule or reason behind its selection could be surmised.

In these dreams, whether or not the dreamer himself was a character, often one or more other persons appeared, too. The dream may have been primarily concerned with the other person. Take for instance a case like the following, which illustrates the sort of dream in which a second person is involved.

"I dreamed I was bathing the children and left the bathroom a minute to run to the kitchen to get the towels, where I had placed them in the oven to warm. While in the kitchen I thought I might just as well do the breakfast dishes while the children played a few minutes in the tub. When I got back to the bathroom I was horror-struck to find little Brad lying underwater at the bottom of the tub. I grabbed him, he was unconscious and his finger tips and lips were blue. I put him across my lap with his head down and started working feverishly over him. At this point, as dreams so often do, it faded.

"I had no recollection of this next day as I went about my chores. At lunch time I put a couple of towels in the oven to warm and then went on to the bathing of the babies. Before taking them from the tub I went into the kitchen to get the towels and did a thing I had never done before—I started tidying up and as I did a feeling came over me that I had lived this moment before. It was a strange feeling and as I tried to analyze it the memory of the dream came back. I flew into the bathroom and found Brad exactly as I feared I might; he was lying absolutely still under the water. I had him out in a flash and even though I was filled with terror I noted the blueness of his lips and fingers. I followed the same procedure of the dream and brought him around. His cry that morning was one of the most thrilling sounds I ever heard."

Of the two people involved in that experience, the one primarily concerned really was the child, even though a tragedy to him would surely have been one for the mother, too. Still, in making a survey like this it was necessary to distinguish between those instances in which the dreamer himself was the one mainly concerned, and those in which it was someone else. As it turned out it made a difference in the general kinds of subject matter, whether the dream was primarily about the dreamer's own affairs or those of other people. And the other people were not only those in his immediate family, but some dreams concerned distant relatives and acquaintances, even total strangers.

The dreams involving people on various levels of relationship to the dreamer varied so much that it seems best to present them separately here.

HIS OWN AFFAIRS

In the entire group of over 2,500 dreams, 33 percent, or a full third, concerned the dreamer's own affairs. Either no second person appeared in them, or else the dreamer was the main character. This episode, told by a woman in Chicago, is one such incident.

"I dreamed I was on an operating table in a hospital. My doctor was bending over me with a worried look. I felt no pain when suddenly I heard him call out to my husband, who was just outside the room. 'Oh, Joe! Oh, Joe!' I felt weak and seemed to faint away. I awoke then quite frightened, but I never mentioned this dream to anyone. A few days later my back molar tooth was bothering me. I went to the dentist and he pulled it out. The bleeding wouldn't stop, so the dentist packed it with gauze and sutured the gum. A few days passed and during the middle of the night the packing and suturing broke loose, my mouth and pillow were filled with blood. It was 3 A.M. I awoke my husband.

"He tried to get the dentist at home. No one answered (later we found he had gone out of town for the weekend), so he called our family doctor. The blood was still oozing out of my mouth even though I had a roll of cotton in it and was biting hard. The doctor advised me to go to the hospital. After two hours in the emergency room the intern there finally stopped the bleeding. I had lost so much blood that they gave me a room at the hospital. But the next day I was hemorrhaging again. They called my doctor and he came. I found myself being wheeled into the emergency operation room exactly as I had seen in my dream. I became uneasy. I hoped they could stop the bleeding; I was feeling weaker. The doctor came over to me and started suturing the gum. The suture was breaking. It wasn't strong enough. He tried two more times. He began to look worried. Suddenly, just like in my dream I heard him shout out to my husband who was just outside the door. 'Oh, Joe! Oh, Joe!' I felt faint. I prayed. My husband came in and the doctor told him to get on the phone and keep dialing for the dentist, until he got an answer. It was about 4 P.M. Sunday afternoon. My husband finally got the dentist about 5:30 P.M. The dentist hurried over. Two more hours passed before they finally stopped it. What were the results? I spent twenty-six days in the hospital."

Quite obviously the main character there was the dreamer herself; the doctor, the nurse, and her husband were only secondary.

About a quarter of all the experiences involving the dreamer's own affairs were crisis cases, like that example. Along with illnesses and hospital experiences like that one, many of these critical events were accidents of various kinds. Perhaps those occurring in traffic were the most numerous of all, as for instance in the case of a woman in Florida. She says:

"This dream occurred in June of 1945. I thought I was riding in an automobile when dim lights of an oncoming car appeared in front of us, crashing into us. I saw crowds of people about us, low voices, the clang of an ambulance. I felt myself being placed in the ambulance rolling away—and oblivion.

"The next morning I told the dream to my son, home from college. He said, 'Mother, you have been reading of too many airplane crashes.' I put it out of my mind at once. He returned north to school. Since the next day was Father's Day, my daughter and son-in-law came to call. A ride was suggested after supper. We were about to get into the car when I noticed my husband was wearing his house slippers. I said, 'Aren't you going to change your slippers?' He said, 'Why?' I said, 'What if we should have an accident. Wouldn't you look queer walking about the street in house slippers?' He said, 'You would think of that.' He changed the slippers. (Incidentally, in forty years of driving he had never had even a traffic citation, so why should I have said that?) Returning from the drive we ran into the rear of an extremely dimly lighted car. I was thrown through the windshield. I heard the crowd about the car, the muffled voices, the clang of the ambulance. I was placed on the stretcher. I blacked out in the ambulance.

"The next morning I told our family doctor I had relived every situation of the dream—even to the fact my husband did much 'walking about the street.'

"The only discrepancy was in the direction the other car was going. Instead of 'crashing into us,' 'we ran into the rear of . . .' "

Also in the list of topics of crisis cases that of pregnancy and birth comes up again and again. This would be expected since easily twenty or more times as many women as men report ESP experiences. Of course, one can think of superficial reasons for this imbalance. Women may have fewer mental preoccupations than men, greater readiness to report, and such. But in addition the difference may very well go back to something more fundamental, something both cultural and genetic, which makes the feminine mind more open than the masculine to the impressions of ESP. Whatever that something may be, it is probably the reason that women have been called the intuitive, men the rational sex. The culture tends to make it this way, whether heredity does or not. But rationality and ESP do not mix well. For ESP messages, spontaneity is needed. And so there we have it. Even though little boys and little girls show very little difference in ESP ability, as they grow their circumstances, their natures, too, take on the characteristics of adulthood. Considering then the frequency of cases from women, topics special to women come up often in the lists of psi experiences, as in this instance:

"Three weeks before my fourth child was born I had a dream so real and in a way quite amusing. I dreamed my fourth child was born exactly as my first. I went into labor at the same time, I checked into the hospital at the same time, the labor progressed identically; and then my water broke and I delivered a boy, a small boy though. My first son was 8 lbs. and 10 oz. I dreamed they called my doctor into the delivery room, and he turned out to be a woman doctor. Also, I dreamed there was something wrong with my baby.

"The part about the woman doctor was so funny to me that I told my husband of my dream. I also told him of the timing, that he was to be born at 8:45 A.M., etc. Assuming the mind can control the body to a certain extent, this can be explained away. However, one week after my dream, my doctor left on vacation. He assigned my case to Dr. A. When I entered the hospital (at the same time) and labor progressed (identically), Dr. A. (a male doctor) checked me periodically, and I assumed he was to deliver the baby. I went to the delivery room (at the same time as with my first), and they called my doctor. He had gone off duty, and Dr. W. delivered my boy (6 lbs. 13 oz.) at 8:45 A.M. And a *prettier* doctor you have never seen! I had told of this dream to my mother-in-law at least two weeks before my baby was born. All except the last part about something being wrong with him. This unfortunately was also accurate—he has suffered with a genetic skin disorder from birth, been hospitalized, and is still under medical care."

One cannot help noticing that all of these dreams in which the dreamer himself is mainly concerned are about events still in the future. But that does not really mean that people tend to be unduly anxious, and go ahead inordinately to borrow trouble. After all, a person cannot have ESP experiences about his own crises *in the present*. He already knows them, without any ESP.

Another reason why it does not appear that this kind of dream really means that these dreamers in the aggregate are unduly anxious about their critical experiences is that the total number of crisis cases is not larger than it is. It would seem as if more than a quarter of their "previews" would be crises, if the dreamers tended to be morbid. Of course one has no certain way of deciding how many are too many. Still, if one stops to think of it, everyone has a crisis of some kind in store for him sooner or later, and presumably if ESP worked that way, these could all be picked out ahead of time, instead of only a quarter of the times when future experiences are foreseen.

In contrast, half of all the dreamer's dreams about his own affairs were on fairly important general topics not necessarily of anxiety producing kinds. But these general topics did concern almost every kind of event under the sun. They ranged so widely over the spectrum of personal interests that it is difficult to generalize. One of the recurrent themes, however, was that of finding missing objects. The importance of the object runs the gamut of human values. A fairly important "find" is reported in this account:

"About a year ago my mother drove her Oldsmobile to church and parked in the churchyard. After mass, she discovered the car missing, so there was nothing else to do but ride home with friends and phone the police. After searching, the police told us to resign ourselves to the fact that the car must have been taken over the state line. At that time there was quite a racket going on with stolen cars. They were taken to a different state and 'stripped' and painted.

"My mother's car was a beautiful job with all the accessories imaginable; also it had an expensive jack and two brand-new tires in the trunk. Because it was such a gem, the police doubted we would ever get it back. Although I have my own 'Olds,' I was especially sick about the whole thing because I used to drive it myself.

"Two nights later I dreamed about the car and just what street in Cleveland it would be located on. At that time I was living in a suburb about fifteen miles outside of Cleveland. After telling my husband and phoning my parents about the dream, I drove to this certain street in the center of Cleveland and found the car. As you know, Cleveland is a very large city with hundreds of streets; yet I knew exactly which street to drive to.

"The car had been driven over a hundred miles, and had been involved in an accident, but was still in top form. The neighbors in the vicinity told me that the car had been parked there only five minutes before I arrived. I called the police to make out a report so this incident is in the police files of Cleveland."

Another well-represented theme is that of winning bets, games, races, and contests. Of course, these are all precognitive experiences. One such case is reported by a man in New York.

"I had a dream in October, 1947, which came true. Naturally I am puzzled by it. I have no explanation for it. There is a question in my mind; just how do these things come about? I am inclined to believe in supernatural, mysterious forces of some kind.

"I was dreaming that I was in a horseroom with all the entries posted on the wall. I saw an entry for the second race in Jamaica by the name of Ringo's. A long time before I had this dream I had made a bet on the races now and then. I am sure I had never heard of a horse by the name of Ringo's; as a matter of fact, I had no horses in my mind at all.

"When I woke up in the morning, that dream was fresh in my memory. I told my wife about it, saying to her, 'Imagine me playing the horses in my dreams!'

"That same morning I had to go out of town to another city to take an examination for a job. I arrived at that place too early. In order to pass the time, I went to a lunchroom to have a cup of coffee. While I was talking with the man behind the counter, he said to me, 'In case you are interested, we have a horseroom in the back room.' It was right there where my dream came to life. Just as I had dreamed, I walked into the back room, and there were all those entries on the wall. I looked for the entries for the second race at Jamaica, and there was Ringo's at 20 to 1. I had dreamed I bet $10 on the nose. When I saw the first part of my dream come true, I had the idea I should make some kind of bet, but not $10 on the nose. To me it was just a dream. I couldn't afford to waste $10 on the nose so I bet $1 to show. All during the race my horse Ringo's was never mentioned; I was then convinced that I just had a bad dream. But when the race was over, Ringo's was declared the winner. I received some $15."

There is also a wide range of topics that can only be generalized as events connected with the person's job or profession. Some of them have to do with getting a new job, many with incidents that occur while at work. One of this kind comes from a man in Florida.

"About six years ago I had an experience which puzzled me to the extent it frightened me.

"I was an interior decorator and paperhanger in New Jersey. It was perfectly natural that I should dream of approaching a house, being met by an elderly woman, and introducing myself (according to my actions, but words were blanked out in a silent interlude). Then I walked up a flight of stairs, turned, proceeded down a short hall, noticed an umbrella stand, and entered a small room. The dream ended there, and I thought no more about it.

"Months later I made an appointment to look at a job. As I approached the neighborhood, I sensed something familiar, (no, not familiar, but strange) about it. Turning a corner I was aware I had been where I was going, but I knew only too well I had never been there. By this time, I became somewhat curious and agitated, indeed interested. I hesitated, and began to try hard and recall the details ahead of me as they appeared in the dream.

"Pressing the doorbell, I waited, saying to myself, 'This is going to be funny.' An elderly woman appeared and this explains why the conversation was blanked out in the dream—because it was not my usual introduction. I told the woman the peculiarity of the circumstances and just how I felt; she looked at me aghast. Continuing, I said, 'And is this room on the second floor after a right turn beside an umbrella stand?' She replied, 'Yes, it is.' This also interested her very much, and I told her also how I could sense the entire chain of events with increasing awareness as the address was approached, that I could have described her. We were spell-bound. I never mentioned a word about papering the room, turned and walked away, almost glad to be out of the 'range of famili-arity' as I called it. It was too much for me."

Nearly all of these on-the-job cases are precognitive; fortu-nately for business, few individuals are so upset by them as that one.

Among the many kinds of jobs and professions represented, one that stands out among the rest is that of nursing. An instance is reported that would classify as a crisis case, except for the fact that the emphasis of the dream seemed to be on the dreamer's experience, even more than on her patient.

"I was a student nurse at a hospital where I was taking my training. Upon getting my pediatric training, I was given as one of my patients a little boy, six years of age, who was in for an exploratory operation for a stomach ailment. Upon opening him up, the surgeons found a rapid-growing cancer, and he was sent back to the room on limited time to live. His parents were in-consolable and stayed with him day and night, showering the room with toys and food and everything to try to make him happy. One day while I was off duty, they suddenly decided to take him by train to a hospital in New York where they felt he would be cured. I had finished my day shift and was on night duty about a month or more later when I had this dream.

"We had 7 to 7 shifts and two nurses would work together—one leave from 1 to 3 for two hours sleep and upon her return, the second nurse would leave from 3 to 5 for her rest. This night I went off duty to my 1 to 3 period and fell into a deep sleep. I dreamed that when I returned to duty the phone would announce that I was to get a room with a certain number ready as a very ill patient was to be admitted. I would get everything in readiness and the phone would ring again and tell me to go down to admit the patient; and when I went to the front entrance, there would be my six-year-old patient in a pitiful condition. He would have on a pink-and-blue bathrobe and cap and insist that I carry him per-sonally up to the room. He was so near death I didn't want to carry him, but I would do so and everyone would be very sad and emotional as his condition was so grave. I knew he would pass away before 1 P.M. the next day.

"Now, several things were against ethics in this dream. First, the student never left a floor alone as all patients were admitted by night emergency or ambulance orderlies and anyone that ill never came in through the front door. Also, I never had been asked to personally carry any child at the age of six years and had never seen a plaid cap made like that one was.

"The whole nightmare left me unnerved, it was so very vivid and frightening. I went back on the floor and told the entire dream to the nurse, but we both thought it farfetched, and were sure he had passed away long before. I described the color plaid in the robe and cap, the mode of headgear, the room number, everything in detail, even the hour of his death.

"A few minutes after the nurse left, the phone rang; upon answering it, I knew beforehand what it would be—the night supervisor asked me to get the room ready for a very ill patient who was to be admitted by ambulance any minute, but even she didn't know who it was. I told her who it would be—and the whole story. Even when I described the robe and the front entrance and my meeting them myself, she didn't believe it; said the patient would be admitted as usual through the emergency entrance and by the usual nurse or herself and that I was allowing an ordinary dream to run away with me.

"About ten minutes later, the telephone operator called and said I would have to leave the floor and come immediately, as a patient very ill just arrived at the front door and was so ill she was afraid of the commotion, etc., in the entrance hall. The patient's parents had arrived from New York by train. The ambulance had been sent out in time, but many relatives had been to meet the train and they thought they could bring him to the hospital quicker than the ambulance could. The trip had been too much for the child.

"I went down, and there it was just as in my dream. The parents and relatives crying, the child in a terribly pitiful condition. He was glad to see me and put out his arms for me to take him, which I did and carried him up to his room. By that time I was so unnerved, I frightened myself. I couldn't understand it, nor could anyone else. They all looked at me as if I was queer. The supervisor couldn't explain it and when the day shift came on, I told them he would pass away before 1 P.M. the next day, even before he was examined by a doctor. That turned out true also as he fell into a deep sleep and when the doctor arrived the parents wouldn't allow him to disturb the child and he passed away without having the doctor thoroughly examine him.

"The night emergency and the supervisor were both involved in a sudden emergency operation and were unavailable at the time the child was brought in, and that was the reason the operator called the floor for me to admit him."

The liberal number of ESP experiences from nurses suggests that theirs is a profession that either creates situations made to order for ESP or else a subtle selection of personality types occurs with nurses so that they tend to have ESP experiences more often than the average.

Another large group of dreams about a great range of specific topics can be called "Scenes from Later Life." These pinpoint some event or place in a single scene that is later experienced in actuality. They are like cutouts from a setting just thrown on a screen seemingly without a reason. One such comes from California.

"I had this dream in November of 1936, while living in Kansas. I was a school girl of about fourteen—going on fifteen years of age. Mother wrote the dream as I related it to her. I was too shaken by the vividness of it to speak in very coherent sentences, but I told it to her immediately upon awakening, while it was quite fresh in my mind:

"It is a hot night, not a breath of air is stirring. I am older than fourteen and a half, but I do not know what I look like. I am standing at the kitchen sink in a strange but pretty house and I can see only black night out the window. Reflected in the window is a clock, and I must turn around to see what time it says. The time is 2 A.M. Around me are many people, drinking coffee, and letting tears roll unchecked down their faces. I hear a baby crying, and then Anne [my cousin] walks in holding a tiny baby. At the sink I am washing baby bottles and measuring Karo syrup, while at the stove behind me, water is boiling for formula. That is the end of my dream.

"At the time of dreaming this, Anne was perhaps further from my mind than any cousin could be, for she was living in California, and I had never known her very well. No one hearing about my dream could doubt that Anne and her husband were finally going to have a child. They had been childless for fourteen years and (after all!) some of my dreams had come true, so perhaps this one would too!

"Seven years later, in August of 1943, our family, too, was living in California, having moved there in 1937. In the years between, I had married and was now the mother of a tiny baby girl. One evening my dad got sick suddenly, and the baby and I made a rush trip two hundred miles to my parental home. In the hurry, I didn't take time to make enough formula for a twenty-four-hour period, and after arriving at my parents' home, hurried to the hospital along with everyone else. Cousin Anne kindly came over to spend the evening and night, taking care of my baby. Dad died at 1 A.M. and we all went back to the house. Anne told me the formula was all gone and I would have to make some more, as she didn't know the proportions. While standing at the sink in Mom's recently remodeled kitchen, I happened to see the clock reflected in the blackness of the window, the people crying, and Anne walking into the room with a crying baby.

"The dream of seven years before had come true in its entirety, right down to the details of the paper on the walls! Just for my own satisfaction, I reread the episode in Mother's journal and knew that I had, indeed, foreseen the night's occurrences."

This experience is very typical of this group of cases. Many such dreams show places where the dreamer will later live, or with which he will for some undisclosed reason have a meaningful association. But each, like a picture without frame or title, tells only as much as its details can show. It is not until the event occurs that its full meaning becomes evident.

Besides all these already mentioned themes, there are those involving ceremonies in which the dreamer will participate—

weddings, graduations, speeches, and occasionally natural catas-
trophes, fires, floods, or earthquakes. Nearly every kind of
occurrence a person might be involved in turns up as the subject
of an ESP experience.

But they do grade off in importance. The final quarter of the
dreams concerning the dreamer's own affairs dealt with quite unimportant topics. They were in the form of "Scenes from Later
Life," but were casual little snatches, incidental little glimpses at
times and places of no particular significance to the person. Some
of them covered long time intervals, like this one from Missouri.

"I had a dream one time neither dramatic nor prophetic. It was
an experience neither pleasant nor unpleasant, but I was to relive
that dream not next week or next year, but fully thirty years after.

"This silly insignificant dream had no particular meaning that I
could ever fathom, but anyway it was pretty odd, I think.

"I must have been fifteen. At any rate, I was 'the big girl' in the
dream. And I was down in some sort of place kind of different
from any place I'd ever seen and some children were with me,
three or four, and as we walked along, we came to a delightful
rustic bridge that arched over a tiny stream and we walked across
it together. That's all—nothing happened.

"Well, some thirty years later I was in my forties and living in
Denver when I decided to take a trip to Carlsbad Caverns. So
there I was spiralling down the path to the depths, and there were
six hundred people with me. I was traveling alone; and as I entered, I fell into company with a couple of families who were
taking their children. At the bottom of this first hill we went
through a kind of narrow opening and out into a great enclosure
that was the biggest place I ever saw except outdoors. Well, this
place was somehow familiar. Where had I seen it? I walked on
kind of dizzily; and suddenly I was on a little rustic bridge over a
shallow stream; and believe it or not, those kids, three or four of
them, were on that bridge beside me. When I looked around and
saw this, I knew why everything looked familiar. I had dreamed it.

"In my dream just the children and I were going through this
place. Now we had adults. But they were in front and behind us.
No adult stepped on that bridge while we were on it. But! That

bridge was put there by the government when they made it a national park. *And that was many years after the dream!*

"I understand that many people dream an experience and then live it afterward, but think how long afterward this was. This dream is maybe too mild to interest you; but if it does, use it any way you wish."

Of course it is partly the very "mildness" of a dream like that that makes it significant. One wonders by what trick of the unconscious such a trivial momentary scene would be picked out and reproduced so long ahead. And what tremendous problems about the structure of the universe it raises, when the significance of such foreknowing, as shown not in this one experience only, but in many, is faced! It may be that the very magnitude of these implications helps to keep the significance of such precognition ignored or that it is easier to say that such experiences are based on chance if they occur. But even that subterfuge is not easy for anyone who reads the hundreds of accounts in a group of experiences like those represented here.

Among all the kinds of dream experiences that mainly concern the person himself, the point to emphasize seems to be that they cover a range of topics from the greatest to the least, with the important topics not even especially favored; the unimportant ones are just as plentiful. It looks as if the psyche is interested in practically any kind of event that will turn up in his own personal experience.

But what about the events that will occur to people in his immediate family, those with whom his emotional ties are strongest? What kind of events involving them does he select?

HIS FAMILY'S AFFAIRS

The dreams that concerned affairs of the dreamer's family were somewhat more plentiful than those about his own affairs, making up forty percent of the total. But of course his family circle can include a lot of people—his parents, children, husband or wife, brothers, sisters, friends—while he himself is only one. Thus, on the basis of the number of people included in the forty percent, his dreams about his own affairs far outnumber those about any of the members of his family.

A striking difference in the distribution of topics of dreams concerning the dreamer's own experiences and those about the affairs of family members showed up in the frequency of crisis cases in the two groups. Only a quarter of the dreamer's own affairs were crisis cases, but two-thirds of all these involving family were about either deaths or physical injury. This may look as if the dreamer were more concerned with family crises than with his own, but here too, numbers can be deceptive. Two considerations can change this interpretation.

One of these is the time factor. While all the experiences concerning the dreamer's own crises have to be precognitive, those about family members can concern present events too, and about half of these did so.

The other consideration involves the topic of death. Nearly half the crises of the family group were deaths, and they included those in the present and in the future, too. Very few dreamers dreamed about their own deaths, and of course if they did, the experience had to be precognitive. A few cases were included in which it looked as if a scene at his own death or funeral had been precognized, but these cases were almost necessarily secondhand and usually were only recalled by others after the dreamer had died. Even so, the number is so small that it looks as if this is a topic that the unconscious tends to steer clear of.

Occasionally a person who has had a dream come true on some topic other than death then dreams of his own death. Naturally it disturbs him for he tends to fear that it too may come true. Such cases can readily be dismissed, however, as "anxiety dreams." They are not likely to be the result of ESP, but of unconscious mental processes making material out of hidden anxieties. The few such dreams reported that seem likely to have had a basis in ESP were usually not recognizable by the person himself in the same obvious way these pseudo ones were. Therefore it is seldom that such dreams need be taken seriously.

With two-thirds of all the dreams about the family circle devoted to crises, only a third remains, and these are practically all on fairly important topics. This is a much smaller total number than the comparable one in dreams concerning the dreamer himself. The range of topics they cover, too, is much more restricted than when his own experiences are involved. These about family members come nearer having only a few general themes, even though there still is considerable diversity. Of course a basic general situation governs this. In all these cases the dreamer is separated from the family member he dreams about, and so the ESP experience is one that brings information about the distant one. It may show scenes at his location, it may bring news about his troubles and tribulations, and often about his return or visit to the dreamer. The seriousness of the topic varies, of course, but trivial or unimportant topics are so rare that their total number is almost negligible. It is easy to see that the dreamer does not concern himself much with nonessentials where his family is concerned.

All of this shows that the rules of selection of information are different for the person's own affairs than for the members of his family circle. With his own affairs selected on a very wide basis of interest, he is surely ego-centered, but not morbidly so, for he tends to underplay his own troubles of the more serious sort. At the same time his ESP messages involving his family circle tend to center on their crises, which of course concern him deeply. Even with the less serious topics one can notice that those that impinge on his own interests are picked out more than other possible themes. And those on the small day-to-day level of their affairs, he almost entirely ignores. On this level, he does not intrude into their lives. Here he is preoccupied at home, and often with trivialities which he would ignore, if they are not his own.

But now what about the dreams involving people who are outside his family circle, those with whom his emotional attachment is slight?

AFFAIRS OF REMOTE RELATIONSHIPS

ESP experiences involving distant relatives, neighbors, business associates, and mere acquaintances made up only 14 percent of the dreams. However, it seems likely that experiences concerning people as remotely connected as some of these might often be overlooked. The person might not find out that his dream came true, and this would lower the number that would be reported. In any case, however, fewer dreams occur about those with whom the emotional bonds are weaker.

On the other hand, many strong ties exist, even when the actual relationships are not so close as the immediate family. For instance, grandparents and grandchildren, and also uncles and aunts and nieces and nephews are in this category, and perhaps this is one reason it is as large as it is.

The general proportion of distribution of the topics of these cases was about the same as in the immediate family group. Over half were crisis cases and almost none were unimportant. But in the crisis cases involving mere acquaintances, it seems that a new basis of selection came in, in place of the strong emotional interest that one supposes accounts for the selection of events concerning close family members. For instance a New York woman reports a case in which no emotional connection existed. She says:

"The evening of December 23, 1958, I dreamed a coworker of my husband's (both servicemen for a Long Island oil and coal co.) had a 'head-on' collision on Port Washington Blvd., in the late afternoon of Christmas Eve. The dream was accurate in every detail. I did not dream how or where he was taken to the hospital or, if I did, I can't recall. I did, however, 'see' him in a hospital and could 'see' that he had sustained head injuries.

"Since my children and I had a great deal of last-minute shopping to do, we were 'up and out' early Christmas Eve morning. Exhausted by noon, we stopped at the village luncheonette and accidentally ran into my husband and another of his coworkers. Upon seeing him I automatically asked him how 'Whitey,' the man I 'saw' in the accident, was. He was rather surprised at my inquiry, and I proceeded to tell both him and his coworker about the odd dream I had had.

"Late that afternoon my husband called me to tell me that on his way 'in' from a job, 'Whitey' had a head-on collision and it all happened exactly as I had dreamed it. I can't begin to tell you what an odd feeling this news gave me.

"I must add there was no bond between myself and 'Whitey.' On the contrary, I probably have seen this man six or seven times in the past six years or so, not more than twenty minutes at a time; and while I would hesitate (out of sheer politeness) to call him a complete nonentity, I can't in all truth find another word to describe him, both physically and mentally."

For the selection of topics with such slight emotional connection as that, one must suppose a low level, or perhaps one could call it a general level, of interest suffices. It is the kind represented in the frequently heard phrase, "Did you hear that so-and-so died —or is in the hospital—or was in a wreck?" In place of the strong personal and emotional interest of the cases involving the person's own experiences or those of his family circle, this kind is so general as scarcely to involve emotion at all. And yet, obviously, it can be sufficient. It is the new basis of selection introduced by these cases involving remote relationships.

AFFAIRS OF STRANGERS

This final group of cases is the really nonemotional one. If emotionally toned relationships were necessary for the selection of ESP topics, no cases should appear here, yet 13 percent of all the cases concern strangers, persons the dreamer has never met. And here again, most of the topics are crises. But the figures alone do not give any hint as to why the topics of these cases should have been selected.

Here, in order to see how really "far out" some of the topics of ESP messages are, it is necessary to analyze the kind of relationship that did exist between the dreamer and the stranger.

Before trying to do that, however, it should be observed that the strangers in some of the dreams appear in experiences which are essentially the same as those in "Scenes from Later Life." These, too, are scenes from the later life of the dreamer, and in some of them the stranger plays no distinctive part. He is just a detail, a part of the scenery, as it were. An experience that illustrates such a situation is this one from a man in Oklahoma.

"I am a parcel postman or mail carrier. As you know, on delivering parcels in tall buildings we put the parcels on the elevator and put them off on each floor that they belong on as we go up, then walk down and take them to each office. Well, I dreamed that I was delivering my parcels in the tallest building on my route and when I got to the second floor, I stooped over and reached down to pick up the parcels I had left there to deliver, when the elevator door opened and out walked a little girl, dressed in white, with blond, curly hair, followed by a short, chubby lady dressed in white-and-red plaid with an apron effect with a darker red trim nearly like a heart on a valentine; then another girl got off and I knew her. She used to run that elevator, but she was all dressed up in a solid-color blue dress. That is the way of my dream.

"Ordinarily when I have a dream, I hardly remember it past breakfast time, but this morning after I had the dream I thought about it several times for some cause or other and because every detail was so vivid in my mind. Well, that morning on my rounds I had placed the parcels on each floor and was delivering them. As I got to the second floor and started to lean over to pick up the packages, that elevator door opened, and out came the people just as I had dreamed the night before."

Just part of the scenery, the strangers in such experiences are scarcely on the level of actual personalities. However, the line that shows just when they are more is a vague one.

The closest connection of the dreamer to the stranger in any of these experiences was when he did know of the existence of the other. This included dreams about celebrities, political personages, and the like, and also, sometimes, private individuals. In a case like the one below, for instance, the dreamer knew the stranger existed.

"In 1939 my mother rented a furnished apartment to a young married refugee woman and found her to be a pleasant person. It was about two months later that Mother related the dream she had that night. The dream was that Helen Brown's (the roomer) husband knocked on our door and asked for his wife. Mother described him in detail. She had never seen a picture of him and did not know anything of his looks. Told of his stocky build, ruddy complexion, baldness, etc., Helen thought it strange that Mother could describe him so accurately, but she laughed off his coming as his last letter told of a long wait for a visa in England. She felt it would be at least a year before his coming. After Helen left for work, Mother told me she didn't like the husband as he wasn't a fine person.

"That afternoon about 4:30 there was a knock at the door, and Mother and I were dumbfounded to see standing there a man fitting the description of her dream. He asked for his wife, Helen Brown. We invited him in and soon after Helen came home. After the welcome, her husband explained that the visa had come through unexpectedly soon and he flew in without anyone knowing of his plans.

"Soon after the welcome, he asked Helen, 'What did you do with the money you earned here?'

"Mother couldn't tolerate him and asked them to move."

However tenuous the line may be between two persons when one merely knows of the other, still if all the cases had this connecting link, one would probably say a link like this must be the necessary minimum. But in other instances, the dreamer does not even know that the other person exists, yet he may appear in the dream clearly enough to be recognized later. A woman from Indiana tells of such a case.

"When I was nineteen, I had a dream that was so real I related it to Mother the next morning. In my dream I saw a young man, tall, fair, blue-eyed, and with curly black hair. I told Mother he was the man I would marry, although I didn't know who or where he was.

"About six months later, while at my work at the cabinet factory, I had an experience I shall never forget. The table I worked at was against a wall with a doorway into another room at my left, so there was much traffic past my table and I very seldom paid any attention to who passed through the doorway. As I worked I always faced the wall so that I never saw who was coming down the hall back of me. That morning was the same as any other until I had the strangest feeling of a force drawing me to something. I didn't know what. Then two men came past me and through the doorway and I looked up just in time to see their backs vanishing into the other room. One back was my boss's but I didn't know the other one. That evening while setting the table for supper, I said, 'Mom, I saw my man today.' Then she asked if he had blue eyes and black curly hair. I told her I didn't know as I only saw his back and he was tall and wearing overalls and a cap. But a few days later I saw his face. He looked just like the young man in my dream, except he had his cap on and I couldn't see his hair until later, and it was black and curly. Three months later we were married."

Dreams like this one that seem to envisage ahead of time the person the dreamer will marry are not uncommon. But perhaps in these, too, one can suppose a link, if not that of a person already known, at least that of a motive for finding out who he will be. The office is known, let us say, but not the candidate.

In other instances, however, the stranger may be someone who has no already existing role to fill. He may be an individual of whom the dreamer is quite unaware, and yet he may be etched out distinctively in a dream. A man from North Carolina had such a dream.

"An incident that occurred during the last war may not be unusual, but I relate it for what it may be worth to you in your work. Before telling the details of the dream and its results, I wish to say that at the time of the dream I had not heard of the man in the picture, and had not heard the slightest description of the city I visited.

"I was living at that time in Athens, Georgia, and one night I dreamed I was making a trip to my home town of Sanford, N.C., as I had received a message my mother was ill. I traveled to Sanford on the S.A.L. railway, and after finding Mother was doing well, I was returning to Athens via Fayetteville, N.C. While waiting for a bus connection out of Fayetteville, I noticed a young lady attempting to make a telephone call without much success. After each unsuccessful attempt she would sit near me until she made another try. Finally she asked me if I knew how to get a call through to Fort Bragg as she was having trouble and was getting her calls routed to the wrong section of the base. I gave her the desired information, and she got her call through. About this time my bus was called; and as I started to board the bus, I happened to notice the girl standing behind me in line to board the same bus. We sat together during the trip to Athens; and before the trip was over I asked for a date, which she granted. She told me her name was Barbara Jackson and that her home was Macon, Georgia. She gave me her street address, but she said that inasmuch as I might have trouble finding it, she would meet me in the lobby of the main hotel of the city—the name of which I have now forgotten.

"At the appointed time for the date I went to Macon; and upon my arrival in the business section of the city was impressed with the rows of trees growing along some of the business streets, as it is a little unusual. I went to the hotel; and upon entering I noticed it was 'T'-shaped and at the end of the vertical line of the 'T' was the registration clerk's desk; and over this desk was a huge portrait of a young soldier. Barbara met me and took me to her home. Wanting to be honest and aboveboard, she told me she had a boy friend in the service, but that if I wished to be friends it could be that way and nothing more. I accepted the conditions as I was not interested in getting serious at that time. End of dream . . .

"Upon awakening next morning I remembered the dream but thought nothing more of it at the time. The following day I received a message my mother was ill, and I made the trip exactly as in the dream.

"I did not connect the trip and the dream until I was boarding the bus at Fayetteville. All events of the dream came to pass exactly as I remembered the dream. I doubt that I would have connected the dream to the actual occurrences had it not been for the fact that a trip via Fayetteville to Athens is a little out of the way and I would not have gone via Fayetteville on the return trip had it not been for a bad tie-up on the railway due to military traffic at the time.

"The girl I met in Fayetteville was named Barbara Jackson; she lived in Macon, Georgia; she looked exactly like the girl in the dream. I met her in the 'T'-shaped lobby at her request and the portrait of the soldier—a local military hero—hung over the desk. Also, in the dream I would not be able to obtain a room at the hotel where I met her, but did get a room at the Sidney Lainer Hotel—this also occurred.

"At the time of the dream I had no reason to think Mother might be ill."

In both situations, the dreamer later came to have a personal relationship with the stranger. However, if the fact of the personal involvement was in any way a cause of the dream, then it was a "future cause."

In the general run of precognitive experiences, material is admitted to the unconscious presumably because it is of some degree of interest to the person. That interest is already existent, even though the fulfillment of the event precognized is in the future. But here the reason, too, is a precognitive one!

Even so, how big is the reason? Is it just that this stranger will sometime come to have at least a passing interest? How small can such an interest get? In some cases, slight indeed, according to occasional experiences like this one from a man in Jersey City.

"While in high school I dreamed of meeting a man in a blue suit at a social gathering in a brightly lit room. Well, I was friends with a history teacher who was helping me with a bit of extracurricular study of social sciences. I became interested in consumer cooperatives, so he arranged for me to attend the meeting of a local cooperative. The incident happened exactly, true in every detail.

"When the event happened with Mr. Blue Suit (that's all I remember about him now), I was filled with a sort of numb shock. I felt as if I were set apart from myself watching. The man came forward, I met him, and we shook hands exactly as in the dream. My own movements seemed to prevent me from taking any deliberate action which wasn't in the dream."

Obviously in such occurrences even the future reason for contact with the stranger was a slight one. It was just the oddity of the introduction, with no meaningful sequel whatever.

But even this is not the end. Next are experiences in which the dreamer not only had no previous knowledge of the stranger, but he never meets him personally, and only hears of him eventually in connection with the episode of the dream. The situation reported by a woman in Ontario is of this sort.

"My experience occurred in the year 1910 and centered about a very gruesome dream that left me a little unnerved. I related to my husband that I had had a horrible dream the previous night. He looked at me inquiringly, and I said, 'I dreamed of a man and a woman with a team on a wagon. One horse was a big bay. They drove onto a bridge which had sides like an inverted 'V.' When they got to the middle of it, the bridge went down. The bay horse reared and tried to go backwards. I saw the man. He had a piece of board right through his chest.

"We discussed the entire incident for what it was; as we thought, a very bad dream. As a matter of fact, I explained to my husband that I knew neither the man nor his wife and did not recognize the road.

"The next day my husband went to town. When he came home, he looked at me with a strange look and said, 'Your dream came true.'

" 'What do you mean?' I asked.

"He said, 'Mr. and Mrs. ———— came into town to the mill to get grain ground. They left about four o'clock to go home. The ———— bridge collapsed with them. Both were killed. There was a piece of wood driven through his chest. The one horse was a big bay. There was an eyewitness to the tragedy.'

"This occurred at least twelve hours or more after my dream. I did not know the people or the locality where it occurred."

It would appear that here a new factor is introduced in the selection of the item. No longer is there any trace of personal connection, past or future. Instead, the dreamer's interest in the stranger is on a quite impersonal level, just as it is in reading newspaper accounts of accidents and calamities happening to strangers. In fact quite a few cases are reported that later are found to coincide with a news account, whether in newspaper, television, or radio. For instance, it may be an experience like one reported by a California woman.

"In 1940 or 1941 there was a news story in the *Stockton Record* about a missing rancher. It was suspected that he had been murdered, but they couldn't find his body. One night I dreamed of a ranch. The house was roughly built, and it was set onto blocks of wood which kept it off the ground. On the outside back wall hung an old-fashioned tin washtub. I entered the house. It was very dirty; on the table there was a clutter of dirty dishes and a large jug of wine which was almost empty. There were two bunk beds that had been built onto one wall. In the lower bunk a man dressed in long underwear was lying with his face to the wall, and there was a bullet hole in his back. One foot was bare, but the other one had a wool sock on. Then a young man entered the house; his hands, shoes, and clothing were covered with damp earth. He walked to the dead man, picked him up and carried him out to a newly dug grave not too far from the barn door. He placed the dead man in the grave, face down, with his face resting on his left arm. He covered the grave with dirt, then he went to a cement mixer and mixed cement, and then he covered this grave with the cement. He made a regular driveway into the barn door from this grave.

"I told my husband about the above dream, and he said, 'Let's wait and see what happens.' Not long after, the young man was apprehended in the dead man's car. He confessed to the crime. From the details in the paper all the things I had seen in my dream were identical. This was the first time I had dreamed of anyone outside my family circle."

Presumably, the account of the murder may have triggered the dream, but the significant part of it is that it covers the "gruesome details," not brought out until the murder was solved. In all such instances, the only possible connection seems to be not only a future one, but one as slight as simply the reading of the episode in the news. This, then, must be a sufficient reason, at least sometimes, for the item to be admitted.

The number of experiences involving strangers at this extreme of obvious connection is small against the general background of total subject matter of ESP, but here again figures can well be treacherous. Dreams about people with remote or no personal connection could very well go unnoticed, and no recognition of them in consciousness, no checkup would ever show that they were meaningful. This thought opens up a wide range of speculation. Does ESP sometimes touch the real objective world, but without the person's ever finding out that his impression was true? It just could be. But speculation in that direction here would lead off into the wild blue expanse of "maybe." Instead, it is more profitable to step back onto the level of reality from which this discussion started, and ask what all this has shown about the rules of admittance of information in the unconscious.

The obvious fact about the spread of the information included in the dreams surveyed above was that it was so wide as to seem practically unlimited. Nearly every kind of imaginable event that could make a news item turned up as the topic of an experience, and affairs of people at all degrees of relationship to the dreamer did also. But the great variety of topics was confined largely to those that were or would be items of the dreamer's own experience. The topics selected when strangers were involved were much less varied, and more entirely crisis cases. This seemed to be a matter of obvious orientation toward the dreamer's own interests, and that idea was augmented by the fact that a goodly number of the experiences involving the family were definitely so oriented. In fact the general panorama of topics takes on that of the perspective of the dreamer. It reflects in a broad and general way his involvement with the world he lives in. It also gives a picture of the typical dreamer of ESP dreams as a person of wide and comprehensive outlook, ego-centered but normal, alert to the welfare of his family and friends, and with considerable general interest in people, even when they have no personal relationship to him. In short, the picture given here is not really any different from one of Mr. Everyman, as it might be shown by his sensory instead of extra-sensory experiences.

The rules of selection then appear to be the rules of personal interest and involvement. In each individual, those rules of course are specific for himself alone. Thus, even though the list of topics of all these dreams is such a long one, the number of experiences of any single individual is relatively small. The topics of the study were divided among the many people who reported them. Some reported more than one, a few reported many, but always there was a definite limitation and no person had an unlimited perspective down the years of his own experience, or that of others. Even though presumably each one might have selected any given topic —death, illness, accident, or even triviality—there was some limitation so that only certain ones were chosen. That limitation one can only suppose was made up of the combined result of the persons' inherent interests and the complex of personality and circumstance through which his ESP could be expressed.

CHAPTER 8

The Range of Targets (*Laboratory*)

DOUBTLESS, the first experiments that had a bearing on ESP were undertaken because certain human experiences suggested the existence of an ability to get knowledge without the intermediation of the senses. But in those days, now fifty years or more ago, the kind of experience most generally reported was the so-called crisis case, which involved mainly the dying or deathbed situations. If the early experimenters, for instance, those in England in the last quarter of the nineteenth century, or those who followed after, even the first experimenters at Duke, had been guided by this kind of case, however, they might well have failed to try out the simple digits and symbols that soon became routine as target material. They might well have assumed that only significant personal events would suffice for targets. But an inclusive list of spontaneous life experiences like that referred to in Chapter 7 shows that simple, even unimportant topics can be the subject matter of ESP, too, and hence could be used in testing. The list shows that at least in spontaneous experiences, material may be included that falls into almost every level of significance for the person involved. It suggests an extensive range, and indicates that trivial items can serve the purpose too. As a matter of fact, when experiments in this country began they were not really modeled closely on spontaneous material of any kind. Instead, the idea then was to simplify the test procedure sufficiently that no question about interpretation and evaluation of results would arise. The aim was to investigate the possibility of an extrasensory way of getting information in as thoroughly impersonal a manner as possible, with no foolishness about evidence that was no stronger than that of the human testimony in case material.

It was lucky indeed that the requirements of modern research methodology did not entirely preclude the operation of a process as fragile as that of ESP, and that it could operate to a detectable degree, even before the experimenters understood what a delicate unconscious process it is.

And so targets like those offered Linzmayer, numbers and other symbols, were the kind of impersonal item used most often. The emphasis was not on the item itself, but on the subject's ability to identify it. However, with this procedure the freedom of choice of material in the unconscious was gone. Subject matter *per se* had lost its importance. Even a box of almonds or a white penknife, as in the semiexperimental tests with the Creery sisters, were in themselves more interesting than the series of intrinsically unimportant items the subject now was asked to identify.

But even so, as results have shown, meaningless targets can be accepted in the unconscious to a sufficient degree to give a statistically measurable effect. For instance, when the child Lillian came to think it highly important to get twenty-five ESP cards in their correct piles and thereby please Miss Pegram, she managed to do it. It was above her ordinary level of success, but with special effort, she succeeded.

On one particular occasion, the subject Hubert Pearce, strongly challenged by J. B. Rhine, was able to call the entire twenty-five card ESP deck correctly.[1] It was not his ordinary level, either, but he could do it when pressure was great enough. And for him just then it was important to satisfy the experimenter. Also, too, he himself was deeply interested in finding out just what that mind of his could do. For reasons such as these, and probably others too, equally difficult to specify and quantify, experience shows that sufficient importance, interest, and meaning can be injected into the identifying of monotonous and undistinguished lists of symbols to make them acceptable, and hence accessible. They can be selected in the unconscious mental depth where ESP begins.

It is necessary, however, for the requisite pressure of motivation to be created, or no selection will occur. The end of the experi-

[1] Rhine, J. B. *New Frontiers of the Mind.* New York: Farrar & Rinehart, 1937, p. 94.

ment will show results at chance, and nothing more. As experimenters know too well, the easiest result to get in ESP tests is a "chance" score, an average of five per run. After the study of the subject matter of dreams of Chapter 7, and the personal interest that envelops even the more trivial topics that are sometimes involved, it is not too difficult to see the reason why.

Another artificiality demanded by good test procedures is a forced timing of response. The unconscious selection of the target is required at once, not at some indefinite time when a quirk of some unusual kind may produce a spontaneous readiness. And even more than that, the demand is to do it repeatedly, for test procedures usually consist of a series of calls, and not only a single one as in spontaneous cases. This feature becomes necessary with the introduction of methods by which the results can be evaluated statistically. And in spite of the fact that repeated guessing of symbols in a deck of cards is not in itself of interest to the subject, and in spite of the monotony and lack of spontaneity it entails, it has proven to be a favorite method, and one used in nearly all experimental projects. It is the easiest way to get quickly a lot of data that can readily be evaluated.

The material used in the greatest number of research projects has been the ESP card deck. This has been favored for several reasons. One is that the number of choices it offers has proved to be rather optimum: a larger number than five tends to tax the subject's memory, a smaller one is more likely to increase his tendency to "pattern" his calls. In addition, five is a handy number to handle mathematically. The result of it all is that, with the cards, successful results have been secured by many different experimenters.

Other kinds of targets besides cards and symbols, however, have been used from time to time. In England in the 1930s several projects were carried out with quite different kinds of target material.

One investigator, Mr. G. N. M. Tyrrell, found a special subject, a Miss Johnson, who had shown what seemed to be spontaneous ESP. In an article he wrote later reporting an experiment he car-

ried out with her, with rather unique target material, he explains
how he came to select it for his test.

In October 1934 I was particularly struck by a feature in Miss
Johnson's faculty, viz. the extreme satisfaction—one might almost
say the excitement of satisfaction—which accompanied the finding
of any lost object. If one could create such an excitement, even in a
mild way, and make the condition of its satisfaction the performance
of some experiment on a measurable basis, it seemed it might be
possible to harness it in the work of demonstrating ESP.[2]

The way Tyrrell succeeded in harnessing Miss Johnson's ability
to find things was by preparing a series of five small boxes, or
compartments, so arranged—under a screen which concealed the
two persons from each other—that the front of the compartments
faced Miss Johnson, the back, Mr. Tyrrell. On Miss Johnson's
side, each of the compartments was closed by a lid that could be
raised. At the back they were open, so that the experimenter could
insert an object in a selected one of the five. Miss Johnson's task
was to find the proper box, and open the lid, thereby letting in
light, so that the experimenter would know her choice and could
record it. At first he simply inserted a pointer. With this her success was striking. It was so high, in fact, that critics thought
perhaps she got an auditory cue.

Although Tyrrell was convinced that no sound was made to tell
her which compartment he had chosen, the possibility of auditory
cues was difficult to rule out absolutely. He, therefore, changed
the apparatus and inserted little electric lights in each compartment. Each of these was lit by its own particular key, which he
could turn behind the screen. Miss Johnson's task was just the
same as before. She simply had to lift the lid of the box that she
thought contained the lighted bulb. Her successes on this task
were lower than before, but still highly significant, for in 2,300
trials she made 551 hits, a gain of 91 over the 460 to be expected
by chance, a CR of over 4.7.

Although Tyrrell's success with this apparatus and this subject

[2] Tyrrell, G. N. M. Further research in extrasensory perception. *Proceedings of the Society for Psychical Research,* **44** (1936–1937) 103.

was so convincing, no one else has repeated the particular technique and type of target. But Miss Johnson's results can be taken to show that a subject can "find" a hidden object, for essentially, of course, it was a test of *location*.

About the same time Tyrrell was working with Miss Johnson and the locating of targets, another Englishman, Whatley Carington, a psychologist, was planning a very different experimental project with very different target material.[3] He had been reading of some historical attempts to get evidence of "information without the senses," and was so impressed with some of the weaknesses of the work of his predecessors that he decided to make a "perfect" experiment.

In order to avoid the monotony of card symbols he chose to go back to the old practice of using drawings for targets. To break the monotony of using the same targets again and again, as in card tests, he would have all of the target drawings different. Of course this was stepping backward into the use of "free material," but he thought he could overcome the drawback of not having any mathematical basis on which "chance" could be reckoned. He decided to do it by an elaborate system of judging the results against a control set of drawings.

With Tyrrell's experience with the pointer and the possibility of auditory cues freshly in mind, Carington determined to plan his experiment in such a way that later no one could even whisper that any kind of sensory leakage could have occurred. He therefore selected his subjects entirely without regard for their location; some were even across the Atlantic at Duke University. None of those in London were ever permitted in his office when his target drawings were displayed, and as he says, few were even in the building.

On ten successive evenings, of five different series of experiments, Carington drew a picture of the first noun given on a page of the dictionary. The page was selected by a randomizing technique. The drawing was then displayed overnight in his office in London. Each evening at their own convenience in their own homes his subjects, about 250 in all, made drawings designed to

[3] Carington, Whatley. Paranormal cognition of drawings. *Proceedings of the Society for Psychical Research,* **34** (1940–1946) 151.

match the one displayed, and mailed them to him next day. At the end of the experiment, although a few drawings had not been contributed, a total of 2,200 were on hand.

By a complicated process these drawings were matched and scored by judges not informed as to which targets and drawings were supposed to match. The result was most unexpected.

The actual number of hits on a night-to-night basis was disappointingly close to chance, but there was a surprising number of subjects' drawings that markedly reproduced one or another of the originals. Only they were not drawn on the proper night. Some came later, some before the target which they hit. Of course no one had been prepared for an outcome like this.

It was so outstanding, however, that an additional way of judging the results was devised, just to double-check the method of evaluating the hits that Carington's judges had used. For this a "control" series of fifty other drawings, all different from the originals, was made, and the items in it were numbered alphabetically. A new judge was selected, one who did not know how the already completed tabulation had come out. He was asked to find the number of hits, just as before. Presumably if some of the original response drawings had been like the target set, *just by chance,* then some of them could be expected to resemble some of those in this new set of targets, too. But they did not. His results showed no significance. Neither in totals nor on successive nights was there any more hitting observed than could easily be accounted for by coincidence. It therefore seemed that Carington's subjects had been "affected" by his list of targets. But it was also true that they had not responded according to the expectations of *timing.* It was rather as if, let us say, all fifty targets had been displayed at the same time and as if the subjects had simply tried to match as many as they could. As it was the results were displaced chronologically, some falling before, some after the date on which the given picture had been selected.

At that time the possibility of displacement of results was a new idea, but its occurrence has since been repeatedly observed upon occasion by other experimenters. When it occurs, usually for some reason the subject is not making many direct hits and it appears as if his aim is systematically displaced. This is a phenomenon which is related to the effect known as psi missing.

In 1939, when Carington's experiment was performed, the most puzzling part of it was the series of hits in his material made *before* the corresponding original had been drawn or even selected. These are now recognizable, of course, as precognitive hits. But then, although results of precognition tests made at the Parapsychology Laboratory had been published, it was too soon for them to have been really digested. Carington, however, did recognize that these hits of his seemed to say that precognition had occurred. But it is doubtful if he or many others then appreciated fully the extent to which results like his illustrated the fact that to ESP, time is not the barrier it is in the world of sense perception. The idea of precognition was still too new, too unassimilated, for its implications from results like this to be taken with full seriousness.

In its entirety, Carington's mammoth experiment contributed mainly the idea of displacement, but of course, at the same time, it showed that drawings of nondescript objects used as target material could to a point be successfully identified. Whether the method as such had anything to recommend it is doubtful. Naturally, the judging of hits was a very laborious and complicated process. It takes pages of Carington's report even to describe the method he devised. Compared to checking an equal number of card calls, anyone would say that a method like this had better have a definite superiority over the simpler one if it is to be justified. The verdict of history seems to be that it does not have such superiority. At least it has not been used in other experiments when cards could be substituted. However, it did have a degree of value for a few subsequent experimenters in cases in which cards could not be used as in those that call for the evaluation of "verbal material," like the sayings of mediums. But the number of mediumistic studies has declined sharply in the years since 1939. Only very recently, however, in certain dream studies has the method been resurrected and used somewhat again, in spite of its cumbersome nature.

After Carington's displacement discovery, researchers in general were naturally alert for signs that ESP was operating in other ways than in direct hits on target. Carington's results had suggested that the ESP process may be somewhat like rifle practice, in which if the hit is not a bull's eye, still it will tend to be near it.

Acting on this suggestion, in 1953, another Englishman, Mr. G. W. Fisk, and his collaborator, A. M. J. Mitchell, tried a novel type of target for his ESP test in a further attempt to discover what kind of process the phenomenon of ESP really is.[4]

Fisk's resulting idea was a method by which the degrees of success could be determined in order to find out if misses did tend to aggregate near the bull's eye. For this a circular arrangement of targets seemed desirable. Fisk then made target cards which like a clock face consisted of twelve places arranged in a circle. On each of a dozen of the "clock cards" an hour hand was drawn pointing to one of the numerals, which would be the target on that particular card. Using a stack of these cards, enclosed in opaque envelopes, his subjects guessed the "hour" on each. Afterward, their hits around the circle could be checked; not only could the exact hits be checked, but also the distance of the misses from the target. In the initial tests, several subjects took part and their results showed individual differences in hit patterns. One subject scored high on direct hits, but in contrast a total of sixteen subjects produced scores significantly high on the places next to the target.

In the scoring, however, a complication for mathematicians developed. It turned out that human subjects have innate preferences: they choose certain hours more than others. The calls were so uneven in numbers around the clock, that it was necessary to correct for the tendency, which had disturbed the expectation of one hit in twelve on each, just by chance.

However, after this correction was made, it still looked as if the rifle analogy had some validity. Even if the designated target was missed, the response tended to be near it. And even though the test, like Tyrrell's, used position or location for the target, it was broader in that the "spread of missing" could be determined.

Sometime later, and in an area quite different from that of

---

[4] Fisk, G. W., and A. M. J. Mitchell. ESP experiments with clock cards. *Journal of the Society for Psychical Research,* **37** (1953–1954) 1–13.

Fisk's, another clock experiment was carried on.[5] But the target in this was time rather than location. In Johannesburg, South Africa, Professor A. E. H. Bleksley, head of the Department of Applied Mathematics at the University of Witwatersrand, had for years been interested in ESP, and had written about it so that his interest was widely known. Thus it was that in 1960 a stranger to him, a Mr. W. van Vuurde of Cape Town, wrote him saying that he was convinced that he could waken himself at a time chosen before he went to sleep. He wanted to find out what process was involved, whether that of a "built-in alarm clock," or ESP.

An experiment between the two was set up. In the main part of this Bleksley determined a target time, between midnight and 8 A.M., and set the hands of a nonrunning clock accordingly. He did this each evening, and some thousand miles away, in Cape Town, his subject alerted himself to waken at the time indicated on Bleksley's clock. The subject was provided with a clock that could be stopped by pulling a cord, so that he could waken, pull the cord, and go back to sleep, leaving until morning the taking of the record from the stopped clock. In one experiment a total of 161 trials were made in this way, and the record was sent to Bleksley. He checked it against his list of target times and in a certain experiment found that when the chance of a hit was one in 480 trials, on three nights a direct hit had been made. In addition, seven hits one minute off were made. The number expected by chance on these was one in 240 trials. This result was striking and presumably would have been even more so if the subject could have avoided a tendency to waken too soon. If he stopped his clock, then, he of course had no chance of making a hit that night. But even so, the experiment showed that, for this subject at least, apparently a built-in alarm clock existed that could be triggered by ESP. Although possibly Bleksley's clock hand was the target, it was also possible that the result meant that a *time* as well as a position could be the target of ESP.

Still a different kind of target was used by an experimenter from another quarter of the globe. The experiment was performed at

[5] Bleksley, A. E. H. An experiment on long-distance ESP during sleep. *Journal of Parapsychology*, **27** (1963) 1–15.

the Parapsychology Laboratory at Duke University while the experimenter was a research assistant there.[6] This experimenter was Mr. Jurgen Keil of Hobart University, Tasmania, and his work was the basis of his Ph.D. thesis. In it the novelty was that the ostensible target was a piece of recorded music.

Keil asked his subjects to select favorite excerpts from records and transfer them onto a tape. Then in the test, several rooms away from a subject, he selected by a randomizing method a single excerpt from the tape and listened (with ear phones) as it was played back. At the time it was being played, the subject was guessing which piece it was. The music thus could have been the target.

A checkup showed considerable variation among the subjects, but one in particular succeeded very well. The experiment of course left unanswered questions, for it was in effect a general or GESP situation in which the target could have been the experimenter's mental experience, and therefore a telepathic one, or a direct awareness of the sound, and thus clairvoyant. At any rate, it suggested that music can be added to the list as possible target material for ESP.

During all the years covered by these various projects, in the mainstream of research, the ESP cards were being used in spite of the continued criticism—mainly by those outside the field—that these cards were too impersonal, too uninteresting. As a matter of fact, with the repetition of calls in experimental situations, any novelty or special interest a target may have initially soon wears off and the test again descends to monotony. This must be offset by means other than the simple one of providing an intrinsically interesting target.

One of the first introductions of novelty, or rather of an adaptation of the card test, however, was made not because the subjects needed a new stimulus but because the *experimenter* did, for he himself declared that he was "sick of" the cards.

And well he might be. The experiment goes back to a time even earlier than Carington's experiment, when Dr. S. G. Soal, a mathematician from the University of London, began to test for

[6] Keil, H. H. J. A GESP test with favorite music targets. *Journal of Parapsychology,* **29** (1965) 35–44.

ESP, using the ESP deck.[7] He had read the reports of work going on at Duke, and he was trying to repeat it to see if he too could get evidence of ESP.

By the time Carington discovered the displacement effect in his picture tests, Soal had been testing subjects off and on for five years. He had worked with 160 of them, and made a total of 128,300 trials—*with no results!* Or rather with no results significantly different from chance. Understandably he was discouraged. He was about to conclude either that the reports from the United States were phony, or else that Englishmen do not "have ESP."

It would have been difficult for him to realize that a subtle element in the spirit or atmosphere of the testing situations might have accounted for the difference in results. In the United States, Linzmayer, Pearce, and the rest of the subjects who had a part in the establishment of ESP were students caught up in the interest and enthusiasm of pioneer research being conducted by a researcher who was dedicated to getting the answer to a question which he felt was of great importance. In order to guard against mistakes that could lead to a false answer, and thereby first of all, mislead the researcher himself, careful methods of procedure were worked out as a matter of course. They were important, but incidental to the goal of the research. The general atmosphere in which the subjects were tested was one of high adventure; of real first-hand interest in discovery. Restrained but definite excitement and enthusiasm were in the air, and could scarcely fail to be contagious. Like the experimenter, the subjects were interested and personally involved in the answer.

Soal's subjects, however, came to him mainly in response to advertisements. They were strangers to him, but willing to take the tests that were given in orderly, routine fashion by a careful and earnest experimenter who was doggedly trying to repeat someone else's test. After all, he was not carrying his own torch into the exploration of the unknown. His attempt accordingly was a repetition, but actually, one in name only. It was like a car without a spark plug, and ESP happens to be an ability also like a car in that the spark plug really is essential. Unconscious mental levels are not

---

[7] Soal, S. G. Fresh light on card guessing. Some new effects. *Proceedings of the Society for Psychical Research,* **152** (1940–1946) 152–198.

concerned with the external world when a strong reason for such concern is lacking.

It was still too early when Soal was making these tests of his for investigators to realize fully that in ESP experiments the subject's attitude and involvement is all-important, that ESP is not something just waiting to be turned on by a switch; that instead conditions favoring it must be created. Without a situation that creates the necessary attitude, no test is a test of ESP. More than that, no ESP test is or can be an exact repetition of another because even with the same individuals the atmosphere changes, the people are never quite the same the second time. Situations can be recreated in which the essential factors are produced, but in the laboratory they do not create themselves. The skill and artistry of a good experimenter is necessary, but just what all that means is still difficult to put in words. The art of producing evidence of ESP in test situations is much like the art of teaching, something that can be improved, but not inculcated.

Thus, Soal's long search yielded him nothing. About to give up, in correspondence with Carington he learned of displacement, and that ESP may not always consist of direct hits on target. Carington urged him to search his data for it. And so he did. He found no trace in the records of the majority of his subjects, but in those of two, there it was!

With one of the two, Soal was able to work further. She became an outstanding subject, and Soal, quite convinced now of the existence of ESP even in the English, worked with her long and fruitfully.

About the same time Soal found another outstanding subject. This one called upon Soal and asked to be tested, because he was confident of his ESP ability. And with him Soal worked in succeeding years even more. Results from both did much to advance the cause of parapsychology in England. In the "forward displacement," among other effects shown in some of their scores, much was done to advance the recognition in that country of precognition as a human ability.

But all of this preamble leads up to the simple fact that Soal, in working with these two exceptional subjects, did not use the ESP symbols, but instead substituted cards bearing pictures of four animals and a bird, with the name of each printed below. There were a lion, an elephant, a zebra, a giraffe, and a pelican. Of course one cannot tell if the results he got were better or worse, or in any way affected by this switch of target. As a matter of fact, the names were soon considered too long and cumbersome to write out in the records, and their initials, *l, e, z, g,* and *p,* were substituted so that in effect the targets really soon came to be letters of the alphabet. But whatever one chooses to consider them, animal names or only letters, they worked. Soal's research with the two special subjects is outstanding among all the experimental research that has been done in England.

From a report published in 1950, a novel target variation was used in an experiment by Morris Skibinsky, a graduate student in statistics and also at the time a part-time research assistant at the Parapsychology Laboratory.[8] Going on the assumption already mentioned, that emotionally toned targets ought to produce higher ESP scores than the ESP symbols, he devised a target sheet on which names and symbols both were used. In alternate rows, the names of relatives—his three sisters, his father, and himself—were randomly arranged, in the other rows the ESP symbols were randomly arranged. The test was a GESP type in which the experimenter in Durham looked at the target sheet at an arranged time, and the subjects, who included family members as well as nonrelatives, in separate homes in New York City, wrote out their responses.

The result showed a significant difference between hits on names and on symbols. But it was in the opposite direction from that expected, the scores on names were negative, those of relatives the lowest, those on symbols slightly positive. In fact the averages per run of about three hundred runs each, when five was expected by chance, were 4.72 on names, 5.16 on symbols, a significant difference. The fact suggested by these deviations was that, as the experimenter expected, the use of emotionally toned targets seemed to have an effect, but as he did not expect, it was as a depressant rather than a stimulant. That it should be such will perhaps seem less inexplicable after reading the discussion in

[8] Skibinsky, Morris. A comparison of names and symbols in a distance ESP test. *Journal of Parapsychology,* **14** (1950) 140–156.

Chapter 12 of the factors that affect the way ESP is expressed in various circumstances.

In various other ways, in succeeding years, changes have been made in the general technique of using ESP cards. For instance, in a primary school in France, from 1954 to 1956, the teacher, Mrs. Christiane Vasse, made an innovation toward a more emotional or personal relation between the subjects and the targets they were asked to guess.[9] She had long been interested in ESP and took the opportunity her pupils presented to make some tests with them on the general topic of finding optimum conditions for ESP. It was not primarily concern with different kinds of targets but something closer to necessity that led to the feature of her work that is especially interesting here. As she reported, because "We did not have the regular ESP symbol cards," she decided to have the children make their own target cards. She thought it might make the test more interesting, too.

Each of forty children made five drawings. Then the class—by vote (in the first grade!)—chose five out of all the two hundred. These were pictures of a man, a house, a train, a boat, and a flower. The teacher then had these drawings printed on cards and used five of each kind to make up a twenty-five-card deck. The number that could be expected to be correct by chance alone when this deck was "guessed" was five—just as in the ESP card deck. In the tests made that year the children guessed so many of these cards correctly that no doubt could be raised that ESP had occurred. In fact, in both tests made individually, and those made in groups, their scores were high enough to yield in each case CR's of over four.

The next school year the ESP cards were available, and in some of the tests made, the two kinds, ESP cards and the children's own, were used in circumstances in which they could be compared. Forty runs were made with the ESP deck and sixty-three with the children's deck. For both decks results were secured that indicated ESP. The difference was slightly in favor of the children's deck, but not significantly so. It looks as if other conditions in this experiment were so good that unconsciously these little children

[9] Vasse, Christiane, and Paul Vasse. ESP tests with French first-grade school children. *Journal of Parapsychology*, 22 (1958) 187–203.

picked the proper target often enough to show that the secret door had opened, but that the difference in the two target decks was not an important one.

Another experiment on the effect of emotionally toned targets was carried out in 1961 at the Parapsychology Laboratory by Dr. John Freeman.[10] In this the subjects were college students instead of primary school children, and instead of drawings, each subject brought in five objects of his own toward which he felt an attachment. Using these alternately with ESP cards, some subjects scored better on their objects; others did better on the ESP runs. The conclusion was that emotionally toned targets do not necessarily produce higher scores.

From these and other ways in which the characteristics of targets have been tested, it seems that in experiments it is not the target itself on which the selection in the unconscious depends. Instead it is something in the total situation. Somehow the total situation must be such that the subject becomes personally involved. And this, if one thinks about it, is exactly what the ESP cases are saying. The *target* in them is a complex thing; it is an objective fact, like a broken windshield, a woman doctor, a stolen car, a winning horse. But ever so much more than that. In each case it is something that has a personal meaning for the person. It was his own experience and still it is his own, even if only about a stranger of whom he will read in the newspaper. Somehow, in the laboratory the attempt to reproduce this quality of ownership by trying to give the targets personal meaning is not sufficient. If any preference is induced that way it is slight and evanescent, for it tends to disappear when the *repetition* of testing is involved.

When this attitude, this personal involvement, has been created, then apparently any of the various kinds of targets used can serve the purpose. It would be difficult to find an unsuccessful experimental attempt in which failure could be laid to the nature of the target material, easy to find those in which it seemed to lie in the experimenter's inability to create the necessary psychological effect within his subjects.

The fact that stands out strongest is that it is important in ex-

[10] Freeman, John. An ESP test involving emotionally-toned objects. *Journal of Parapsychology*, **25** (1961) 260–265.

periments to arouse the personal motivation of the subject. Somehow he must become involved himself, and take the task for his own. Although simply trying, or even trying hard, to identify the target may not be enough, since other factors can prevent success, still, success will not come without such motivation.

If all other conditions are favorable, then strange or novel targets may be an added asset, but the experimenter must manage so to stimulate and motivate the subject that the selection of the targets will occur regardless of what they are. This can be difficult, but it is not impossible. The psyche is broadly interested in the world as it touches directly the narrow range of personal involvement. If it does that, then the target need not have intrinsic significance, but can be an item of only peripheral importance, whether mayhem and murder in the news, or a series of test symbols in the laboratory.

CHAPTER 9

The Form of the Experience

THE workshop of the unconscious is a busy place. Activity there apparently seldom ceases. Evidence of it comes out in people's actions when awake, and in their dreams when sleeping. Now that the operations of ESP can be recognized and added to the list of unconscious activities, they too must be fitted into any general concept of the mental processes that go on there.

When ESP begins, it means first that decisions must be made about material to be admitted. A choice must be made. But more than that—once an item of information has been accepted, something must be done about it. It must be disposed of; at least disposal of it is made, for certainly messages do get to consciousness. Whether or not the ones that do so are all of those admitted, no one can say. But these were definitely admitted into, or perhaps propelled into, consciousness. Inspection of them shows that they arrived there in one or another of four different ways or forms.[1] Occasionally they arrive in combinations of the four, but for simplicity at this stage of discussion, let us forget about the combinations.

Three of the forms that ESP messages take in consciousness are as familiar as bread and butter. These are intuitions and realistic and unrealistic dreams. Only the fourth form is relatively uncommon (and incidentally, for that very reason has often been misunderstood and given an aura of mystery beyond its due). This is the pseudosensory kind of experience known as the hallucinatory.

The significant point here about these four forms is that they are not bizarre or peculiar to ESP or even uncommon as mental processes, nor are they special outlets created for ESP alone. In-

[1] Rhine, Louisa E. Subjective forms of spontaneous psi experiences. *Journal of Parapsychology*, **17** (1953) 77–114.

stead, the familiar ones, the intuition and the dream forms, are humanity's old friends, and even the less familiar, the hallucination, is not unknown.

But what are intuitions, dreams, even hallucinations? They are devices of the mind—"constructs," as psychologists have called them—that serve the purposes of conscious life. They are part of the basic mental equipment of the personality, ready-made methods of carrying messages into consciousness, including those originating by ESP.

Ordinarily, as everyone knows, intuitions are the result of past experience—memories, wishes, hopes, and fears already stored unconsciously. As a background process in the making of an ordinary non-ESP intuition, these stored remnants, of course, are not consciously scanned and added up, but are worked over unconsciously, rearranged perhaps, and then the result—all by itself it seems—appears in consciousness, an intuition or a hunch which may prove right or wrong according to circumstances and the efficiency of the preceding unconscious mental action. The intuition comes as an idea only—no imagery, no rational introduction, no explanation. As such, the person believes it in a general way, of course. But if facts prove otherwise, what of it? The hunch was wrong and easily forgotten.

ESP intuitions, as distinct from the ordinary kind, bring new information—not the reworked product of stored remnants of the past. They too appear in consciousness as ideas, imageryless, unintroduced, unexplained, but *there*. And probably registered there initially, as shown in Chapter 5, with strong conviction.

A woman now living in Australia had an intuitive experience of which she says:

"I am sending you an account of my experience. It happened a long time ago in Russia, but it puzzles me still—like the invention of radio or TV.

"If machines can receive and transmit events from far away, why not the human being? We are more sensitive than machines.

"I was married for eighteen months only when my husband went to our estate for a few days while I stayed in town. It was seven hundred miles away, and we usually went only when there was some business to be attended to. The big house was occupied by the administrator, and we used a small cottage consisting of two rooms, kitchen, and verandah.

"On this particular occasion my husband had gone alone to the estate while I stayed with my mother.

"It was a Wednesday evening when I started to feel uneasy, sensing danger for my husband's life. My mother noticing my mood asked what was the matter. 'George is in danger,' I blurted out, 'danger from fire.'

" 'Now don't get such ideas into your head. What can happen to him? He can look after himself.' My mother seemed slightly annoyed.

"But my restlessness only grew. I got up, wished her good night and went to my room, saying I was tired though it was only just past nine o'clock. How could I warn George, I asked myself. The cottage had no phone. A telegram would only reach him the next morning.

"Suddenly I hit upon the idea of warning him by telepathy. I sat down, put my elbows on the table, my head in my hands, visualized the bedroom in the cottage and concentrated on my husband's head. Mentally I repeated over and over: 'Beware of fire, beware of fire, . . .' on and on, until I was exhausted. After relaxing for about ten minutes, I started again. It was by now ten o'clock.

"After that I felt peaceful and went to sleep.

"On Friday I had a telegram from my husband telling me he would be back on Saturday morning.

"When he arrived, he told me a lot about the estate—not a word about a fire—and I only hoped my mother would not mention my anxiety. Suddenly she said, with a smile, 'And there was no fire?' 'What do you mean?' asked George, but I sensed directly he had grown tense. And then my mother told him. George did not laugh, but turning toward me, asked, 'Which day was it?' 'Wednesday night.' 'What time?' 'Between nine and ten. George, what happened?' And then he told me that on that same day he was very tired as he had worked hard. At 9 P.M. he had started to write letters, but soon decided to go on to bed and get up early the next morning to finish his correspondence. When on the point of falling asleep, he had suddenly been aroused as if somebody were calling him. He had sat up in bed, and not knowing why, had inhaled the air deeply. Was there an odd smell or not? Nonsense, he thought, what could there be, and lay down again.

"Again he was on the verge of falling asleep when he was again roused energetically. This time he got up and opened the door leading to the kitchen. He quickly shut it again as there was no fire but a terrible smell of charcoal gas.

"The woman who came to do the household and cooking had, before going home, put out the fire in the fuel stove by pouring water on the burning wood, then closed the air pipe. The charcoal gas would have filtered slowly into the bedroom, killing my husband in his sleep . . . and he was seven hundred miles away."

The experience began without logic, without reason, and without awareness of detail. It was just an impression in consciousness that carried with it an unreasoned certainty. This factor of certainty is part of so many ESP intuitions, as to be almost an identifying mark.

The mental device used in more ESP experiences (according to the numbers reported) than any other is the dream. The intuitive form runs a close second. Of course, since people sleep about a third of their lives, it would be expected that many ESP experiences would occur in sleep, provided of course that unconscious mental activity does not also "sleep," which it obviously does not all the time.

One way in which dreams are different from intuitions is that they feature imagery while intuitions do not. But here again the person is unaware of the process by which his dream is formed. He does not know how his dream is made, nor does he feel that he himself is making it. The work of its construction goes on in levels far out of consciousness. All he knows about it is that a dream appeared—and sometimes not even that, since awareness of it depends upon recall, which can be a quite unreliable process.

Ordinary dreams, like ordinary intuitions, are constructed from materials already in the storehouse, and sometimes too from current sense experience, if sensory stimuli happen to be present at the time. In certain dream experiments, for instance, external sounds can be shown to affect the character of a dream. The imagery may be modified accordingly.

ESP dreams, like ESP intuitions, seem to differ from ordinary ones only in the origin of the material. In the ESP variety, new material is worked into the dream imagery.

The imagery of dreams, although mainly of the visual type, varies from the extremely realistic to the highly symbolic. People differ as to which kind they feature, but in general each person seems to show considerable consistency in the kind he uses.

When a person with a tendency to dream realistically has a dream that carries an ESP message, the imagery is true to an objective situation. Details are included and are generally precise; often the whole dream is somewhat like a view seen from a specific angle, as is illustrated in the dream reported in the following case.

"This dream remains a vivid picture, even after six years, for to me it was a definite reality. . . . The fact that I have never been subject to disturbing dreams and am seldom aware of having dreamed at all has caused me to place special emphasis on the few which were forceful, like this one of a June night six years ago, a few days after my son's graduation from elementary school.

"Suddenly I was aware of being in a very very large room, such as a small auditorium or large gymnasium. There were so many people within this enclosure, individual faces were not distinguishable. The crowd was so large all seats were taken and, in the dream, it seemed there was not room for another person to stand. I was seated not far from a wall. In glancing over the throng, somewhat casually, most forcibly and suddenly across this vast room (also near the wall), my attention was focused upon a young man. He was taller than anyone there, so tall indeed I wondered whether he might be standing on some box or bench; his face was clearly defined, half profile view: he was wearing a white short-sleeved shirt—neither casual nor dress—with tie. The trousers were dark—I could see only this much because he also was standing behind other people. I awakened with a keen sense of this having truly occurred, for in the dream somehow I approached him and said to him, 'Why, you are taller than Doctor W.' Until the dream Dr. W. had been the tallest person I had ever noticed.

"After that realistic dream, I searched for the young man in every large, crowded place—even in the supermarket. On Sunday afternoons during the summer we were in the habit of attending the Albert Coleman 'Pops' concerts, which were at that time conducted in the Fox Theater. I scanned the crowds there. All summer I searched. No one even remotely resembling this young man ever materialized. But I knew he was in existence.

"Then my son entered the eighth grade at Southwest High School, Atlanta, in September. As always, the first PTA meeting was attended to overflowing. We were there along with all the other first-time high schoolers—a little late, so we sat near the back doorway, midway up on the 'bleacher' seats, which are folded against the wall of the school auditorium-gym, when not in use.

"As one so often is inclined to do in such gatherings, I was glancing over the vast turnout of parents in a sort of bemused way when, shockingly, there all the way across the room, almost in direct line, was my young man. He was looking down, speaking with someone in the exact attitude in which he had appeared in the dream. He was a new teacher in the area, a basketball coach as well as teacher of English and science. He was six feet, eleven inches tall. My son had been assigned to him for homeroom and for English and science.

"Nothing more has developed from this phenomenon. He was kind enough not to discredit my account of the dream, although he did smile in a way. His remark was that he had an aunt who had similar experiences."

The profuseness of true detail that sometimes apparently rivals that of photography is, of course, the identifying characteristic of realistic dreams. The viewpoint may not always be so precise as in the case above, but may nonetheless be implicit. The amount of detail, too, may vary, as it does in the numerous examples in Chapter 7, all of which are realistic dreams, but the general characteristics are the same.

In unrealistic dreams, as the name implies, the imagery is fanciful, or dramatic, or bizarre; and the message is carried by the meaning of the fantasy, not by the trueness or exactness of the imagery. Sometimes a combination of realism and unrealism may be shown in the imagery as in the dream below, for instance.

"My son had been home on furlough from Mississippi, and I had taken him to the depot late at night to take a train back to camp. He asked me to go home and get some sleep. He didn't mind waiting alone.

"Two nights later I was sound asleep when I thought I heard a loud knock on the kitchen door. I got up and turned on the kitchen light, then opened the door. There stood my son. He had bandages on his legs and tears in his eyes. I said, 'Come on in.'

" 'I got lost from the other boys tonight,' he said. 'I was in a swamp. I just wanted to come home and see you once more. Now I have to go back and see if I can find them.'

"He turned and went down the steps toward the garage. It was raining a little—foggy—he just disappeared in the fog. I shut the door—*and woke up*.

"I stood there frozen in my tracks. I knew it was a warning or a vision. I went back to bed after praying for my son's safety.

"Two days later I received a letter from him. He said, 'The first night after I got back we went on night maneuvers. I was sent back to camp for something we forgot. I took a shortcut and got lost. I was really lost for hours. I didn't think I would ever get to see you again. I prayed I would find my way out of there. But I followed a light, like a star, and finally came back on the road."

"Was this a dream I had, or a vision, and did my prayers help him?"

Without attempting to answer the final question raised in that person's letter or more than commenting on the sleep-walking aspect of the experience which had nothing to do with the element of ESP that appears to have been at the basis of it, one can note that although the imagery seemed to be realistic, it was not true. Her son did not appear at the door and tell her of his dilemma.

Therefore the experience is easily classified as one in which the dreamer merely reoriented the information into her own perspective. That reorientation originated as a dramatization in the unconscious, but it came to the dreamer as if from the exterior.

When an ESP message is carried by an unrealistic dream, the difficulty of identifying it as such increases the farther the imagery departs from realism. However, it is sometimes possible to identify it with a reasonable degree of assurance if the unrealism seems to carry a symbolic meaning, as in the following instance.

"When I was in college I had this dream: I was standing in a field completely familiar to me. And Elaine (my fiancée, who was then attending college 1,500 miles away) was at the perimeter of this field. She flung out her arms as happily we ran toward each other, calling, and eager to embrace, when quite suddenly a deep gorge between us appeared. From nowhere it came and naturally kept us apart. We ran up and down it, trying to make a crossing. Impossible. She was left on the other side weeping hysterically. And I could only call out to her in frustration and complete defeat and bewilderment. It was incredible that this deep, forbidding chasm could exist in this field I knew so well. I woke writhing with the problem.

"To make the story short, a few weeks later (three, I think) Elaine's letter came telling me we were through—that we could not marry. Although heartbroken I somehow felt that there were underlying currents I didn't know about and that poor Elaine was having troubles. I met her a month after that, and she tearfully broke down and confessed she had been forced to write the 'Dear John' letter to me because a member of my own family had been writing her abnormal love letters. She just had not known what else to do. My reactions to all of this are unimportant, but at least my troubling dream and this unaccountable gorge and barrier in a field I *thought* I knew were explained. The symbolism was direct, and the message accurate."

In occasional extreme cases it sometimes appears that the imagery of an unrealistic dream tends to be "stamped in," sufficiently that it becomes, as one might say, a habit and is used repeatedly to carry similar ESP messages. Such appears to be the case in the dreams reported next.

"Although this experience was not my own, I was present at the follow-up and can vouch for the authenticity of the full story.

"During the war (1945) my sister, Muriel, was a WAVE stationed in Washington, D.C. She became ill and was hospitalized. Muriel was very ill, and one night dreamed that she was sitting on a high wall—if she lived, she would have to manage to stay on the wall; but if she fell, she would die. Thankfully she lived.

"Several weeks later our father contracted pleurisy and was dangerously ill. He was confined to a hospital. The family, knowing Muriel would worry, and she had been so ill herself, decided not to call her home unless it was absolutely necessary. One night after our nightly visit to Dad, the door opened, and there was Muriel demanding, 'Where is Dad and *how* is he?' It seems she had had that same dream, but this time Dad was the one on the wall, so she went AWOL and rushed home, knowing instinctively that Dad was very ill. He recovered, and Muriel was not found out to be AWOL—so we were all happy."

Through varying degrees of fantasy in unrealistic dreams, the underlying information is usually discernible, as the basis on which the dream imagery was freely and imaginatively constructed. When no such underlying basis for the symbolism is obvious, it is still possible that unconsciously the dreamer "had a reason," but here is treacherous ground for any attempt at reliable interpretation. Reliability goes down the drain when possibility of a checkup is excluded. It is probable that as much fantasy is included in much "dream interpretation," as in the symbolic dream itself. In studies of ESP in dreams, fanciful interpretations have no place.

With a large proportion of all ESP messages appearing in consciousness either directly as intuitions, or less directly as dreams, only a small part of all the experiences reported remains, and these come to consciousness by the mental construct of hallucination.

In a hallucination the person thinks his senses, usually those of vision or hearing, are involved when no objective cause is present; no object to reflect light rays to the retina, or airwaves to the ear drum.

In their external characteristics, hallucinations are somewhere between intuitions and dreams. Like intuitions, they occur when the person is awake; like dreams, they carry their meaning by means of imagery. But even though that imagery seems as real as seeing or hearing, it is no more so than the mental pictures made while dreaming. This imagery is ready-made to be misunderstood and misinterpreted, for it fits right in with the real scene, and the person gets no hint that these images are not real sense impressions, that, instead, they are made up in his own unconscious.

Since the hallucinatory form, like the rest, is a device by which material from the unconscious may be expressed in consciousness, the effect may be made up entirely of stored remnants of past experiences, and as such have nothing to do with ESP. An example of such a "regular" hallucinatory (not ESP) experience is described by a woman from Iowa:

"In October, 1939, my husband sustained a broken neck and severe head cuts in a car accident. After a few days in the hospital, our doctor felt he would be better off at home, so I had him at home in traction until the end of December. At that time he was allowed up while wearing a head-and-neck brace.

"January 15 it was necessary for me to enter the hospital for major surgery. During this time he spent part of each day with me. After ten days I was home, but with orders to be up only half a day. I noticed that he seemed nervous and had changed completely toward me. We had always been unusually close and more so if possible after our girl arrived after a wait of five years.

"Monday morning, February 12, he announced he had to go to Omaha on business. I didn't want him to go, but he left, getting back that night completely exhausted. The next day he said he was going to Minneapolis with some man from a neighboring town. He expected to be back late that night.

"About midnight he called (I was beside myself wondering what had happened). He said he was calling from a hotel in a town about a hundred miles from our home, and he was so tired that I suggested he stay all night and come in in the morning. He said he guessed he would.

"I went to bed and to sleep. I had planned on his being there for dinner, and he didn't come. By the middle of the afternoon I knew something had happened. We checked with the highway patrol, etc., to no avail. To complicate things it began to snow (it had snowed some during the night).

"About 11:30 I looked out our front window and I saw our car come past the house—round the corner on the way to the garage. I told our hired girl I'd go open the door, for I knew he shouldn't. I hurried out, opened the side door, and there was the car inside; the door was shut, and he was slumped over the wheel. How I ever opened the door, I don't know. I knew he was dead and had been for some hours—the gun on the seat beside him.

"I called our doctor, he in turn the coroner. Their opinion was that he had driven home after he called me that night—put the time of the death at about 2 to 3 A.M.

"What I saw was as real as any time I'd ever seen him come home."

Direct and indirect remnants of earlier experiences in that case included the memory of earlier times when the husband returned home and drove to the garage, his wife's hope and wish that he would so return, her anxiety that he might not. Somehow these together "triggered" the optical impression of his return. But the person herself had no more awareness that she was the author of the experience than she would have had about a dream or an intuition. It was all done unconsciously. It took the form in consciousness, of a hallucination.

Auditory hallucinations operate just like visual ones. Ordinarily they too result from stored memories, hopes, anxieties. Sometimes with these, too, the distinction between stored and new information is difficult to make—especially when details are not specific. The following account is one in which this distinction is unclear.

"My oldest boy ran away from home, leaving no trace. I was unable to locate him for over two years. Needless to say, while contacting police departments, worrying and praying, and asking radio programs to help, I spent many sleepless nights. But some nights I really slept, as I was working steadily and did get very tired.

"One night I was in that semiconscious state one is in just as he falls asleep. At that time I was sleeping on the porch. Suddenly I was wide awake at the sound of my son's footsteps coming down the street. I was sure they were his. I would have known them anywhere and they were outstandingly clear in the stillness of the night. So overjoyed was I that he was coming home at last that I jumped out of bed with a loud cry and peered over the porch railing, sure that I would see him turn into our gate. There was nothing. There was not a soul in the street. I couldn't believe it. I went inside, donned my robe and slippers and went downstairs and looked both ways. I was heartsick with disappointment and unbelief and a little angry. I marked the date on the calendar and when he finally did return a year later and we discussed many things, he distinctly recalled having had it very strongly on his mind then to come home, so strongly that he said he could picture himself walking the street and turning in at our gate and my calling to him and running to meet him with a glad welcome."

With two persons yearning for each other, the sound of footsteps may have been only a "stored remnant." No one can be certain that it was more.

In cases with visual imagery, the hallucinatory effect is usually that of "seeing" a specific person who generally is later found to have been undergoing a crisis at the time. In many of the reported cases, the crisis is death, but frequently other kinds of crises are involved.

"In December, 1951, my husband was drafted into the Marine Corps. We had only been married three months and of course were very close.

"He had been down in Parris Island about a month; it was a very cold spell and according to weather broadcasts even the South was having bad weather.

"I stayed at my mother's house several nights a week as I was lonely. On this Friday night I fell asleep and about 1:30 A.M. I woke up and Richard (my husband) was standing in the room next to me. It was as clear as this paper. He didn't speak but just stood there as if sort of pleading.

"When I got up the next morning I told my mother I was very worried that something might be wrong. I didn't hear from him that day—but the next day, Sunday, I received a long-distance phone call from Charleston, S.C., Navy Hospital. He had pneumonia.

"At the time he appeared to me on the Friday night he was standing 12–4 fire watch. As you know, Marine-Corps boot training is pretty rigid, and when he complained of being sick, they thought he was trying to plead out of fire watch and he was forced to stand it anyway.

"He had a fever of over 104 and was very sick, and at those moments when he appeared to me, he told me that he was walking the watch, just praying so hard that he could be home with me.

"He was wrapped in a blanket and even so the damp coldness of the night was still making him shiver and brought him almost to tears. Somehow—I don't know how—he spanned those eight hundred miles and came to me."

The person's vision of her husband, of course, gave no clue as to the kind of crisis he was undergoing. She had to find out later by ordinary methods that he was ill.

As is very typical in such experiences, the person in that instance was quite convinced that somehow the other "came to me." However, had it been a dream instead of a hallucinatory experience, the dream image would more likely have been interpreted less realistically. By the long habit of believing sense impressions as originating "out there" from whence they appear to come, it is quite natural for people to interpret hallucinatory experiences that way too. The *internal* origin of the imagery is not self-evident, and the opposite impression is very convincing.

Auditory hallucinations in their most common form are those that can be referred to as "call cases." In these, the person hears himself called, and it turns out that the one who he thought called him was undergoing a crisis at the time. Such is the following case.

"In February, 1922, my mother had a nervous breakdown and went to stay with a friend for a two-week change. I was twenty-one at the time and working; my brother was overseas. My maternal grandfather had lived with my folks about thirty years at the time. He adored me. I was his 'Love,' a Lancashire term of affection. He was eighty-six at the time, going senile, and his whole concern and interest lay in keeping all the stoves well banked to have a nice warm home upon my and Father's nightly return. But he'd forget to check the dampers when the fire started drawing well, and we'd find the stoves at white heat. To protect him and house it was necessary to place him temporarily in a 'home' hospital, until Mother's return, if we expected to have any house left for her to return to.

"February 22, a holiday, I visited him and promised him he would be home as soon as Mother returned. He looked at me with the saddest faraway look in his eye and said, 'Eh, me Love, yer so much like yer grandmother. You've 'ur [hair] just like hers. Well, it won't be long now afore I'll be seeing her.' I consoled him. Told him how much we all loved him and it would only be a few days more and he could come home. The nurses treated him wonderfully.

"It was a terrible day and worse night. The worst blizzard, sleet and ice storm in years raged. Unaware of the situation at home, an old family friend had come up from Providence for the holiday and slept with me that night. At 1:10 A.M.—February 23—a voice woke me, calling my name twice, very clearly and distinctly and evenly. 'Ruth?'—'Ruth?' Thinking Mae had called me for some reason I answered, 'Yes?' and asked what she wanted. No answer. I shook her and woke her up. I told her someone had called. She said I must have been dreaming and go to sleep. But the voice seemed to be still vibrating in the bedroom. The storm was terrible. I was restless. I put on the light, went into the sitting room to check the clock. It was then 1:10 A.M. I returned to bed and no sooner fell asleep than the phone rang. It was 1:30. The Sisters in the nondenominational home were reporting that Grandfather had gotten out in his underwear while they were occupied with a dying man. Fire laws required that locks on institution doors lock on the outside only, and always open from the inside. After I left he had become possessed with the idea he should get home to keep the fires going and the house warm for his 'Love.' In his sly, senile illusion he waited for a chance to slip out. We called the police to search for him. At 6 A.M. they found him frozen to death in a nearby field. He'd gone out the back door and wandered over a sparsely settled area, slipped on an icy stone near a brook, struck his head against a jagged rock edge, stunned himself, and froze before regaining consciousness."

As in the visual cases, the implication is easy—that the person actually did call, and that somehow the other heard the call. But whether or not an actual call was uttered—as for instance in the earlier case when the girl clerking in a store "heard" her mother call—seems not to matter, for calls are "heard" whether or not one was uttered.[2]

Another kind of hallucinatory effect that superficially seems rather different from any of those above is reported fairly often. This one features general bodily sensations. Instead of seeing or hearing something that is not there, a person feels something, often pain or other physiological symptoms that turn out to have no ordinary cause. In a deeper sense these are hallucinatory too, for they seem to be rough or general duplicates of similar feelings being experienced by someone else.

Such an experience is reported by a woman from Virginia.

"My mother and aunt had lived together in Indiana for a number of years. Although they were both near eighty, they were quite well and active for that age. My aunt had no children, so her nieces and nephews have always been very close to her. I am the only daughter in my family. Consequently I spent as much time as I could with my mother and aunt, and wrote them regularly. They depended on me for many of their decisions, and our relationship was very close.

[2] Rhine, Louisa E. The relation of experience to associated events in spontaneous ESP. *Journal of Parapsychology,* **17** (1953) 187–209.

"On November 8, 1961, shortly after I had arrived at the school where I teach, I went into the office. Suddenly an extremely severe pain struck my shoulder and chest, so intense that it made me cry out. The principal and other teachers who were in the office were alarmed. However, the intensity of the pain did not last, and I went on with my work.

"About an hour after this, my principal came to my room to tell me I had a long-distance call. My aunt had suffered a heart attack, as she and my mother were going downstairs. She had died instantly, with only my mother there. As well as we could estimate, it had happened about the time the severe pain had struck me."

Another kind of experience occasionally reported is the feeling of labor pains at the time when a child is born, even though the person who has what one might call a pseudoeffect is unaware of the timing of the birth. A woman in Washington had an experience of this kind.

"Seven years ago we adopted a daughter. The doctor had assured me that the baby was expected in September, a month away.

"I was especially anticipating this event, as we had had several heartbreaking failures in our attempt to acquire another child. I had been informed after a complicated delivery that I could never bear another child.

"The night our 'gift' baby was born was a night of torture for me. I was unaware that the mother was in labor, but I most assuredly knew something physical was occurring to me. I had severe abdominal pains which caused me to pace the floor all night. When our physician called at 5:45 A.M. to tell me the baby had been born, my exact words were, 'Why didn't you tell me I was in labor!'

"Perhaps this is not a phenomenon, but I will always feel that I wanted that baby so much I had to help to get her born."

Usually, when pain or other physiological effect is "shared," the two persons are very close emotionally, but in the situation in the experience above, presumably it was the significance of the birth rather than the relationship of the two persons that afforded the connecting link. Much more commonly the one who has the "pseudobirth" pains is a mother, sister, friend, or even husband, father, or other close male relative. But whatever the relationship, nothing about the sensations as such tells the person that this is not really his own pain, but the pain of someone else.

These various modalities—visual, auditory, general bodily, and even olfactory and tactile sensations—are all occasionally reported.

This survey of the forms which ESP experiences take answers the questions about the way information received by ESP is disposed of in the unconscious. If the person is awake, his experience will usually be in the form of an intuition, but occasionally it may be a hallucination. If he is asleep, the information will be incorporated into dream imagery, which is more often realistic, but can also be symbolic. These are the forms or constructs which are used in life situations when conditions are free and unrestricted so that natural proclivities, many of which are still essentially uncharted, can run their course.

In experiments, however, the situation is not free. It must be restricted in a number of ways, including the range of possible forms the response can take. Usually it is not that a particular one is specified by the experimenter; rather the conditions he must impose do it. For instance, it is easy and simple to work with subjects when they are awake, but it is complicated and cumbersome to experiment with ESP in sleeping subjects. Consequently in all the advances so far made in parapsychology, subjects have been used when awake. The dream forms thus have been almost automatically excluded.

It is true that recent developments in techniques for the study of dreams have made it possible to include ESP tests in dream studies, and early reports indicate that attempts to induce telepathic dreaming have shown some success.[3] However, the testimony of spontaneous cases already indicated quite strongly that ESP does occur in dreams, so this finding is scarcely a surprise. Instead it is something like an accessory after the fact. Even so, it is not a finding arrived at easily. The technique to date involves expensive

---

[3] Ullman, Montague. An experimental study of the telepathic dream. *Corrective Psychiatry and Journal of Social Therapy,* **12** (1966) 115–141.

equipment, and the necessary procedures for collecting the data are slow and laborious. In addition, even after it has been secured its evaluation presents another problem. The dream records are in the form of narratives, of course, for people do not dream series of calls of symbols, as in the responses of waking subjects. The narratives then must be judged as to the degree to which they reflect the idea, picture, or whatever item was used as target.

Judging the degree of fit of verbal material, as already mentioned in connection with the research of Whatley Carington, is a cumbersome procedure, and one which at best lacks the definiteness, concreteness, and speed with which the responses of waking subjects in conventional ESP tests can be judged. Compared to that simple procedure, the method of evaluating verbal responses is a hundred times more difficult. It is not likely therefore that the method will be used in any ESP research not directly connected with the dreaming state or its physiological accompaniments.

Thus it was that when Linzmayer and the other subjects who have taken ESP tests when awake were asked to name the cards in a concealed deck, the only forms their responses could take were waking forms, either hallucinatory or intuitive. Under the circumstances and in view of its rarity, the hallucinatory response was hardly to be expected. Thus the circumstances practically dictated that the intuitive form be used. Assuming that the new material, the information about the card symbols, was admitted into the unconscious, the situation required that it be transferred to consciousness by a series of intuitions. Considering that in life situations four avenues are available, but in experiments like this, only one, success would appear to depend on whether or not unconscious forms of expression can be thus commanded.

The question then is, Can the unconscious employ *any* form or construct, and are there reasons why a specific one is chosen in a specific case? From numbers of spontaneous experiences, as they are reported, it seems likely that some of the four forms are used more often than others, however, and this fact may possibly have a degree of meaning. Of course figures in connection with reported experiences are very unreliable. In the first place, certainly many occur that are not reported, and among those that are reported, much selection occurs, for when strikingly important events are concerned, they are more likely to be remembered and be thought worth recording than when less important ones are involved. But in spite of this the numbers of experiences of each of the forms may have some reliability. There is no reason to think they would be too unevenly reported to give a clue as to their actual frequencies of occurrence.

The cases in the Duke collection are now numerous enough, it would seem, to give some testimony on the point. At the last count (made in 1963), 10,066 cases were classified in the four forms; and the percentage of them in each was, intuitive 30 percent, hallucinatory 13 percent, unrealistic dream 18 percent, realistic dream 39 percent.

A distribution so unequal suggests that reasons must exist that lead to the selection of some forms more often than others. What could those reasons be? It is impossible now, and perhaps forever, to say for sure. But at least now the question can be asked, and the possible implications of these numbers discussed.

In both waking and dream experiences one of the two forms seems to be used much more than the other. In the waking experiences it is the intuitive; in the dreams, the realistic. There are some obvious reasons in both groups that might lead to a difference, but they are not the same in the waking cases as they are among the dreams.

As already mentioned, the hazards of reporting lead one to expect the more outstanding, spectacular kind of experience to be overreported in relation to ordinary little humdrum affairs. In fact, this may be one reason that collections of reported ESP experiences like the realistic dreams of Chapter 7 include as high a percentage of crisis cases as they do. Crisis cases, however, are not limited to any one form; they occur in all forms.

The first contrast in numbers here, 30 percent of intuitions to 13 percent hallucinations is the reverse of what one would expect if the fact that the more spectacular kinds of cases are reported most often were the only thing involved here. Surely hallucinations are more spectacular than intuitions, and also less likely to be taken for "ordinary." Still, these percentages say there are twice as many of the ordinary as of the extraordinary kind. One

can say then that something tends to inhibit the use of the hallucinatory form.

In dreams it is just the opposite. Here the most spectacular, or
at least, the most easily identified kind is also the most numerous.
Realistic ones are more easily identified as bearing an ESP message than are the more fanciful and inexact unrealistic kind. But
in the Duke collection, all cases with even a slight amount of
fantasy were considered unrealistic, although often they had realistic elements too, so that the number of unrealistic dreams on this
particular score was increased in proportion to the realistic ones.
And still the realistic are more than twice as frequent. It seems as
if a selective factor may be operating here too, but probably a
different one than that in the waking cases.

The difference between the frequency of reports of dreams and
waking experiences is also interesting and suggestive, for it seems
that dreams predominate considerably. Yet most of the reasons
that one might suppose would affect the reporting of the two
kinds, would favor waking experiences. In the first place, people
spend less time asleep than awake, so that if ESP experiences were
equally likely to occur at any time of day or night, one could
expect fewer of them to be dreams. Next, waking experiences
would tend to be believed and remembered; to make an impression on the person and so get reported more than dreams. It is
easy to say "just a dream," but not so easy to laugh off something
that occurred when one was awake. As a matter of fact, this very
conviction of the truth of waking experiences more than of dreams
was shown in the relevant cases in the Duke collection. In these,
by actual count the waking experiences gave evidence that the
person believed and took them seriously over three-quarters of the
time. But less than one-quarter of the dreams were so believed.
Thus on this matter of belief and consequently of impressiveness
too, waking experiences would seem more likely to be reported
than dreams.

Another aspect to consider is that of the timing of the person's
experience in relation to the event it seems to concern. In the
majority of the examples mentioned in earlier chapters, except
those of Chapter 7, the experience and the event occurred at about
the same time. Naturally, more of life's experiences occur when

people are awake than when they are asleep, and if ESP experiences depended on timing, again one would expect the majority to come during waking hours. However, on the matter of timing the cases are divided nearly equally, so that no strong connection is shown between waking and contemporaneous experiences, or between sleeping and precognitive ones. Taken the other way around, however, the contemporaneous experiences are about evenly divided between dreams and those that occur when the person is awake. But three-quarters of the precognitive experiences reported are dreams.

In trying to understand what figures like these tell, it is necessary to remember that in precognition the experience is not timed to coincide with the event. Presumably a precognitive experience could occur at any time of day or night. Thus the great preponderance of dreams seems to show that when one is sleeping the mind tends to run ahead into the future more than when awake, so that for precognition dream constructs are favored. However, a preference for the dream form also seems to be shown by the figures in the contemporaneous group. Here, nearly half are dreams. But surely not that proportion of events occur at night. Thus a preference for dreams even aside from precognition is showing in the background. Or it may not actually be a preference. Possibly dreams are more effective or more efficient carriers than intuitions or hallucinations, so that their message gets there (in consciousness) to be counted more efficiently than those of the waking forms do. This matter of the efficiency of the several constructs will come up again in Chapter 11, but here it is only necessary to note that it may well be that dreams are the more productive—in a way, the "easier"—channel of the two.

If dreams are easier, must one then suppose that realistic dreams are easier than unrealistic ones? It seems possible that a different influence could come in here, but impossible to say whether, in fact, it does. That influence could be one relating to the type of personality. Unrealistic dreams are those that in their imagery show a tendency to imagination or drama; the realistic ones are more like photographs, in that the imagery is a reproduction of reality. It seems possible that the two different tendencies, one to create fanciful, the other matter-of-fact imagery, might reflect habitual thought patterns, which in the unrealistic dreamers would be more imaginative, and in the realistic, less imaginative. If this is true, and if it should be only that a realistic type of personality is the more numerous, it would explain why fewer unrealistic than realistic dreams are reported. A possible straw in this wind may be the fact that in ordinary life only an occasional person has strong poetic or dramatic tendencies and can create plots for novels or short stories. Certainly by any count the great majority of those who write show descriptive, realistic, and matter-of-fact, rather than dramatic tendencies.

Perhaps the difference between the numbers of intuition and hallucination cases also goes back to personality structure. It is obvious that the hallucinatory form is not easily available in the unconscious, since it does not occur regularly to everyone even for stored material as dreams and intuitions do. Instead it is restricted largely, although not entirely, to people in unusual mental states; states like those induced by illness, drugs, or extreme emotional crises.

It is therefore only logical to suppose that for the fresh material as well, the hallucinatory kind of expression is not as readily available as the intuitive. In fact, it may well be that only an occasional person has an inborn tendency for unconscious impressions to trigger the senses, and that only those with a well-developed tendency of this kind can have hallucinatory experiences. This question, whether only occasional persons can even have a hallucination—like the question about the difference between realistic and unrealistic dreamers—presumably could be answered by the proper kind of psychological inquiry. Perhaps in time it will be.

This discussion of the varying numbers of times that the different forms of experience occur has settled nothing. If it had seemed to do so, it would have been because a complex situation had been treated too simply. And there is another complication which shows that the suggestions made so far do not yet point to an answer. That is the simple fact that individually people vary greatly in the forms of experience they have. Some report only realistic, some only unrealistic, dreams; others, only intuitive experiences; a very few, only hallucinatory. Then the combinations begin with those who have mostly dreams but occasionally an intuition and vice versa. Now and then an individual appears who has had experiences in each form of the four.

Reports from individuals show personal variations that cover the complete range. The general suggestion is that each individual has his own range and that he probably remains true to type, but the difficulty is in knowing just what his type may be. He himself may not be aware of all the times when he has had an ESP experience, and may overlook innocuous and insignificant instances regardless of whether dream or intuition. For this reason alone, reliable estimates are impossible, but still the very confusion of indications shows one important thing.

This lack of unity in people's reports of the forms of experiences they have had shows that in some cases at least the unconscious is not limited to using just one kind. This may be one reason experimental procedures can succeed; at the same time, the restriction of the form in experiments may be one reason they sometimes fail.

Was Linzmayer a success because he happened to be an individual who in life situations would have used the intuitive form of expression naturally and well? Or, was he one who could express ESP upon occasion either by intuitions or by dreams, so that when conditions said intuition, intuition it was?

These questions and others like them are stirred up by the original one, What disposal is made in the unconscious of the new material, once it has been admitted? They are stirred up but not answered. Answers could be guessed at, of course. But guesses, even informed ones, can be wrong. Here they cannot as yet be based on actual inspection, as the main answer is. It is not a guess that disposal is made of the information by the use of the ready-made psychological constructs. It is an answer arrived at by a survey of actual experiences. These are the constructs, the forms, that in actuality are used.

Inspection of actual ESP experiences tells more than just the different kinds of forms they took. It tells something about the origin of the messages they bring, the way they are made up, and how they come to consciousness. They do not simply appear full-blown as if by magic. Instead, they represent mental processes that follow their own well-developed patterns and work according to their own internal laws; or perhaps it would be better to say they travel their separate but specific pathways into higher mental levels. Many of them show traces of the paths they took and these remain and say to all inquirers who read the signs, "Kilroy was here."

These traces make sense. They show the effect of turns, twists, and pitfalls along the way, and some of the reasons why the messages of ESP are sometimes unclear, imperfect, or incomplete in meaning; why they may be wrong or only hint at but not really tell their story. For their characteristic limitations and imperfections, the traces of influences along the way, are different too. As in any good detective story, adding up the clues and traces gives a plausible idea of the way Kilroy went—in this instance, from the inception of the message at the point of initial judgment until it appears as an ESP experience, recognizable in consciousness.

However, the detective's job includes the running down of all clues—not only the most obvious and unquestioned ones. In this particular sleuthing job the traces left upon the four psychological constructs of ESP are not quite all of those that must be considered. In addition to experiences involving ESP are those others that consist of physical happenings that seem to have no ordinary physical cause, like the picture that fell or the clock that started unaccountably. These too have a story to tell that seems to fit in with the processes by which unconsciously received information manages to get to consciousness.

CHAPTER 10

The PK Component
(*Mind Over Matter*)

No list of the activities that go on in the unconscious, even aside from those of ESP, is yet complete. Psychologists and psychiatrists in whose fields such listing falls would be the first to say so. They know that the study of the unconscious levels of mental life is still in its infancy.

The parapsychologists too still have a lot of unfinished business in connection with unconscious mental processes. But they do know now that information secured by ESP is processed or conveyed to conscious attention by the psychological constructs; intuitions, dreams, and hallucinations. Only recently has it been realized that another method may sometimes be used in this processing; one of which psychology knows nothing.

As discussed previously, ESP is but one of the two general classes of phenomena which have been labeled psi. The other is that of psychokinesis, or PK: the ability of the mind to influence matter directly. It well may be that PK too is sometimes involved in the processing of information received in the unconscious, and its transfer to conscious attention.

It is involved, if certain occurrences of a physical nature sometimes reported can be taken seriously. These are cases that to an extent appear to be analogous to ESP experiences. They come as overt physical effects, however, instead of as subjective experiences as in ESP. But like ESP experiences, those of PK too can be taken as having meaning for the human beings concerned. They too sometimes seem to bring messages, and when they do so, the physical effect is usually observed by someone to whom the occurrence seemed to be directed. This "experiencing person" finds no ordinary reason why the effect occurred, but he is closely related to another individual who is absent, usually at a distance, and who, it develops, is undergoing a crisis at the time. This other person is in effect then, the target person. The physical happening thus appears to be a communication informing the experiencing person about the crisis the other is undergoing.

Two examples were given in Chapter 1. In one, a picture of a friend of an experiencing person fell from the latter's desk at the time the friend, the target person, was struck by a train and injured although not killed. In the other, a clock that had long been stopped started to tick the day the distant target person was killed in battle. In neither case did there seem to be an ordinary cause, and so each occurrence could be taken as if in some way connected with the human situation. That situation in both cases was one which at the time the experiencing person did not know.

Another case involving a time piece, this one rather more typical because it stopped, rather than started, is reported by a woman in New Jersey.

"I lost two brothers in the First World War, one day apart. My youngest brother had enlisted when he was 17. He survived every battle but the last, the Argonne Forest. He was killed the day we received word that my older brother was dying of influenza. He had been in camp only five weeks. My mother, a widow, and sister were seriously ill with influenza too at the same time.

"It was up to my husband and myself to try to get my brother, if possible. As you know, the roads in those days were not as good as today's, and everything that could happen to delay us, happened. The ride I called my ride to hell. I will never forget it.

"We left home at six o'clock that night, riding all night until four o'clock the next afternoon to get to Alexandria, Va.

"I had asked my mother before I left to let me carry my brother's watch which he had left at home. I had forgotten I had it in the belt of my blouse until 2 A.M.

"My husband had gotten out of the car to find some water for the radiator, which had sprung a leak, when I heard this loud ticking. I took the watch out. As I did so, it gave one loud tick, and stopped at 2 A.M.

"At that moment I felt as if my own heart had stopped with a knife through it. I told my husband, 'It is too late, John just died.' No one will ever know the feelings I had. Of course my husband did not believe it, but the records show that John died at 2 A.M., October 9, 1918.

"I had wound the watch when we left home at 6 P.M. After I told my husband that John had died, I looked at the watch again, and it was running. I wondered myself if I was imagining things until I found out later what time my brother had passed away.

"The watch was an Elgin railroad watch, which had to be kept accurate, as my brother was employed by the railroad. It was his first watch and he was very proud of it."

Although in each of these three cases, this one, and the two in Chapter 2, the specific physical effect was different, they still were alike in that in each, the target person was undergoing a crisis. In one it was an injury, in the other two death. In all three, the possible significance of the episode lies in the timing of the effect to coincide with the human crisis.

In somewhat different instances the target person is someone who is deceased. This introduces a variation, for in this situation, of course, no crisis of the target person can be supposed. Instead the significance here depends not on timing to match a human crisis, but on the occurrence of the effect at a time when the experiencing person's mental state makes it seem to be particularly relevant to a particular target person.

An example of this kind is given by a man in Illinois.

"Last year after coming from my sister's funeral, and walking into the hall of her home, a hat that was on the clothes rack jumped off and hit me in the face. I had not touched it.

"I turned to my brother-in-law and said, 'It must be Mabel's; she wants us to know she is with us.' My brother-in-law was so full of grief I don't remember if he replied. I too was in a strange state of mind. I just cannot explain it.

"There were no vibrations of the floor or from any other source, or I would have noticed it. The hat had been there for days with people passing by it, and had not fallen off the hook.

"My wife did not go to the funeral as her health was not good. When I got home and walked through the doorway into the small hall, a hat that belonged to me also jumped off its hook and hit me. I turned to my wife and told her that a hat did the same thing when I walked into the hall at Harold's. She thought it was strange, and then we both forgot it as we were so sad about the death of my sister."

The experiencing person in that case, having just come from his sister's funeral, was still in a mental state particularly focused on her. The fact that the hat fell then, apparently without any ordinary cause, gave the episode its significance, made it seem to convey a message.

In all cases of this kind, an occurrence that appears to have no ordinary explanation happens under circumstances that seem to connect it with some human situation. At face value, the physical effect can be taken as a "sign" of it, or as information about it.

The main reason a question arises about whether to take such occurrences as these seriously is the difficulty of being certain of all the facts. Sometimes, for instance, when timing is the important point, the physical effect may have occurred unobtrusively, and was neither noticed or timed until too late to do so accurately. Also, in cases like the examples above, if an unnoticed vibration or gust of air caused the hat to fall, or if in the case of the watch, a momentary aberration of sight made the person think the watch had stopped when it had not, then neither episode would have the significance it seemed to have to the experiencing persons. Even ESP experiences are often difficult to identify, but these thus have a built-in extra weakness in that the circumstances themselves may be unclear, or only partly known. All one has to go on in trying to assess reports like these is the fact that the individuals themselves were forced to conclude that the ordinary cause was absent, and therefore the occurrence seemed significant to them.

This uncertainty about the reporting itself made it easy in the past for critically minded persons to dismiss all such reports as presenting no real problem. If the occurrences might have been the result of malobservation and coincidence, then there was nothing to explain. On that possibility the episode could be discounted.

At the opposite extreme, many persons took such unexplained physical effects at face value and considered them to be evidence of communication from the dying or deceased. If it turned out that the target person was dying at the time the clock stopped or the picture fell, as in many cases he was, the sign was taken to mean that he sent back a farewell message; if he was already dead, it meant that his spirit had survived its separation from the body at death and by this message was indicating it. The manipulation of physical objects seemed like a miracle, and it could only be supposed that at the time of death, and afterward, special abilities which the living do not possess could be acquired.

To many people such a general interpretation has been a welcome and easily accepted one. For them it was strengthened, because, as in several of the above examples, the target object often had close association with the target person. It was his clock, or picture, or the dish that he had given. Logically the question of whether the deceased would have an ability to move physical objects should remain unasked until the primary one, Do the deceased survive? has been answered. But even if that question were answered in the affirmative, and even if it were known that the deceased have the power of manipulating physical objects, still this explanation would not fit cases like the one in which the target person did not die, but was only injured. However, these were reported much less frequently than those involving the dying. And so they were ignored, or simply thought of as a coincidence or other kind of puzzle like occasional anomalies of other kinds.

A new factor which has to be taken into consideration has been introduced, however, now that the ability of living human beings to exercise PK has been established. And the ability has long since been established much more firmly than the earlier dice-throwing tests mentioned in Chapter 2 could indicate. By 1943, publication of the researches which had demonstrated it was beginning in the *Journal of Parapsychology,* but readers were urged to wait for the full report before trying to evaluate the evidence. However, Rhine could say in an editorial that year:

This is the human *mind* doing *physical work*, but with its own peculiar forces. It is as simple as that so long as we do not ask, "How is it done?" But that question we have long been used to being unable to answer in matters concerning the mind.[1]

The tone of conviction expressed then was the result of a new line of investigation which had only shortly before been carried out. This, it developed, not only confirmed the conclusions to which the earlier dice-throwing experiments had led, but clinched them so securely that in another editorial in 1944 the same writer could say:

> When the first report on the PK research was published a year ago, the critical reader was urged to suspend judgment on the PK hypothesis until he was acquainted with all the work that had been done. Now, however, the situation has changed; and suspended judgment, we believe, is no longer necessary. The issue of the PK hypothesis can be decided within the scope of a single article.[2]

The single article was a report of this new investigation. It was an investigation which had come about more or less inadvertently. In 1941, the Second World War had had an effect on the busy scene at the Parapsychology Laboratory. Up until then, ever since 1934, some of the young people engaged there in psi research had been throwing dice in PK tests as well as calling cards in tests for ESP. The outcome of these dice-throwing tests gave ever increasing evidence of PK, and by 1941, large numbers of results had accumulated; but publication of them had been held off for various reasons. One was that such an unorthodox discovery as a mind-over-matter effect, would certainly cause eyebrows to be raised, and heads shaken. And to make matters worse, this idea would come from the very Parapsychology Laboratory which had so recently strained the credulity of the scientific world by announcing that it had proof of ESP.

[1] Rhine, J. B. Significance of the PK effect. *Journal of Parapsychology,* **7** (1943) 142.

[2] Rhine, J. B. The PK research at the point of decision. *Journal of Parapsychology,* **8** (1944) 1.

In the face of this it had seemed best to wait a while before throwing a second bombshell. It was also more prudent because on so "far out" a topic, it was wise to continue experiments even to the point of redundancy in order to be doubly sure. Therefore, no publication about PK had yet been made when, at the close of 1941, the war called away nearly all the staff of the Parapsychology Laboratory. Rhine himself was eager to go; the old First World War Marine-Corps training still had its effect. But some men had to stay home—particularly those over age, with family and professional responsibilities such as his.

At home then, and at the laboratory with only a skeleton force left, the new line of PK investigation was undertaken—mostly by Rhine himself and his assistant, Miss Betty Humphrey.[3] This investigation was not one of further actual experiment. Instead, it was a kind of pencil-and-paper job. Its importance (because it *was* a different approach) was fully recognized only later. It started because the two investigators wondered if they could find the same pattern effect in the records of PK experiments that had already been found in ESP records. It was the so-called "decline effect," which reflected a tendency of most subjects to score best at the beginning of their experimental sessions and then to taper off to almost nothing but "chance" toward the end. So many of the general characteristics of circumstance and result in ESP and PK tests had seemed to be similar, that a common relationship of the two had been suspected almost from the first. Now that most of the laboratory's working force was gone, it seemed a good time to check the records of the PK experiments which had been carried out earlier to see if this matter of declines was common both to PK and to ESP.

Luckily for the projected study, the records of earlier PK experiments had to a large extent been made according to a prescribed pattern. Almost at the start of the research it had become the custom to take down records of each experiment on sheets of paper or pages of notebooks in one particular way, regardless of the specific object of the individual experiment. Usually an ex-

[3] Rhine, J. B., and Betty M. Humphrey. The PK effect: special evidence from hit patterns. I. Quarter distributions of the PK page. *Journal of Parapsychology,* **8** (1944) 18–60.

perimenter recorded the number of hits of each throw of the dice his subjects made in a column down the page with twenty-four throws per column. A typical record page had space for ten such columns. When a page was filled, both experimenter and subject knew it; and in some more or less incidental way, felt that a unit of the experiment had been completed.

The columns on the page were thus always progressive records of a task, beginning on the upper left and ending on the lower right. But the number of dice per throw might vary in different experiments.

It had early been established that twenty-four throws of a single die would be considered a unit performance—a "run," as it came to be called—for which the average number of hits to be expected by chance was four. In many of the experiments six dice had been thrown at once. In this case usually only four throws were made per column, so that the average expected by chance at the end of each such column would of course still be four.

At the top of each of the record sheets pertinent data was always recorded: what the target was, the number of dice used, the date and time and names of subject and experimenter.

Now old records of experiments, some of them dating back as far as 1934, could be studied and compared to see if hidden in them might be "position effects" of which no one had been aware at the time the experiment was made. The totals on the various pages had of course been known as each was made, and their "extra-chance hits" evaluated. Now, it turned out that the records which could be used in this survey, because they had been made in comparable fashion, covered a total of 651,216 die throws, or 27,134 runs. And these in their totals gave a combination of CR's with odds against chance occurrence of 10^{115} to 1. Beyond question something more than coincidence had been involved.

It had been realized all along, of course, that the conclusion that that something was PK could be drawn only if all counter-possibilities had been eliminated. For instance, loaded dice would give extra-chance results, and so, presumably, would certain skilled ways of throwing. It was taken for granted that experienced gamblers have many tricks by which they can control the dice they throw sufficiently to "beat chance." And the subjects in these experiments had "beaten chance." While it was clear enough to the PK experimenters that neither they nor any of their subjects were experienced gamblers (they were mostly Duke students, and with the exception of those enlisted for the divinity versus gambler contest, not even student gamblers), still the need for precautions had been recognized.

Controls against faulty dice had been built into the early experiments by rotating target faces so that die bias could not influence results. Measures to prevent skilled or tricky throwing had been taken, first by requiring the dice to be thrown from containers, rather than by hand, and later by various releasing devices, and even by electrically driven rotating cages in which no one touched the cubes from trial to trial. Controls against spurious effects thus built into the design of the experiments had been efficient and effective. But they required explanation to be appreciated, and a skeptical public was not very patient when it came to explanations and could always discount them with a, "Yes, but. . . ," only half accepting the adequacy of the conditions.

But position effects on a record page, and those only discovered long after, were obvious testimony of something other than chance. They were open to no "Yes, buts." If the extra-chance results had been caused by any kind of artifact, a chance distribution of the positions of hits on the record page should result and not a consistent pattern of distribution of a kind unthought of, either by subject or experimenter, at the time of recording.

And so these many record pages were examined to see whether the hits were patterned. Each page was quartered, in effect, by dividing it into half, both vertically and horizontally. In the upper left the first six throws of the first five columns were isolated; in each succeeding quarter, the next; so that the final quarter at the bottom right recorded the hits of the last six throws of the last five runs. The total number of hits in each quarter was then obtained.

The result of all the surveying, given in a single unqualified statement, is that the first quarters included so many more hits than did the last quarters that the odds against such a distribution occurring by chance were about a hundred million to one. Further, the two quarters in between the first and last supplied intermediate data; the second quarter, on the average, was lower than the first, the third lower than the second but still higher than the fourth. The page quarters made, in effect, a fairly regular series of descending steps. This meant of course that the subjects throwing dice to fill a record page succeeded best at first and then their results declined in a systematic way. And this had happened in the results of over a dozen different experimenters in eighteen different experimental projects. Now, long after, the trend unnoticed earlier was disclosed for all interested persons to see.

These generally pervasive decline effects not only established PK all over again quite independently, but they also told something about the nature of the phenomenon. The pattern was like the one that occurs in ESP and like those of such general psychological processes as memory, learning, and sense perception.

As psychological declines these performance declines make sense. Apparently, and understandably, subjects try harder or more effectively when they start out on a task like learning a series of words, observing a series of pictures, calling a deck of cards, or throwing a series of dice for a target. As they make repeated efforts, their efficiency runs down as they approach the end of the task. To the PK subject, each column of the record was a sub-task in the entire task of filling out the columns of the page. If repeated for another page, it all happened over again. The fact was now clear that PK was very much like ESP in position effects too, even though the overt phenomenon was different. In the years since, the scope of research has broadened and the PK effect has been measured in various ways, but it has remained an area needing to be integrated more completely with ESP.

Once PK had been established, and parapsychologists were convinced that it was a human ability that was widespread at least if not universal—for many different subjects had given evidence of it in the tests—it was only natural to suppose that it must occur spontaneously in nature as well as in laboratory experiments. But when?

It was not like the situation in ESP with its dreams, intuitions, even hallucinations which were familiar processes well known by everybody. To say that those forms can carry ESP messages was only introducing a new kind of content into old familiar vessels.

But when PK had to be recognized as part of the same scene, it seemed to be an entirely new phenomenon. No one recognized it as something that happens every day—or any day. Both ordinary people and psychologists could say they had never heard of an actual effect of mind on matter without physical intermediation.

It is a good question, however, whether this may not be another case like grandfather's lost spectacles, which, on his nose, are so close to him that he cannot see them. It is a really intriguing thought that the very body-mind situation of every man and animal may be essentially one of PK, one in which a mental impulse moves a physical system with no physical intermediation.

The idea that the normal relationship between mind and body may be one of PK was recognized early by parapsychologists. In 1943 Rhine said,

> The mind in its domination of the body exercises a causal influence which cannot be otherwise than kinetic. Thus, psychokinetic action . . . is the basis on which every man interprets his routine experience of daily life.[4]

And then a few years later the idea was advanced by the English psychologist Dr. Thouless, already mentioned.[5] In an article in the *Journal of Parapsychology* in 1948 he showed that, granted a mind unit, a "me," as distinguished from the human body, a force like PK is necessary in order for the "me" to will the body to act. Logical as such deductions are, they do depend upon the assumption that mind and body are different units. This view, the dualism of philosophy, is out of fashion now in scientific circles. In the opinion of many scholars today dualism is about the same as superstition. The prevailing mechanistic view will have none of it. And yet the fact of PK would seem to call for a kind of dualism whether or not ESP itself does so. If the mind has force directly, then the mind again is in the driver's seat, the body only what is driven.

[4] Rhine, J. B. The mind has real force. *Journal of Parapsychology,* **7** (1943) 70.

[5] Thouless, R. H., and B. P. Weisner. The psi processes in normal and "paranormal" psychology. *Journal of Parapsychology,* **12** (1948) 192–212.

However, regardless of the philosophical implications of PK, the experimental results lead to the conclusion already mentioned; they are evidence of the *human mind* doing *physical work*. They also give evidence of a relationship with ESP, one which produces basic similarities as well as differences. And they make it necessary to ask where and when this PK ability operates spontaneously in life situations. It is logical to suppose it must do so sometimes, just as ESP so obviously does.

The searchlight then goes at once to the cases of physical effects that appear to lack ordinary causes, and to be connected with the affairs of human beings; just the kind illustrated by the examples of this chapter. Among these must be instances of the spontaneous action of PK in life situations.

And so, in collecting reports of psi in life situations at the Duke Parapsychology Laboratory, instead of rejecting all reports of such occurrences as spurious, because the facts might not be entirely accurate, or, on the other hand, believing them entirely and accepting them as evidence of a miraculous means of communication from the dying or the dead, they were collected and examined carefully to find out what their general characteristics were.[6] If these were instances of PK in action, it seemed there should be basic similarities among them as well as the obvious differences.

The physical occurrences as reported were of a number of different kinds, but were mostly effects produced on household objects. Among these, pictures and clocks were involved most often, and dishes next. Clocks stopped, started, chimed, or chimed aberrantly, and like pictures, fell from walls or shelves. Dishes fell and broke. Doors opened, shut, locked, unlocked, lights came on or went off, chairs rocked or moved—and all these effects occurred, as it were, "by themselves." In all cases, no ordinary cause for the occurrence was found. But still, aside from that negative attribute, no common similarity seemed to unite them either, nor were any of them connected exclusively with persons in any one condition, living, dying, or dead.

However, behind some of the variations a few general, if not universal, similarities could be seen. One of these was that the

⁶ Rhine, Louisa E. Spontaneous physical effects and the psi process. *Journal of Parapsychology,* **27** (1963) 84–122.

experiencing person was always acquainted with the target person, and in fact always had strong feelings for him. In the majority of cases, but not quite in all, it was reciprocal, for in the majority of cases the two individuals were close relatives. In a few instances, however, it was a one-way affair, and the target person did not know the experiencing person. One such instance was that of a clock that stopped in the home of a devout Catholic family at the very time of the death of Pope John.

The fact that the experiencing person was always emotionally concerned with the other, however, did not mean that he was always thinking of him at the moment the physical effect occurred. The common thread instead was that the relationship was such that he would have had a degree of constant, though at times unconscious, concern for and interest in the target person. Probably a good illustration of this would be the mental state of a mother at home with a son away at war. He of course might not be in her conscious thought at all times but unconsciously her state of interest and concern for and about him would be unremittent.

The situation of the target person was not a constant, like that of the one who had the experience. Much variation of course resulted from the fact that in some cases he was living, in some dying, and in others dead. Also, he might be near or far, in the same room or halfway around the world from the one who had the experience, and from the place where the physical effect occurred. The experiencing person, however, though not always in the immediate vicinity of the effect, was always within a relatively short distance from it, and usually at least in the same building.

The fact that the effect did usually occur near the experiencing person was the main reason why, in the past, and without knowledge of PK, these effects had been taken to be communications from the target individual. Now, with the idea that PK could be involved here, they still looked as if they could be phenomena bringing information about him to the person who had the experience; but not because the target individual sent it as a message, for although in some cases he may have been thinking of the experiencing person, in others he was not even aware of him. It apparently did not matter if the target person was not thinking of the other; the experiencing person could get the information just the same. All of this raises the question whether the physical effect might have been his own "sign" of information unconsciously received. If so, then the fact that the effect occurred near him would have a new interpretation. It would mean that the physical effect was another method, besides those of ESP, by which information is unconsciously processed, and by which it comes to conscious attention.

However, if these physical effects in life situations are indications of the same PK process demonstrated in the laboratory, two circumstances about them seem very different. One is that in contrast to the great array of kinds of effects reported in the cases, in the laboratory thus far satisfactory results have been achieved only with objects which, like falling dice, are already in motion. Whether a greater range can be achieved experimentally, no one yet can say. Reports, mainly from mediumistic circles, and mainly from earlier days, that static objects have been moved by the power of thought have never been confirmed beyond question even though reports of such effects have been sufficiently recurrent to deserve further inquiry before the question of their occurrence is settled.

The other difference is that in these cases no one knows he does it. When the target person is living and therefore able to report, he is quite unaware that any effect occurred, nor does the experiencing person know anything of it until the moment he sees or hears what has happened. In the laboratory, however, the subject is always trying, quite consciously willing, to make the object behave as he desires. If the process in the two different situations, experimental and spontaneous, is the same one then it must mean that the conscious willing of the experimental subjects is not actually necessary. It must mean that it is only the part of the process, comparable let us say in marksmanship, to taking aim, but that the trigger pulling occurs on an unconscious level.

The situations in life and in the laboratory seem alike, in that in both PK is fundamentally a mental function, or at least it begins that way, and in both, clearly it is one that operates unconsciously. In dice tests, like those in the contest between the divinity students and the student gamblers, not one of the participants knew how he influenced the dice. And none of the people in cases like those of the examples in this chapter knew how the effects they puzzled over were produced.

At first it looks as if a major difference between the cases and the experiments might come in in the fact that in the former, two persons are involved, both the target and the experiencing persons; in experiments only one, the subject. He is the one who does it. But in all experiences all signs point to the experiencing person as essentially the subject. He is practically always in the vicinity; always interested in and concerned about the other and about any crisis that befalls him. And if the object involved—the clock, the picture—is one that was associated with the target person, that association is always in the mind of the experiencing person also. Further, the experiencer is usually in the vicinity of the effect, while the target individual is often at a distance, frequently a great one.

No conclusive experiments on distance and PK have yet been made, although short distances tried have given results that encourage the idea that distance may not preclude PK.[7] All the successful PK experiments have been made with subject and object fairly near each other. Thus if both the experiencing and the target persons have PK, it is as reasonable to suppose the former one exercises it as the latter.

If the experiencing person is the one who himself causes the phenomenon, then it must be in effect his own "sign" to himself of the distant event. It would be visible evidence that information about this event was admitted at the secret door. But, when it was, instead of being processed as a dream, intuition, or hallucination, it led to the operating of his PK ability. Just how this could be, and how it could fit into the psi process, is a topic to discuss in the next chapter, when the clues and traces of the paths that the different forms take to consciousness are added up.

By close inspection of certain cases, the detective work involved in tracing the possible connection between the PK effect and the experiencing person is not too overwhelming. Clues that can be

---

[7] Nash, Carroll Blue, and Alice Richards. Comparison of two distances in PK tests. *Journal of Parapsychology,* **11** (1947) 269–282. McConnell, R. A. Remote night tests for PK. *Journal of the American Society for Psychical Research,* **49** (1955) 99–108. Fahler, J. Exploratory "sealed" PK placement tests with nine college students with and without distance. *Journal of the American Society for Psychical Research,* **53** (1959) 106–113.

very significant are given in occasional cases. For instance, in one experience in Chapter 2, the writer says, *"Suddenly I felt a surge of blood racing through my veins;* and at the same instant a picture of a close friend hanging on the wall above my desk dashed to the floor . . ."* and in another, this one in the present chapter, the writer says, "When I heard this loud ticking, I took the watch out. As I did so, it gave one loud tick, and stopped at 2 A.M. At that moment *I felt as if my own heart had stopped with a knife through it.* I told my husband, 'It is too late. John just died.' No one will ever know the feeling I had."

These are clues that will help to outline in more detail this area of parapsychological unfinished business in the unconscious.

CHAPTER 11

Influences Along the Way to Consciousness (Life)

IN the workshop of the unconscious the several forms in which ESP information can be processed are available to carry it to higher levels. But they are not objects like carts or cars standing around waiting to be loaded. They are processes ready to be activated, for although the messages arrive at their destination without a tag or any obvious indication of their source, they are not simply "there," instantaneous, pristine, and unchanged from start to finish. They do not come like a streak of lightning, clear, immutable, or not at all.

They are the result of processes that operate in the secret recesses of the mind and cannot be directly observed. They do go on long enough, and in such a manner, however, that circumstantial evidence can show something of the way they operate.

Most of this telltale evidence is to be observed in the nature of the forms themselves, and in signs left on some of the messages they transmit.[1] At their best, messages can bring true and complete items of information. In most of the experiences given in earlier chapters this was the case. But less than perfect messages are reported. Some of these do not entirely agree with the real situation; some even include outright mistakes. The kinds of defects they show often betray their causes, so that from them one can get suggestions about the kind of process it must have been, and of the influences and difficulties that affected it.

To begin with, as soon as the new information is admitted and

[1] Rhine, Louisa E. Psychological processes in ESP experiences. I. Waking experiences. II. Dreams. *Journal of Parapsychology,* **26** (1962) 88–111; 171–199.

the form it will take determined, the meaning will have to be translated into a message appropriate to that form. If it is to be an intuition, it must be a short, concise abstract of the meaning; if any of the other ESP forms, their imagery must be constructed; and if PK, then the tendency to action must originate.

Then, either at this original translating stage, or soon after, and well before the final conscious end of the process, an opportunity for secondary influences to operate comes in. Here the memories, anxieties, hopes, fears, desires of the individual can color the message and change the original true information accordingly.

Each of the forms—the intuitive, the dream forms, the hallucinatory—at times yields imperfect messages but some of them do so more often than others, and each in its own specific way. Consequently each must be traced separately. Of course these tracings, these analyses take time and will constitute a slow-motion description of processes which in reality are probably as quick as thought.

Perhaps it will not be out of order here to emphasize that the *form* of an ESP experience is quite distinct from its type. In type it may be clairvoyant, telepathic, or precognitive, but each of these types may occur in any of the four forms, as an intuition, realistic or unrealistic dream, or as a hallucination. It is the form, not the type of ESP, which gives the hints of the kind of process this is, by which the information makes its way to consciousness, for the type shows only the kind of target, thought, thing, or future event, but the form shows the psychological manner in which the information got into consciousness.

IN INTUITIONS

It would be logical in tracing the development of the forms of psi to begin with each at its very inception and follow the process to the end. But as in any other detective job, one must take the clues where they can be found most plentifully. That place is not always at the beginning, but varies from form to form.

In the intuitive, imperfect messages give the most clues because of the nature of the most common imperfections. It so happens that nearly all the intuitive messages which are defective are simply incomplete in meaning. The impressions they give are not wrong, or at variance with the objective facts, as might result from deep-lying personal influences, but instead only a part of the total item is included. Often a kind of blockage is suggested, something like that in memory and recall, perhaps, when someone may say something like, "I cannot recall the name . . . it is a word of two syllables . . . it begins with *K*." In ESP, however, the actual conscious attempt to recall is lacking, and it seems as if instead pressure from within is building up, which may or may not eventually cause a breakthrough. Some of the expressions of cases already given show this "blocking" effect, and the signs of increasing pressure. For instance, in a case in Chapter 2, the person says, "I had an uneasy feeling . . . this feeling grew until I could endure it no longer." In another case, this one from Chapter 5, the phrasing is, "I awoke with the slight feeling . . . this feeling persisted . . . I was made very restless by it . . . the knowledge hit me like a thunderbolt . . ." In a third in Chapter 6, "I found myself restless . . . the feeling of uneasiness increased. . . . Then it happened . . ." One can almost see the struggle in a case like this one:

"It was Election Day, Nov., 1932, and the general atmosphere was one of mild excitement and of tension. But as I went about my morning work I had a feeling of something very different and very personal, as though some disturbing message was trying to get through to me. By noon this premonition had become so strong that I told my husband and a neighbor about it.

"By mid-afternoon, I knew I would receive a death message. I became as positive of this as if I had been ordered to wait for it. The day wore on and my husband who was a policeman went to work. He had to work all night, a normal procedure on election days.

"After putting the children to bed I sat down to rest about 8:30. Soon the family that lived upstairs knocked on my door. They were going out and asked if I wanted anything from the store. I said, no, but I wanted to ask a very unusual favor.

"I explained my foreboding to them and as I had no telephone, but used theirs for emergencies, I asked them to leave their key with me so if their phone should ring I might answer it.

"They gave me their key and I sat down to wait. About 10:30 they returned, picked up their key and left. I tried to read until midnight. Then still very wide awake—and still waiting—I decided to do some sewing. I cut out a dress and was basting the parts together when I heard the telephone upstairs ring.

"I looked at the clock. It was 2 A.M. The phone kept ringing. As the neighbors were heavy sleepers, they didn't hear it. Finally I took my broom and knocked on the ceiling under their bedroom and eventually succeeded in waking them. I heard the murmur of their voices and waited. Finally I went to the staircase and called up that I was certain it was for me and to please tell me what it was.

"My neighbor came downstairs, put her arm around my shoulder, and told me to brace myself for a shock. It was my sister-in-law calling to say my father had committed suicide about nine o'clock the night before. He lived about a hundred miles from me and I had neither seen nor heard from him for weeks previously."

Seemingly the message of the suicide was almost blocked. Then gradually—it is a death—came clear. But not the rest.

The specific kind or extent of fragmentation of the message that may occur varies from case to case. Sometimes one part, sometimes another, may get into consciousness. It may or may not be the part that makes sense to the individual, but as in the experience of a woman in Chicago, it may be a part that is quite apropos.

"One day while I was riding on the train into Chicago on my way to work I was sleeping soundly when I suddenly awoke and sat upright. I had the feeling my children were in danger. This was before my mother moved in with me, and the kids left for school shortly after I went to work. They had always been quite responsible, and I never worried about them in the short interim. I felt a panic which I had never felt—also a helplessness. What could I do on a train? I couldn't even call home. I just kept saying over and over, 'Don't light a match!' Then I prayed and prayed all the way into Chicago, 'Dear God, protect them. I can't do anything. Protect them!' Then I felt a peace and forgot the incident until that night when I returned home.

"The minute I opened the door the strong odor of gas hit me. They had turned on the gas jet; and when it didn't light after a long time, they were going to get a match. Suddenly my oldest felt he shouldn't light the match, and they went on to school. I might mention here that Gary has read my mind on so many occasions I have long since discarded the realm of coincidence. At the time of my panic I did not know what they had done. I only knew I had to keep thinking, 'Don't light a match!' Then suddenly I knew that everything was all right."

Obviously the idea there was, that gas was escaping. The admonition, "Don't light a match," would follow from it. But consciously, the idea itself was blocked, and only the admonition got into consciousness.

A host of experiences are reported which consist of an emotional state only. No idea whatever to account for it gets into consciousness. An illustration of this comes from Ohio.

"I am twenty-five years old, happily married, and have two small children. My intelligence is average, as is my way of life. If I were typed, I would say I was outgoing and a bit too sensitive. Because of this, I am perceptive to the feelings and moods of others—often to the point where it has been embarrassing to friends and confusing to my husband.

"My first and most startling experience began a few years ago. My husband and I were living in Youngstown, Ohio. I was pregnant with our second child. Our first was in a home for retarded children in Dayton, Ohio. He was ten months old, and I had seen him only twice—both times at the hospital where he was born. From that time neither my husband nor I saw nor heard of him. Although I often longed to see or hear from him, I knew the course we were taking would be best in the long run.

"During my pregnancy with him I knew I would never bring him home, although my confinement had been as normal as blueberry pie. I often said this to my husband who would laugh and say this was a common worry. Common sense told me he was right, but it was a terribly deep concern to me.

"His illness was not known immediately. When I was told I had a healthy baby boy, I knew a mistake had been made. When a day later the truth was found, it came as no shock to me. This puzzled my family because I am not a pessimistic person by nature.

"When I became pregnant with my second child, there was no doubt in my mind that the child I was carrying would be normal—and I continually told my husband this. My second pregnancy was a very happy one. I didn't have a blue day and was happy as a lark. That is why when one night in March during my sixth month the terrible gloom that descended upon me was so unexpected. We had been out to dinner, arrived home early and were getting ready for bed when this heavy unhappy feeling began filling my heart. I tried analyzing myself as I do when something is bothering me, but try as I might, I could not find the answer. My heart was so heavy I fought to keep myself from tears. I had no control whatsoever over my emotions. That night was a mixture of tears, tossing, and turning. When the morning finally came that horrible heavy feeling was still with me. My husband was reluctant to leave me and made me promise to get out of the house and be with someone. I had no desire to be with anyone I knew, so finally at 2 in the afternoon I dragged myself to the grocery store to buy food I didn't need. I remember vividly standing beside the meat counter when all of a sudden a glorious feeling as though a great weight had been lifted from my shoulders—no, that was the wrong word, lifted from my heart. The clock was directly across from me, and I purposely looked at the clock because I wanted to tell my husband everything that had happened since it was such a strange experience. It was exactly 3 P.M.

"That evening I told my husband everything—down to the detail of the time. We had just finished eating when we received a long-distance phone call. It was from the home our baby was in in Dayton. Our baby had been very sick the night before and had passed away that afternoon at 3 P.M.

"This certainly was not an earth-shaking experience, but every word is true. The spelling, grammar, etc., may be wrong; but I feel I have described my feelings exactly as they happened."

In cases like that one, the emotion fits the situation. Obviously if information about the baby's illness was admitted into the deep unconscious, emotion would have been generated too, and apparently it penetrated into consciousness, regardless of whether the idea which generated it did so, or not.

It is of course more difficult to be sure that ESP has occurred when no idea accompanies the effect. Standing alone, such cases could only be thought to be coincidences between the mental states and the actual occurrences. But in the present context, they fit. And what is more, many of them are reported in which, as in this particular instance, the timing is a feature too. This frequency with which such cases, timed so exactly, are reported in itself almost makes them seem beyond coincidence. Moreover, it would not seem unreasonable to suppose that the emotion would be more penetrating than the idea. Many persons can testify to *moods* without ideas, even when the cause is some well-known and easily traced memory or physiological state.

It is not only emotion that gives evidence of penetrating into consciousness, when no explanatory idea accompanies it. Action, or the urge to it, too, may be so displayed. When the item of information in the deep unconscious calls for action, it, like emotion, may be projected. An earlier instance of this was the case of the woman who seemed to know that her small daughter would need protection. Apparently the message may sometimes be even more completely blocked than it was there, and an urge to action may be the only sign of it in consciousness. From Florida comes this illustrative experience.

"I feel somehow I must write you of my experience with ESP. As far as I can tell, this is the only one for me. I do feel it was responsible for saving a child's life. I am also well aware that it was not I, but a power beyond myself.

"I was a student nurse at a children's hospital on this morning of January 18, 1945, when this happened. Due to the shortage of nurses at the time, I was alone on the floor. I had just made the rounds and found all my little charges to be in good condition. I was to be married that day; and of course had my mind elsewhere. It was almost 6:30 A.M., and I was most anxious to get off duty at seven. I was just finishing up the charts for the time. All was quiet; I heard nothing. All of a sudden I had an urge to go into the large ward. I tried to fight it but was unable. I walked directly to a little girl's bed at the far end of the ward. I could not hear until I got within a few feet of the bed. The child, about four years old, was choking. I was unable to dislodge the foreign object and just ran with her (held upside down) to the phone, where I called the resident. He did an emergency tracheotomy in the service room. Needless to say, we worked under much less than ideal conditions. I know we were both crying by the time the child started to breathe again with the help of artificial respiration. This child did recover. I knew the child had been admitted for a bronchoscopy for a bean or something. However, I was not concerned about her during the night—nor was her doctor, for she had shown no signs of difficulty during the evening before. I'd never seen this child before or after that night. I'll admit I do wonder about her at times. I'm interested in ESP and very grateful for it."

The compulsive action taken in such a case speaks for "information under the surface." At least the direction of the action, and the feeling of conviction that it should be taken, could indicate that it was projected because the proper information had been admitted in the unconscious. In such instances one can see that the most important part got into consciousness as if it somehow had the strongest propulsive force. The same seems true, whether the result, like this one, is compulsive action or an admonition like "Don't light a match." In either kind of case the experiencing person got the important element in the situation, even without full understanding.

In most of these experiences, even if the messages were incomplete, one can at least see a kind of symptom that something was occurring under the conscious level. But still other cases are occasionally reported lacking even the awareness of any hidden meaning. And yet it well may be, that they, too, mean "information in the unconscious," but information entirely blocked from consciousness. For example:

"I have always felt that when things like this happen it's God's way of letting you receive the blows in a calmer way by learning ahead of time that something isn't right. Therefore, a person can accept it—and almost expect it.

"Three years ago, June 22, 1958, was another day when something just didn't feel right. My husband had bought a new car and was going to the garage quite often for little adjustments. My son and I always went along for the ride. We'd gone along on Saturday, but Sunday we stayed home. Right after dinner George decided to go to the garage. He went alone, and I didn't even suggest going with him although the other times no one had asked and we had all gotten ready and had gone along.

"That day I sat around, read, and did little or nothing till later in the afternoon. I don't know why I ever did this—there was no reason at all. But I went through everything that George owned. It wasn't snooping exactly because I knew what I'd find in every little tackle box or cuff-link box I opened. But I went through everything in his desk, and everything in his drawers, and straightened things out. I took every gun out of the gun cabinet and held it and put it back. There was no funny feeling at the time—no feeling of being nuts to do it or questioning of why I was doing it—I just did it. I straightened up his workbench that had been a mess for months and knew there was no reason to straighten it because it would be a mess again. But I put all the tools away, swept up the dust, and put an old plastic tablecloth across the bench. My things and my son's things needed straightening a lot worse than George's, but I didn't touch any of our things. I even went so far as to empty out the bottom of the gun cabinet and set everything back in neatly, such as cleaning stuff and flies for fishing, etc. Things that I knew very little about and had never bothered with before, I straightened.

"I didn't start supper although it was quite late. I was sitting at the kitchen table and looked at the clock; it was about 7 P.M. I started for the phone to call the garage (fifteen miles away); and before the operator came on the line, I hung up and decided I'd wait a while longer. About 7:20 I decided I'd waited long enough and would call. I talked to the man at the garage who said George had left about fifteen minutes ago. I hung up and heard the rescue squad or police—I didn't know which, but I thought I didn't like to hear that when I knew someone was on the road.

"Then I thought no more about it. I settled down to watch the end of Ed Sullivan and turned the set off again before the picture even came on. I don't know how much later or what I did in the meantime, but our best friends came to the door. Steve, my son, met them and said, 'Daddy isn't home yet.' Then I almost knew before they could say anything, and I asked if George was hurt bad. Al, the man that came to tell me, said, 'George is dead, Betty.' He was killed in a one-car accident just three miles from home, about 7:15 the doctor's report had said.

"The strange part of that is I've often wondered why I straightened up everything that belonged to him that same afternoon. My friends can verify that part about the workbench. They'd often commented on it. It was quite a mess, and sort of helter skelter; but when Al and Pat came to tell me that George was dead, the bench was all cleared off, cleaned, and a plastic cover over it. The clothes and guns and desk I could understand—maybe I'd just felt wifely and cleaned up some of the things even though they didn't need cleaning; wives get those urges. But the workbench was kind of forbidden territory, and I'd never done that before—even to put a cloth over it. George was alive and well while I was getting everything he owned in order, so I knew right where everything would be from paper to clothes."

What are all these various degrees of incompleteness telling? They seem to be saying fairly clearly something that is no secret in areas other than those of ESP. They are saying that crossing the threshold of consciousness is difficult; that to thrust directly into the stream of conscious thought is no easy feat. In fact, it can take an effort to get an absorbed person's attention even by a sensory stimulus. Many a wife or mother in trying to get a pre-occupied family to the table could testify to this. When the interrupting item comes from unconscious depths the difficulty may be still greater.

Thus it is that the imperfections of intuitive experiences appear to be caused by the difficulty of getting an idea from the unconscious into consciousness. This difficulty in intuitive experiences of crossing the threshold of consciousness is, of course, one that is met at the very end of the process. One learns nothing about its beginning from this evidence.

The only other evidence one gets as to the nature of the intuitive process is in the intuitive form as such. The fact that it lacks imagery may be one more piece of evidence of difficulty at the threshold. At least it is one of the great distinctions between intuitions and dreams, for of course dreams do not face this hurdle of thrusting directly across the barrier. Instead they play below the level of full consciousness and must be recalled on waking. This is obviously a hurdle too, but a somewhat different one. The intuitive and dream forms are, in fact, so much in contrast on this point that the situation in dreams can well be looked into next, deferring until after that the other waking form of ESP experience, the hallucinatory.

IN REALISTIC DREAMS

A dream that is to carry a news item up to or near to consciousness is constructed quite differently from an intuition, although here too one can follow a progression of stages. Of course, there must first be a translation of the item into an appropriate message. But here one often has reason to think that in this translating operation itself, and not at a later stage, personal motivations can affect the truth or correctness of the message and mold it accordingly.

In dreams, the translation of the meaning into an appropriate message means the construction of imagery. And the process of making imagery differs depending on whether the result will be realistic or unrealistic. The difference between the two seems slight at the start, but it can cause very different end products.

Realistic dreams as many earlier examples show, tell their stories by imagery that pictures the event in some detail. They are therefore very good message carriers and tend to bring perfect messages. However, occasionally a realistic dream may be imperfect too. And those that are are important here, for they show that the process of making realistic and true imagery is not quite what it seems. From the realistic dreams that bring complete messages, it would look as if the imagery had been made by something like photography, so that all the details just had to be the same as the reality.

The imperfect cases show that the dream maker has more freedom. He has a choice. He does not simply have to copy; he can select the imagery and modify it upon occasion. Actually he selects the entire scene as well as the viewpoint for his imagery.

In this selecting and constructing of imagery to portray the news item, and in playing freely with it, the actual facts to be portrayed may be changed around, embellished, or obscured in various ways. Often the identity of the person the dream is about, the target person, is changed, omitted, or another person substituted for the proper one. Again, identity may be faithfully portrayed, but the event in which the target person is involved may be unclear or its main meaning missing. Sometimes it is easy, sometimes not, to guess at the personal motivation that caused the defect in the imagery. For instance in this case from Minnesota, one can easily suppose a reason.

"It was five years ago; I was eighteen years old. I woke one morning after a restless night with a very vivid dream imprinted on my mind. I often wake remembering my dreams, but this one bothered me particularly. My mother at that time slept on a Hide-a-bed in the living room, I in a bedroom adjoining. My dream started with Mother and me standing in a certain spot in the living room, looking down at the body of one of our best lady friends lying dead on the Hide-a-bed. Everything was exact. I was standing a certain way, my mother the same. She sobbed five words, 'She was my *best* friend.' The dream ended and I woke up. I simply couldn't get this dream out of my mind, but I shrugged it off more or less because it seemed very unlikely that this friend would be dying anywhere, but particularly unlikely that it would be on *our* Hide-a-bed. She was in perfect health at that time and still is today.

"Exactly one month from the day of the dream it happened, but the situation was reversed. My mother died in her sleep of a heart attack. I awoke to hear her gasping, called the doctor and this friend immediately. The doctor arrived first and pronounced my mother dead. My friend came in, and we both assumed the exact positions as in my dream—and she said the very words in the same tone of voice."

It seems likely that in this situation, when the information was admitted and its unwelcome meaning grasped, the very construction of imagery was affected so as to *obscure the truth*. The dream maker preferred to dodge the fact, and the substitution was the way to do it with very little effort.

But though in that case the dreamer seemed to have a reason, an important motive for not dreaming true, it is not always thus. Take a case like this one:

"I was about sixteen years old and we were returning from a trip to Kansas to our home in Los Angeles. When we hit Holbrook, Arizona, we had car trouble and had to stay all night. That night I had a dream. I dreamed that I was back in Los Angeles and saw our neighbor standing in his front yard by an open grave. I walked over and asked him what had happened. He told me that Elaine (his little girl) had been hit and killed by a car. *Then he held his arm out—palm up—and brought his fingers up in a crushing motion and said, 'Her head was crushed just like an egg.'*

"I told this dream (with demonstration of the crushing motion) to my mother the next morning as we were walking a block to the post office. We had to stand in line at the post-office window. The Mexican just before us was telling the postmaster about an accident that had happened just outside where a Mexican had been hit by a train and killed. The Mexican apparently saw it—or arrived just after. He said to the postmaster (with the very same gesture I had seen in my dream), 'His head was crushed just like an egg.'

"Well, my mother looked at me with her mouth hanging open, and it gave me such a strange feeling that I have never forgotten it. My mother sometimes mentions it too."

Probably that dream was remembered mainly because it had no *real* reason. The only difference between the real and the substituted identity was the slight one that the dreamer knew the one person but not the other.

Just as an identity can be changed apparently for a very slight motive, so, too, sometimes other details are tampered with. An instance in which details were added to an otherwise perfect picture is given by a man in Wisconsin.

"For some time I have wanted to write of an experience I had twenty-three years ago. It is of quite a personal nature and so naturally I have hesitated to recount it, but after much deliberation have decided that you will evaluate it professionally and forgive me if I don't attempt to 'dress it up' and detract from its authenticity.

"In 1938 I lived in Rhode Island, and was married to a very sweet and lovely woman. During the winter months she had the opportunity to drive to Florida with married girl friends, and I encouraged her to go. While she was away, one of the husbands called me and we got together for a weekend and wound up in New York City. We had a fine time on Saturday night with much drinking but conducted ourselves honorably. Sunday afternoon, while at the bar at the Taft Hotel, two very attractive girls came in and we became acquainted. I fell rather hard for one of them, and we went to a nightclub for drinks and dancing; and then since they were from Bridgeport, we put them on the train at Grand Central late Sunday night. We men drove back to Rhode Island Monday, and I called Phyllis (this is not her name) at her home in Bridgeport. She sounded quite pleased to hear from me. I thought about her a lot in the succeeding days. My wife came back from Florida, and things returned to normal. I ran a filling station at the time. I had introduced myself as Ed Tucker to Phyllis—not by my real name.

"Soon after this a single friend and customer of mine came into the gas station on a Friday night and told me that he was driving to New York and asked me to go with him. He was dating a New York model whom he later married. I called Phyllis and told her I would be in New York over the weekend, and she agreed to meet me. I called home and told my wife that I was going to New York for the weekend, and it was quite all right with her. Bill and I stayed at the New Yorker, and I met Phyllis at Penn Station on Saturday night. The four of us had a nice evening with a lot of drinks, dancing, etc. Phyllis and I spent the night together in her room and early Sunday morning we awakened somewhat hungover. She said, 'Good morning, Ed. I had the funniest dream! I dreamed that I was at your home in Rhode Island and you were married and lived on the waterfront. Your house had a concrete wall in front of it with a dock and boats tied to it, and you had three children. Your oldest girl kept running after me saying, 'Oh, you go out with my father.' Your wife was very slim, had dark hair that she wore behind her ears, and a bun on her neck; she was very young, and had a black tooth in the front of her mouth.'

"The only thing that she missed on was the children. I lived on the waterfront, there was a concrete retaining wall with a dock and boats, my wife was ten years my junior (around twenty-two), she was tall and slim, had black hair that she wore behind her ears with a bun on her neck, and she had a front tooth that had darkened due to a dead nerve. I was aghast not knowing what to say, and in a few minutes she said, 'Ed, what's the matter? You're awfully quiet.' I certainly was.

"That afternoon Bill and I dropped her off on the way back to Rhode Island and stopped for lunch. I asked her to tell Bill about her funny dream, and she laughingly repeated it verbatim. Bill's eyes popped, as he knew my wife well.

"This girl didn't know my right name, and we had previously discussed Rhode Island, and she didn't know anyone there. This was truly authentic.

"I saw Phyllis a few times during the summer of 1939, spent a weekend at Cape Cod, another in New Hampshire, and a couple of times in Bridgeport. I was very, very fond of her but decided to bust it up before it went too far. When I saw her for the last time I told her I was married (which I had always suspected that she knew), and she shook uncontrollably. When she regained her composure, I reminded her of the dream, and she couldn't explain it, but said it was the truth, which I'm sure of."

Why should nonexistent children have been added? Had it not been for the telltale, "Oh, you go out with my father," it might have looked as if the reason probably was that in such a home children would be expected. But the phrase put into the mouth of a child tells more. It suggests that unconsciously this dreamer was not taking her association with this man quite as casually as it might seem. It tells also that the dream maker can embroider the imagery, if he cares to do so.

Sometimes the imagery seems simply not to cover sufficient perspective to transfer the complete meaning. It is almost as if a certain part of the situation caught the fancy of the dream maker, and he omitted part of the scene, thus leaving no key for its interpretation. A case like that comes from a woman in Virginia, and incidentally it is one of the rarer ones in which a happy, rather than a sad, occasion is the subject matter.

"One night back in 1953 I had a most unusual dream. Part of the reason it was unusual was that it was so very vivid and impressed me so much and seemed so real that I related it to my husband at breakfast. I had never made a practice of telling my dreams before because I think they are usually boring to the other person. After breakfast I still could not get it off my mind—it seemed like something beautiful that I did not want to fade from my mind as dreams usually do. I then did something that I have never done before or since—I wrote an account, or description, of the dream in my notebook. Here is what I wrote then, exactly as I wrote it—without change:

" 'March 7, 1953. Last night I dreamed that I came upon a clearing in a woods at night; and there was a house, all lit up, with glass doors all down the side toward me opening onto a terrace. I could see inside a long table spread with a white cloth and set as though for a wedding feast. There were many silver candelabra holding as many as six candles each all down the table and be-

tween them small delicate-stemmed compotes of milk glass filled
with small white chrysanthemums. The table was filled with all
sorts of dainty food—tiny, white-iced coconut cakes and little
sandwiches. The candles had not yet been lighted. It seemed that
everybody must have gone to the wedding and left the house all
ready for the return.'

"The thing that puzzled me so much when I was dreaming this
dream was that there was nobody in the room—no servants or
anyone to watch over it. My most distinct impression was that
everything was ready and waiting for some special occasion, but
there was no clue as to what the occasion was or who the people
involved were.

"I went on about my business and naturally forgot all about the
dream. The first part of April, 1953, my husband received a letter
from his company saying that he had been with them for twenty-
five years and that they wanted us to come to Richmond and have
luncheon at a restaurant or hotel there on his anniversary the
latter part of April. My husband thanked them and declined as I
had recently come from the hospital after a serious illness. (I
would like to add here that neither of us realized before they notified him that my husband had been with them twenty-five years.)
Later in the month the manager called my husband and said that
since we would not come to Richmond they had made reservations
for the luncheon at an inn nearer to our home. So, somewhat
against our will, we were forced to go.

"The inn was rather new at that time, and I had never been
there. When we arrived, the men were all there (ten); and since I
was the only woman, and they were all so nice, it was a wonderful
occasion. I wore an orchid and kept having the feeling that it was
my wedding day. (I was married during the Depression and did
not have any frills, and that day seemed more like my wedding
than my own wedding day had.) When we went in to lunch, I had
the strangest feeling that I had been in the dining room before
although this was the first time—and there was the long table
running down the wall, all in white with white flowers. Down the
other side of the room ran windows looking out upon green grass
and trees. After my illness and everything, the day proved to be
one of the most glorious of my whole life. And I kept feeling all

the time that that was my real wedding day. And all the men seemed to enjoy it so much although they said that usually they rather dreaded these occasions—probably because they had to make up the work the next day and maybe because they were usually very dull and something that had to be done in the line of duty. But on that day they truly seemed to enjoy themselves.

"It was not until I got home later that night that it came to me suddenly that the dining room was the room of my dream—only in reverse—as in the dream I had been looking in from the outside.

"Dr. Rhine, this experience has always puzzled me, and I think about it from time to time. How could I have known ahead about all this when I didn't know it was an anniversary, didn't know the company was in the habit of giving these luncheons, had never entered the inn, and besides that we refused the invitation and were literally forced to go. This was an exceedingly pleasant experience."

Just why the dream maker chose to obscure the meaning in that instance would puzzle anyone looking for strong—if not sinister—motivations in the best of dreams.

Occasionally the meaning seems to be transferred, but like personal identity it may be transposed in some way so that the person is misled and fails to understand the dream correctly. An example of this kind, from a woman in New York, shows the details so transposed that probably a question could be raised whether this actually was a realistic dream.

"During the early part of November, 1962, I dreamt that my summer bungalow on Long Island was a veritable shambles from water coming down the ceiling and walls. Night after night for fourteen consecutive nights I had the same dream: ceiling plaster down, walls wet and bulging, furniture ruined, etc. I tried going to bed late in the hope that, being tired, I would not have the dream. One night I took a glass of wine. I never touch the stuff as it paralyzes me. I felt dizzy and numb, but that did not stop the dream.

"I mentioned the dream to my daughter, to my brother—a retired lawyer—to a friend living up on Nelson Avenue in the Bronx.

I even called up my caretaker and, after telling her of my dream, asked her to have her husband check my place and see whether everything was all right. She reported that her husband found my place in perfect condition. She expressed amazement at my superstitious nature.

"I still felt uneasy and called my insurance man, related the dream to him, and made sure I was covered. He laughed, and said he could not believe I was so foolish as to give credence to a dream. Monday, December 31, 1962, I left the office at five and arrived home at six to find my dining room in New York a veritable wreck. Water was coming down my ceiling, down my walls; carpets, floors, and furniture were wet and ruined.

"Investigation disclosed that the tenant above me had installed a washing machine without the benefit of a plumber. The husband did the work himself and the pipes were not properly connected. Again on Friday, January 4, 1963, I returned from work to find my apartment a regular Turkish bath. A leak had developed in the steam pipe next to the radiator along the window *in the same dining room,* and the steam was splurting its hot water all over the place. The apartment was a wreck. The steam in the building was turned off and an emergency crew worked on the pipe which had to be cut. To install the new piece of pipe, threads had to be made above and below the cut part by a certain instrument on which they had to keep pouring oil or grease, and every time that thing went back and forth it spluttered oil, or grease, all over the wall, window, windowsill, floor, etc. As if this were not enough, two days later a fire from a defective wire broke out in the same apartment above me and more water came down. I almost had a heart attack and do not feel too well yet. I am planning to move out in the spring."

The dream was realistic only in what happened, not in the objective details, for the scene of the event was transposed, and the details with it.

The transposition was of locality, rather than identity, but here it did not afford protection from unwelcome news. Whatever the cause, to transpose like that was neither practical nor realistic. But then, perhaps along with its other idiosyncrasies, the unconscious is also sometimes impractical. At least from cases as jumbled up as that one, it is clear that the dream maker is not confined to reality in making his imagery, although it seems likely that concern for property, worry and anxiety about it, figured somehow in that particular mix-up.

In some instances in which the imagery appears to be reproduced exactly, the viewpoint, if not the entire scene, may be such that an important point in the information is not transmitted. In a case reported by a man in California the scene itself was one from which he could not tell which of two individuals was involved. (The intuitionlike "voice" in this case is atypical in a realistic dream.)

"I had a dream that revealed in clear-cut imagery a scene in which my oldest son was killed just before he was to graduate from an advanced course of training in the Air Force, in August, 1943.

"I had this dream about June 20, 1943. A younger son, in the Army, had just been shipped out from San Francisco—destination unknown. In this dream I was standing on the edge of a shallow, dry irrigation channel and looking toward a high ridge of mountains which seemed to be not more than a mile distant, and approximately 6,000 feet high. Above the level of the field to my right were the mountains. The field seemed to be dark on the surface, as if it had just recently been plowed and harrowed preparatory to planting. Scattered over the field at widely spaced intervals were a few large round-topped trees with dark green foliage. The entire area was remote from any place that I had ever seen before. Almost immediately after I was aware, in the dream, of my surroundings, four men in uniform came off the field carrying a stretcher bearing a body, and crossed over the irrigation channel just a few feet in front of me. They did not seem to notice me standing there, nor did I want to speak to them. However, I did hear a distant voice say to me that they were carrying the broken body of my son, but no indication of which one it might be. At this point I awoke and quickly tried to shake off the impression of the dream, but it persisted clear-cut in detail. However, I did not tell my wife or anyone else about the dream.

"About two weeks later we received a letter from our younger son in the Army saying that he was in the Aleutian Islands and that no activity was expected in that area in the near future. This quieted my fears, but the imagery of the dream remained clear-cut in my mind.

"Around two months later, on August 23, 1943, a call came from the wife of my oldest son. She told me that George had been killed in a plane crash late that afternoon. I told her we would come as quickly as possible, and we arrived there shortly after midnight. The next day we went out to the Air Force Base and made arrangements for having the body returned home, and for the services of the chaplain stationed at the base.

"After the funeral I again pondered the dream and its possible association with George's accident. I decided that I would revisit the base and see if I could get permission and an escort to go to the scene of the accident. I found that the topography of the area was exactly as I had seen it in the dream over two months before. I went and stood on the bank of the dry irrigation channel as I had seen myself do in the dream. To my right was the blackened field, with the dark-green live oaks scattered at wide intervals over the area. The blackened surface of the field had been caused by fire spreading from the wrecked plane and not from plowing and harrowing as it had seemed to be in the dream. I asked the lieutenant who had driven me out from the base and who had been there with the rescue crew at the time of the accident—and to whom I had not told anything about the dream—where the stretcher-bearers had brought out the body and where the ambulance had waited. He indicated that they had brought the body from the field and crossed over the dry irrigation channel just a few feet in front of where we were standing. This was again just as I had seen it in the dream."

Certainly the idea that imperfect imagery, substitutions of identity, place, etc., are used by the dream maker as protection against too unwelcome news, falls down in cases like this one. The person's anxiety was not decreased by uncertainty as to which son was involved. As in several other cases, the dream only imperfectly carried its message, presumably because an unfavorable viewpoint was chosen. The reason why, one can only say, must lie hidden in the puzzle of individual psychology.

A noticeable feature of many of the dreams that bring imperfect messages is that the defect of scene or imagery leads the person either to fail to get the complete meaning or to misinterpret it in some way. The misinterpretations are sometimes overinterpretations of the situation, sometimes underinterpretations. In the case of a man in Texas it was overinterpretation.

"I was born and reared on a farm in Minnesota. I left there at the age of twenty and was married in Lawton, Oklahoma, in 1922. Shortly after we were married, I woke up crying. My wife of course wanted to know what in the world was the matter with me.

"I told her that I had a very terrible dream that my father had been killed in a runaway. She assured me, of course, that it was only a bad dream and that we would have heard from home if anything had happened. However, I was pretty badly shaken up and was for several days; but, on not hearing anything from home, the incident was forgotten.

"I had told her of my entire dream, that Dad was driving a team, spreading manure on the north forty of our farm, and that he had dropped one line and the team started running. The only thing he could do was to hold the one line and let them run in a circle until they tired out. In my dream that is what he was doing, but he fell off the heavy spreader and it ran over him, killing him instantly.

"The following year on a visit to Minnesota and the farm home, we were just sitting down to dinner, when Mother told me that Dad was nearly killed last year in a runaway. She said, 'Well, he was over on the north forty spreading manure and the team ran away when he dropped one line. He kept them running in a circle until they finally tired and stopped.' He was not hurt in the least, but was in danger of being killed at any moment. A runaway team is a very dangerous thing.

"Mother's story of the incident was exactly the same as my dream as to location and other details. We were unable to figure out, however, whether my dream was before or after the runaway, that is, to the exact date. We were able to figure that it was in the same month. At that time we were living at least 1,000 miles apart."

Does the dream maker sometimes allow his anxieties to run away with him, and instead of protecting himself from an unwelcome circumstance, overinterpret it instead, and see it as worse than in reality? It looks that way. It looks as if some people tend to face calamities one way, some another. In constructing dream imagery, innate characteristics affect the result just as they do all the other expressions of the personality.

Failure to interpret the imagery correctly sometimes stands out as in itself the imperfect feature of an essentially correct dream scene, although of course the question can be raised whether the scene was the correct one if it did not really disclose the message. Such a case is reported by a woman in Nebraska.

"In 1931, a few days before my second son was born, I was resting on the bed. I wasn't sleeping, yet 'like a dream' a scene or incident was lived by me. I saw a beautiful green parkway with a striped tent a hundred feet or so away; there was a carpet, and I was walking down it seemingly to my wedding on the arm of someone close (although not my father), and people were gathered on either side. I heard them saying, 'How brave, how brave.' I came to and thought to myself, how strange a dream or vision. Why should I be brave at my wedding?

"My son was born October 27, 1931. On December 7, 1931, my husband died suddenly. I returned to Omaha and sorrowfully stepped out of the funeral limousine at the cemetery which I had never before seen. And, I *beheld* the exact picture of *my dream!* It was cold and snowy; there were the carpet, the people, and the striped tent, and people saying, 'How brave!' And I leaned on the arm of my brother-in-law. This time I *felt* like I was in a dream."

In such cases, one must suppose that either the scene itself was mischosen to hide an unwelcome fact, or else the failure to interpret it, to know it was a funeral and not a wedding, was evidence of the same motive. Whichever it was, it worked. The reality the scene represented was touched upon, but not faced, as one can

say, and probably was the result of a personality characteristic
like the one that substitutes identities. Cases like it have often
been interpreted to mean a hidden unconscious wish for the death
of the person involved, just as a slip of the tongue may be taken as
a giveaway of a hidden motivation. Sometimes this kind of interpretation may be correct. But when made without any more evidence than in a case like the one above, such interpreting goes
beyond the facts, particularly in view of the many indications one
gets that a message from the unconscious can be diverted, de-
flected, or misinterpreted for the slightest of causes.

From such examples we see that the making of realistic imagery
is not mechanical, even though the large majority of reported
instances offer practically perfect reproductions. The dream maker
does have a choice, and he can elect to translate the reality into
imagery that reveals the entire situation just the way it occurs, or
he can modify and even obscure it.

The reasons for making other than perfect selections of scene or
imagery are obviously personal ones. They seem to vary from the
very important, like reluctance to face disaster, and its reverse, the
overanxiety that reaches for the worst; from such slight ones as
unimportant inferences about something that might be expected to
a suggestion as casual as that made by some small element of
similarity.

This is the situation then, when realistic dreams are featured.
What is different, when they are unrealistic?

IN UNREALISTIC DREAMS

Unrealistic or symbolic dreams show no need to reflect objective events just the way they occur. In these the dream maker
plays free and selects imagery as he pleases. As a result, the meaning may not at once be self-evident, as it is in realistic imagery.
The degree to which it brings a complete idea depends on how far
removed from the news item itself the fantasy may be.

In most of the cases it looks as if first of all the item of information *suggested* something else to the dream maker, and that influenced the imagery he constructed. It looks as if more than a mere
association of ideas occurred, for the imagery is apparently fash-

ioned according to the suggested idea, rather than according to reality itself. This makes it possible for the imagery to depart from the actuality, to almost any length. It is this freedom that makes it possible for fantasies to develop that give no surface indication at all of their actual basis.

These suggestions, arrived at in the unconscious, can arise apparently for causes as endlessly different as are the specific situations and personalities involved. Take for instance, one reported by a man at sea.

"During the Second World War, I was in the U.S. Navy assigned to a ship in the Third Fleet in Okinawa. I had received letters from my wife, who was in Norfolk, Virginia, at that time. There was nothing in her letters to indicate that anything was wrong at home, nothing to indicate she had not been well.

"One day I had a depressed feeling—a feeling that something was wrong at home or that all was not well. I even remarked to the Pharmacist's Mate on board my ship that I had a strong feeling that something was wrong at home. He asked me if my wife had indicated anything in any of her letters. I told him that was the strange part, that her letters were cheerful and gave all the latest information at home, but not even a hint that anything was wrong.

"That night after I had gone to sleep I had a dream that I was back in Norfolk, that my wife, several friends, and I were in a row boat and we were pulling into the boat landing after a fishing trip. There were a number of boats tied up at this landing, and just as we were going in between two of these boats a sudden swell appeared and my wife (who was standing up in our boat) fell over the side. Her head was mashed flat. I managed to grab her arm and pull her back into the boat. I saw some people on the pier and asked if there was a doctor present, at the same time they helped to pull her body up onto the pier.

"One of the men knelt down and examined her and said, 'She is all right, but her tonsils will have to be removed.' I awoke immediately at this point. I noticed the time by my wrist watch. Sometime later I received a letter from my wife in which she said she had had her tonsils removed. She even gave the date and time she was on the operating table. I compared this time with our time in the Pacific (the time I was awakened from my dream), and at the very moment I was dreaming of her, she was on the operating table."

To a Navy man, what more natural than that an unspecified calamity would suggest imagery having to do with water, drowning, etc.

In a similar vein, though different in detail, an earlier worry or anxiety might well affect the making of imagery, even when the actual anxiety was a thing of the past.

"My story is as follows: I grew up with one of toughest, meanest, most unpredictable horses that any youngster ever tried to handle. He could be as gentle as a lamb. Also, he would kick, bite, or run away at the drop of a hat. It was impossible to work him down and no one could anticipate his next move. We called him 'Brown.'

"In December, 1918, I was returning home from the Army. No one was expecting me. At about 4:15 A.M. the train I was riding derailed and there was a terrible wreck. I was unhurt. I reached home after dark some fifteen hours later. The first greeting from my mother was, 'Where were you at 4:15 this morning?' I tried to keep a straight face and asked why such a question. She then told me that in a dream Brown and I had been in one of our acts which had been unusually violent. Brown had come out of it clear—not a piece of leather left on him—but nothing was clear as to what had become of me. Then she awoke and the clock stood at 4:15; she had been worrying about me all day. Then, of course, I told her about the wreck. This thing has puzzled me through the years."

As already mentioned, the imagery may tend to be symbolic rather than real, and the symbolism may or may not be self-evident. In the case below its origin is not difficult to see.

"A dream I'd like to tell you took place about eighteen years ago. In the dream, I was walking along the street. No one was around, but at a distance I saw a black-draped figure approaching who I finally recognized as a favorite aunt of mine. She had on long flowing black robes and a black hat with a brim and the hat had a heavy black veil over it which covered her face.

"I laughed when I saw her because she is such a neat, well-dressed person that I couldn't imagine her being dressed in such unbecoming attire. I remember I continued to laugh as she came nearer and nearer. I could see her face; and she didn't smile. She just looked at me and then passed me without saying a word. This too was shocking because she and I were quite close, more like mother and daughter. Then, as she passed, in reality someone began knocking on the door. I answered, and it was my landlady telling me someone wanted me on the telephone. It was this same aunt calling to tell me my grandmother (her mother) had passed away."

Sometimes the reason for the suggestion seems to be a memory, a connection that probably only in a dream could be revived and made into an almost living thing. A woman in Tennessee had such a dream.

"My mother died on December 4, 1959. She had lived in my home here for fifteen years. She was sixty-nine, and in perfect health until cancer struck and took her from us suddenly.

"We had set out some shrubbery together the spring before she died. It has grown particularly well this summer, and I have often thought how pleased she would have been to see it.

"Then, last week, on Monday morning, August 28, just before I woke up, I had one of the most vivid dreams of my life. I thought I came home from the office in the late afternoon and found that a very dignified lady—a friend of my mother's from her home town —had dropped by for a visit and decided to mow the lawn. That sounds silly enough. But the horrible thing was that she had also cut to the ground the beautiful holly bushes in our front lawn.

"I was in a perfect fury over it. I stood in the front yard and called to my mother to come to see what had happened (in the dream she was very much alive). But she did not come. So I ran into the house and back to her bedroom where she stood in the center of the room. I saw her so distinctly that I could see the pores of her skin. I kept thinking, as I saw her, how thin and tired

and weak she looked. I felt ashamed of myself for bothering her
with any problems at all (an attitude I had, of course, constantly
during her last illness).

"But I was furious about those shrubs being cut down. I kept
saying to my mother, 'Do you know what she did? Have you seen
it?' She simply shook her head slowly from side to side as if to
say, 'It doesn't matter. It's not worth getting worked up over. It's
not worth losing you temper. Never lose your temper over trivial
matters.' What she meant was perfectly clear, although she was
only shaking her head.

"I was furious. And then I woke up—with the dream so real
that, for a moment, I was rigid with anger.

"Then I realized it was all a dream, but my mother had been so
real that I turned to tell her about the dream. Then it hit me—that
she was gone, that she no longer lived.

"I was so shaken by her nearness in the dream, in the very bedroom where I was sleeping, that I began to realize that—real as
her skin had seemed, and sure as her meaning had been in every
gesture—there had been a certain unearthly grayness about her.
She had a weariness about her that was unspeakable—almost as
if she had been summoned from the grave by the calls of my
dream.

"The dream was so vivid that I wrote my sister (in San An-
tonio) about it that day. I also told another friend about it. I told
them that at least the dream had one great value: it had taught me
to control my temper—not to become angry over trivial matters,
things that could not be changed like a cut-down shrub.

"The following Sunday morning, September 3, a neighbor of
mine called me to the door to tell me that at last he had found a
man who could do some yard work for me (remove some top-
soil). I gave them exact instructions about what to do with the top-
soil (all in the backyard), and returned to my bath. While I was in
the tub, I heard much chopping going on in the backyard. As soon
as I could get out of the tub and into a robe, I looked out the window. Sure enough, they had done it—they had cut down the beautiful forsythia bushes that my mother and I had set out in the
backyard two years ago.

"They had grown beautifully this summer, and I had been much pleased at the way they exactly filled the space we had wanted them to fill. I was furious. Nobody had ever said one word to the neighbor or the man about trimming any shrubbery. I started to go out and say something to the neighbor about it, and then the dream of my mother suddenly came to me. I held my tongue. I kept seeing her shake her head, indicating that I must control my temper. I said nothing to the neighbor.

"This is greatly detailed, I know. But the two situations were so similar that one seemed to forecast the other almost exactly. They were only seven days apart."

In unrealistic dreams too, the dream maker sometimes plays free with the matter of identity. One characteristic that recurs in either kind of imagery, realistic or unrealistic, is the dreamer's tendency to cast himself in the major role—sometimes probably just because he likes to be "in things." Such could explain that feature of the dream in this letter from a woman in California.

"ESP has been much a part of my life to the extent that my husband and I take it as normal for me. I am an ordinary housewife, but have creative talents and am versatile in many fields; life to me is most exciting.

"I dream every night and entertain my husband each morning by telling the dreams to him. We lived in Hawaii before, during, and after the last war. He worked at Pearl Harbor, and we got up at 4:25 each morning so he could drive the long way to work in the blackout. I told him my dream at breakfast so he can verify this tale. He said, 'You have the weirdest dreams, but this is the craziest one I ever heard.' Here it is: My husband, our ten-year-old son, and I were on a picnic on bicycles. (We had no bikes, but that is OK in dreams.) We had stopped to rest and put our bikes on the ground. A busload of sailors stopped and asked us the way to Waemea Caves. We told them there was a Waemea Falls, but no caves. They were disappointed, as they were going to the caves on a picnic. So they dumped all their picnic food into our laps. There were uncooked wieners, buns, pickles, boiled eggs. *And* a gallon jar of mustard—enough to feed a regiment. The dream ended there.

"That same afternoon this is what happened: My neighbor, who lived down our road about a half-mile, came driving like mad into our driveway and was shouting with laughter as she climbed out and handed me a gallon jar of mustard! Then she gave me cartons of buns, uncooked wienies, boiled eggs, and the food I had dreamed of. I could hardly wait for her explanation of this windfall. She said, 'I was driving along in my Ford and was stopped at the Waemea junction road (where we had rested in my dream). It was a huge busload of sailors on a picnic. They asked, 'Lady, can you show us the road to Waemea Caves?' She answered that there were no caves, but they were at the junction to take them to Waemea Falls. They did not want to go to any falls. She invited them to come to her beach house, where they could have their picnic and cook their stuff on her outdoor grill.

"They did that and had a fine time, and on leaving gave her heaps of food left over as they had planned for about fifty men and only twenty had come on the bus. She shared the food with me, her nearest neighbor. She gave me the mustard as her family never used mustard.

"If I had not told this dream *hours* before it came to pass, no one could be expected to believe it."

Many dreams that classify as unrealistic include a deceased person in their imagery, as in the earlier case about the shrubbery. In that example it seemed natural enough that the mother be a dream character. She contributed no new information, but she fitted in because of the associations and memories called up by the situation.

Sometimes the possibility seems stronger that the dead person did in some way play a part. This often appears to be the case if the deceased brings new information to the dreamer, as in an experience like the following from Arkansas:

"On September 11, 1929, my father died. He was a prominent attorney here from before the turn of the century until his death. During our association after the death of my oldest brother, we were inseparable. It seemed that I took brother's place in Dad's heart. At sixty-nine now I still miss Dad and think of him often. My mother, his widow, still lives with me and is ninety-three.

"Thirty days more or less after Dad's death, while still in the stage of shock, but partially recovered—I was notified by the bank of a note Dad had signed in favor of a guardian of a First World War veteran. (The mother of the veteran.) Dad was her lawyer. The bank was the administrator or trustee of the funds.

"I knew there was a contract between Dad and the guardian which protected Dad for the $500 note he had signed. This contract provided that the guardian was to make monthly payments out of her allotments until the note was paid. The note Dad gave her was to replace funds she had taken in excess of that allowed her as her son's guardian, and to ward off prosecution for embezzlement.

"The court knew of it and commended Dad for his part in the solution to protect the guardian whose boy was her ward.

"The trustee, while he knew of it, demanded the contract for his files to clear himself. I searched Dad's files, but to no avail. Naturally, I was worried. When I went home that particular night I had not been able to shake it off my mind. I mechanically ate my supper and drifted into the living room, still haunted by that contract, as time was running short. I picked up the evening paper to get my mind settled. I don't think I read a word. I had a rearback chair. I pressed the button and gradually fell back into a horizontal position. I must have been at the point of exhaustion or something.

"When I sat in that chair, I was fully clothed. Presently a carriage drove up with two white horses pulling it. Dad was in the front seat beside my oldest brother who had passed away ten years previous. My little sister, who died early in life, was in the backseat with a lifelong friend of the family—a noted, outstanding lawyer and close friend of Dad's during their lives.

"Dad got out laughing—showing his pretty teeth. He had all of them when he died. Only one he broke off, but had it put back on. Dad was seventy-four when he died and was very active. He had gone dove shooting with me the day before he died. I marveled at this sight. I asked myself—Am I dreaming?

"Dad walked over—just as plainly—reached out and shook my hand saying, 'How are you, Son? I thought I'd come and pay you a visit. I've been watching you and am pleased the way you have been taking care of Nellie (my mother). I wanted to find out if you wanted to unravel anything I could help you with.' I said, 'Dad, how did you get out of that concrete vault I put you in?' He answered, 'You are not talking to me; it's my spirit.'

" 'Well,' I said, 'there's just one thing I want to know—that is, where did you put that contract you had with Mrs. _____?' (She was the guardian referred to above.) Dad said, 'I can tell you exactly where it is. I was afraid she would steal it. In the right-hand top drawer of my desk you'll find it full of envelopes turned up edgeways and a piece of newspaper folded under them. Raise the newspaper, and you'll find the contract in a large manila envelope. It's got my name and her name on the underside of it.' As he said this, he looked up and said, 'It's beginning to get daylight. I've got to go, but I'll be back.' When he said this, my wife began to shake me, saying, 'Wake up, Honey; you've been mumbling incoherently for I don't know how long.' I was sitting on the side of her bed half-undressed. It was breaking day as Dad had said. I had gotten up out of the chair and taken my shoes off, and how I got into the bedroom, I don't know.

"I didn't lose any time. I put my clothes on and got into my car. I drove straight to the office. I was nervous, but felt relieved as I was entering the office. My mind was in a doubtful daze. Something was telling me to have courage.

"In the past when I got faint messages in dreams, they slipped out of my mind when I woke up. On my way to the office that morning—what Dad had said on his visit was as clear as if it were before he died. I didn't have to stop to think. I unlocked the desk and pulled that right-hand drawer out nearly too far. There before me were the envelopes turned up edgeways. Under them was the newspaper folded smoothly so it would lie flat to keep them even. Under the newspaper was that contract just as his spirit said it was."

In view of all the "finding cases" mentioned in Chapter 7, and also of the experimental results of tests of clairvoyance, by ESP the experiencing person could himself secure information such as the location of the contract, and he could weave it into the dream imagery just as a playwright puts words into the mouths of his characters. The other interpretation, that the "spirit" was actually there, is naturally the one preferred by many. Whether it is the correct one, however, must remain undecided until the question of survival of death is answered. Until then, the complete explanation of occurrences that suggest survival, but which as here can be otherwise accounted for, must be deferred. At least the presence of dream fantasy in all such cases is undeniable.

The main difference between the imagery of realistic and unrealistic dreams is thus shown to be the fact that in the latter it is based on an idea suggested by the news, rather than on direct meaning of the news. The tendency to depart from the exact fact rather than simply to copy it suggests a personality difference—that the unrealistic dreamers are the fanciful, creative ones, the realistic-minded the more pedestrian. Of course, a fault may sometimes be a virtue, and vice versa. For carrying messages, originality and fantasy are likely to be less efficient than good old faithful copying.

IN HALLUCINATORY EXPERIENCES

Since hallucinations, like intuitions, come when the person is awake, one might begin to look for signs that the main cause of incomplete messages may be, as in intuitions, difficulty in getting the meaning into consciousness. But here the evidence points to something else, something that has its origin farther back in the ESP process, although as one traces it out, difficulty at the threshold may come back into the picture after all, in a somewhat different way.

The outstanding shortcoming of hallucinatory experiences is that the message is usually incomplete. Yet the incompleteness does not suggest blockage at the threshold of consciousness, as in incomplete intuitions. Instead it is inherent in the nature of the phenomenon, as shown in some of the cases already given. In several of these, a person heard himself called, but even though he may have recognized the voice, and thus identified the one who called, it did not tell him why. In another, the effect was visual; the experiencing person "saw" her absent husband, and thus identified him. But still the experience was incomplete. It did not tell what had happened. In a different kind of hallucinatory experience, the person felt pain similar, as she later learned, to that which her aunt presumably felt as she died of a heart attack. But at the time she, with the "pseudopain," had no way of knowing to whom the pain actually "belonged."

A fact to note is that in all these examples only one sense was hallucinated. It was somewhat the equivalent in sense experience of being blind or deaf, but with the reverse twist that instead of only one sense not operating, only one is.

The tendency for only a single sense to be involved is fairly general, but sometimes there are two. Even so, frequently the experience still gives only an incomplete message. Take for instance this case reported by a woman in New Hampshire.

"My Aunt Liz had been through a very trying time. Her husband had been committed to a state institution for the insane. She hadn't wanted him to be committed and had only given in because of family pressure. Although she had been through many hair-raising experiences with him, she thought she should take care of him herself. She was on the point of breakdown herself when the family learned he had, as is true of some mental cases, turned so completely against her as to attempt to take her life not once but several times. He was committed for observation. Aunt Liz was quite done in with the whole affair, so it was considered advisable to have someone stay with her. Ann, her daughter-in-law, came to stay. If the following had happened and Aunt Liz had been alone, no one would have believed it, but Ann's presence gave it credence. Ann is a skeptic's skeptic. She believes only what she sees with her own eyes, and then only a small portion of that.

"Uncle W. had been at the institution a week when the following occurred. (During the week, when visited, he had lucid moments. He knew where he was, and he threatened that if he were able to get out he would fix Liz for having him placed there.) Ann and Aunt Liz had retired for the night when Ann was wakened by Aunt Liz insisting someone was prowling around outside. Ann was rather irritated at being awakened and more to quiet Aunt Liz than because she believed her, got up and went to the window in the hall that overlooked the grounds. Looking down she was startled to see a small, short man coming around the side of the house. He had the build of Uncle W. Aunt Liz said, 'It's W. I know it is!' and was all for going to the door and letting him in, but Ann wouldn't let her. Ann thought it was indeed her father-in-law, but she wouldn't give in. Instead she told Aunt Liz to be quiet, that it must be a tramp. The man had a sack done up on a pole such as one sees in old pictures of tramps. This he set down and came up the steps. Then he pounded on the front door. The whole house echoed with the racket he made. Ann and Aunt Liz stood terrified until the sound died away. Thinking he was perhaps trying to get in through some other part of the house, they looked out again. He came down the steps, picked up his bundle and tossed it over his back and disappeared. It was foggy out, and he disappeared into the fog. As he did so, the telephone rang. It was the hospital calling. Ann took the call thinking it was surely news that Uncle W. had escaped. Instead, they informed her that her father-in-law had just died. He had died in a violent seizure, pounding the walls of his cell.

"As I have said, Ann is a practical person not given to superstitious beliefs. She, of course, reassured Aunt Liz that they had just seen a tramp. But why would a tramp pound on someone's door after the house was in darkness? Why, in such a close neighborhood, had he not gone to another house after he hadn't got any response at theirs? Ann, the first thing next morning, went to the house next to theirs and asked if they had heard any noise; and although the family next door were awake, they had heard nothing. Added to this, they were people whom the slightest sound disturbed; a dog barking or any noise at all in the neighborhood was bound to bring them to the door to call to the neighbor responsible for it."

The fact that the effect was both visual and auditory only served to make the mistaken interpretation that the target person was present more convincing. It did not suggest the actuality, that he had died.

And so it is that in the majority of cases, whether one or more senses are involved, the message is incomplete. As a result, an experience that brings a really complete message is such a rare occurrence as to considerably strain credibility when it is reported.

Credibility, however, depends largely on familiarity. It is easy to believe that a familiar kind of phenomenon occurred even if it was inexplicable, but it is more difficult to credit it if it was something both unfamiliar and inexplicable.

Experiences like the following are extremely rare, and therefore at face value both unfamiliar and inexplicable. This is the only one of its kind among all the hallucinatory experiences in the Duke collection.

"Although I have had many of these rather odd experiences, the one which has always been hardest for me to understand had to do with my youngest brother. I was away at school; and as a certain weekend drew to a close, I began making all sorts of preparations for a sudden trip home. I am far from the most orderly person in the world, but I had my clothes, etc., all prepared to pack quickly. Before nightfall that Saturday I had been summoned home by the tragic death of my little brother. I did exactly as I had planned the night before, and was on a train which should have brought me home by midnight. Instead, my train was delayed, and the train with which it should have connected had gone on. I knew no one in this junction city, and I did not know what to do.

"Out of the crowd of strangers emerged a young man who was the close personal friend of an older brother. (Even today this seems like a fantastic story, but it happens to be true.) He said, 'There is no other train tonight; there is a good hotel across the street. I'll take you over and tell them to call you for the five-o'clock train in the morning.' This he did, exactly. I sat in that hotel room full of grief and loneliness, and grateful that this good friend had happened to be there.

"The next afternoon this same young man came to our house after I was home; I said, 'In all my life I never was so grateful to see anyone as I was you last night.' He said, 'But I didn't see you—I was coming down to that same junction to meet you as I knew you'd be coming in on that train, and I knew you could not make connections; but I never got there. My train was late too.' I knew this young man as well as I knew any of the dozens of young people who made up the circle of my friends as well as those of other members of our family. I hadn't then, and haven't now, the slightest doubt that it was he who helped me. What I don't know is, 'How?' "

In a letter several years later, this person reflects further on her unusual experience, thus:

"I find myself in a rather odd state of mind about the events of that night of anguish. I *know* beyond doubt that what I wrote you took place as I described it. But at times it seems 'fishy' even to me. I've often asked myself the question: 'At any time before he spoke to me had I been aware of this young man milling around in the crowd on the station platform?'

"I know I had not. He was suddenly just there, making his way toward me. The striking resemblance to the young man I *thought* he was could be a matter of mistaken identity, I suppose, but that could not explain his knowing where I wanted to go since I had not spoken to anyone."

The extreme incredibility of such an occurrence is thus testified to even by the experiencing person herself. But the same explanation that accounts for the hallucinating of a single sense, can account for an experience like this one too.

Facilitating factors no doubt were the emotional state of the girl, and the fact that the young man was thinking of meeting her. The information about the hotel, which she needed and which was available to her by her own ESP ability, could thus be projected into consciousness, in the form of a (seeming) sense experience, complete in every detail necessary to make it realistic.

The first reason, then, that hallucinations usually bring incomplete messages is that not all the senses are hallucinated. A second reason is that the imagery is restricted by its very nature, for it is confined to the sight of, or sound of, or even, one could say, the "feel" of the person involved.

The reason this can be so is that the people involved in these cases are practically always closely linked and have often seen and heard each other in real life. Now the experiencing person simply "sees" the other as he would expect to see him and as he has seen him; or he hears him call as in actuality he has called in the past. The imagery then is actually based on memory and expectation, and as such is naturally oriented toward the experiencing person.

This orientation is shown in visual cases, in the impression given that the one in the hallucinatory impression "came to see," the other, or called out to him. Even in the "pain" cases the analogous situation seems to be that the pain of the experiencing person is projected more as he would expect it to have been for the target person than as it actually was. In many cases the point is unclear because the target person dies and no one knows just what his sensations were. Occasionally, however, a case like the following one from England, shows a discrepancy between the experiencing person's and the target person's sensations.

"The one special occasion I cannot forget happened on the evening of April 29, 1949, between 8 and 9 P.M. I had been anxious about my youngest daughter. She was expecting her first child and was a little overdue. Just after 8 P.M. I was taken ill suddenly with terrible pains. Anyone would have thought I was in hard labor. My stomach swelled and contracted every few minutes. My children wanted to send for the doctor, but I told them not to worry, that we should probably hear in the morning that their sister's baby had arrived. The next morning we got the news that her son had been born between 8:30 and 9, and my daughter had had very little pain even though nothing was given her to ease it. It seemed I had the pain for her. She was in the hospital at Rockford and I was here in Lynchwood."

The suggestion in a case like that is that the pain of the experiencing person was modeled on her own idea of labor pain, rather than that being experienced in the actual birth; therefore, in such hallucinated sensations as well as in the visual and auditory cases, the imagery is restricted to a reproduction of the sensations the experiencing person would expect the other to have.

These two reasons together then, the hallucinating of only one or two senses at a time, and the restricting of the imagery to the sight or sound of the other person as the experiencing person knew him, seem to account for the incompleteness of hallucinations. But these obviously go back to causes that operated at the very beginning of the process. They are not the result of difficulty at the threshold, but are a part of the very nature of the hallucinatory form.

A suggestion of the way this kind of form may originate is given in certain cases. In these, particularly among the "pain" cases, the hallucination is not the entire experience, but in addition the experiencing person seems to have intuitive information as well. Usually in such instances the hallucinatory part is so much more startling and realistic than the intuition, that the former is emphasized in the recounting, at the expense of the latter, so that it is easily overlooked, as in the following account.

"We had just moved to Kansas, and my mother was visiting in Colorado. At 3:15 A.M., October 11th, I wakened suddenly with a terrible choking sensation, as though I could be dying. My breath was coming in dry sobs; I looked out the window, noted the town clock was chiming 3:15.

"I rushed into my daughter's room, wringing my hands crying, 'Your Grandma is dead.' Daughter ridiculed my crazy dream as she called it. It was no dream. I had not been dreaming at all.

"In a few minutes I fell asleep, exhausted. Getting-up time, Daughter asked, 'What was wrong with you last night?' I declared I knew something was wrong with Mother and I was going to be prepared for a call. I unpacked a trunk to get out my winter clothing; then I called Western Union to let them know where to find me when the message came. The family meanwhile teased me about my nightmare. The telegram came 4:15 P.M. from Colorado: 'Bury Mother 3 P.M. Friday 13th, Auburn.

"I met the funeral party at Auburn Thursday afternoon. My sister was with them. That night I told of my unusual experience —naming the time. They assured me she passed away at 2:15, a sudden heart attack.

"It was sometime later, it came to me, that there was an hour's difference in time.

"I think I know just how it feels to die of a heart attack."

The significant aspect of this case is that the person *knew* to whom her unusual sensation of dying referred, but information as to the identity was not part of the hallucination. From the sensations alone, the pain she felt might have been her own, or that of anyone in her circle. Instead she knew it referred to her mother, and she knew it meant that her mother was dead. This information came intuitively, and so the experience actually must have been an intuition that brought a complete item of information; however, it was accompanied by the hallucinatory effect.

In comparable situations the intuitive aspect may be less complete, as if only part of the idea was able to cross the threshold of consciousness.

"Several years ago I lived in Virginia. One evening after dark, my wife fell down a long flight of stairs, breaking her left arm above the wrist. The next morning my daughter, living in Colorado, complained to her husband that her left arm pained her awfully and that she could see nothing but Mother. I wrote them about the accident. My daughter came immediately to Virginia to care for her mother. She stayed just a month. I took her to the train, which left at 10:45 A.M. She was now on the way back to Colorado. That evening while doing the chores about sundown a wasp stung me in the right eyelid. The next morning my eye was swollen entirely shut and was very painful. As soon as my daughter arrived home, she reported, as follows, 'Dear Mamma, I had a nice trip home and found the folks all well. But what is the matter with Daddy's eye? My right eye is paining me so I can hardly stand it, and I can see nothing but Daddy. I don't think he is blinded, but his eye is swollen shut. Write me at once.' "

In both instances there, the experiencing person associated the hallucinatory effect with the proper individual. But it appears that the information as to the identity was received only indirectly, as a suggestion based on intuitive information; i.e., "I see nothing but Mother." The actual intuition appears to have been blocked at the level of consciousness, and only enough of a suggestion got through that she could infer that the parent was injured; she got the information about the actual nature of the injury by the hallucinatory effect.

Such evidence of the blocking of an intuition when a hallucinatory effect is experienced may very well give a key to what happens when the hallucination is projected in the first place. It suggests that it was closely related to the intuition in its origin. If so, a reexamination of the development of intuitions can show a place where the hallucinatory imagery might arise. The evidence already given on intuitions suggests that at the same time that the intuitive form is chosen, and the meaning of the new information abstracted into a message, several concomitant elements are projected: the conviction of truth, and the appropriate emotion and action, if action is called for. In many of the cases of pain or other bodily effects the reaction is obviously *sympathetic*. It is the experiencing person's imagined approximation of the pain felt by the other. It would be only natural, one might say, that along with an incipient emotional state, there might well be a sympathetic *sensation* too. There might—provided that the person is one in whom a *sensory excitation* can result from an unconscious mental cause.

We must suppose that no great number of personalities are so constructed that this would be a possible response, since hallucinatory experiences are comparatively rare. However, people obviously differ in the degree to which mental effects produce physical reactions. Some can have a conscious experience, let us say, of the sight of another person being injured or in pain, and feel no concurrent physical reaction. Others may be upset, nauseated, or otherwise physically affected by it. In view of this, it seems not too great a jump to suppose that even on the unconscious level, there may be those who would react in kind, let us say, to the pain of a relative's heart attack, when by ESP, information about it was admitted. If so, however, one must suppose a tendency for the intuitive experiences of such persons to be entirely, or almost entirely, blocked, so that the hallucinated effect is the main mark it makes in consciousness. One would have to suppose this because in the majority of hallucinatory experiences no concurrent intuitive aspect is reported.

At this point one goes back again to the question whether hallucinations, like intuitions, suffer from difficulty at the threshold of consciousness. It looks now as if the difficulty affects the intuition, not the hallucination. Just as a blocked intuition may betray itself by conviction, emotion, or compulsion to action, so too, perhaps, it may do so by a hallucination.

All this, of course, seems most to be shown in the hallucinatory pain experiences, but it is easily possible to see that hallucinations of the specific senses could have a similar origin. And right here could fit in the fact that the majority of hallucinations involve only one sense. It seems that only certain personalities are so constructed that they can have hallucinatory experiences even in the normal physiological state. From that, one could easily assume that to hallucinate, one sense would be "easier" than two. Judging by the frequency with which they are reported, the auditory must be easier than the visual.

It well may be, then, that hallucinations are really secondary effects arising in the formation of intuitive experience. They do not seem primarily to be message carriers, even though in a way they do mediate information into consciousness. But the information they bring is so incomplete and fragmentary as to be more a "sign" that an unconscious effect occurred than that a motivated message was involved.

It is, perhaps, small wonder that through the ages this particular form of ESP experience has been mysterious and generally misinterpreted. After all, it scarcely could have been more ready-made to be misunderstood. Without the insight the fact of ESP now gives, without the benefit of today's awareness of unconscious mental processes, with humanity's deep urge to get reassurance on the subject of "life after death," it is small wonder that hallucinatory experiences in the forms known as ghosts or apparitions took on other-worldly connotations. From this present analysis, it still looks as if such effects may indeed be "signs," but signs of ESP messages below the threshold of consciousness.

With the above analysis of the probable origin of hallucinatory experience, the primary forms of ESP experience are actually reduced to intuitions in the waking state, and dreams in sleep. However, since the hallucinatory form does succeed in some degree in transmitting information, it can be kept on the list, even though it probably has a secondary origin.

IN THE PK FORM

After one recognizes the secondary origin of hallucinatory experiences, it is not difficult to fit in the probable place of origin of the PK effect, as an additional form in which information may get to consciousness. In both effects it is necessary to suppose that for occasional individuals unconscious reasons can produce overt responses. In PK, however, instead of a response registering in the experiencing person's own organism, it is shown as a physical effect on an external object.

However hypothetical this idea of possible personality structure may be, it is easily observable that some of the unusual physical effects reported, granting a connection of some kind between them and the human situation, seem less like messages about it than they do like "signs" of it. In some of the cases the person already knew of the event and needed no message to tell him of it. The physical effect thus could have been connected with the human situation in a way *other* than bringing a message about it, as in a series of occurrences reported by a woman in Illinois.

"We have a clock over a hundred years old which belonged to my father before me and to his mother before him. A few years ago my parents were living with us, and the clock rested on the mantel in the front hall. We lived in a home in Chicago, Illinois.

"The day of Mother's death in 1952 the clock stopped at the exact time of her passing. I rewound the clock and the next day it stopped at that exact time. It has never since stopped at that time. The clock uses more than twenty-four hours to run down before stopping, so that would eliminate its second stopping at that exact time from being run down.

"We were living in the same house about three years later when our eldest daughter's first baby was born. When my husband and I returned from the hospital, I noted that the clock had stopped at the exact moment the baby was born. I rewound the clock, and the following day it again stopped at that exact time. It has never again stopped at that time.

"A few years later, in 1956, we moved from Chicago to our present home in the suburbs about twenty miles distant. The clock was placed in the front hall. In 1958 our youngest daughter was married at our church in Chicago. When we returned home, the clock had stopped at the exact time the minister had pronounced them man and wife, as I had glanced at my wristwatch at that time. I rewound the clock, and it has never again stopped from being run down, as time proved it doesn't stop running in twenty-four hours after winding. It takes much longer."

Quite obviously in such a case the clock stopping occurred sometimes at least when no message was necessary. All concerned already knew a baby was being born, or that a wedding was taking place.

However, as mentioned earlier, the fact that a relationship between unexplained physical effects and human situations may exist is still very precariously established. In this area one travels at his own risk, scarcely knowing when a report should be considered as possibly meaningful, when not.

In the past, of course, inexplicable occurrences in this area have been discounted almost without exception. Now, perhaps it would do no harm at least to give them some consideration, while drawing no conclusions about their explanation. In that vein, and because here too, as in hallucinatory experiences, the phenomena are often taken to be messages or signs from the deceased, the following account from a woman in New York is given.

"This incident happened when my daughter, Charlene, was thirteen. That was two years ago. We told her father of it that evening, but I have never told it to anyone else. Charlene has been interested in acting and the theater (*not* films and Hollywood!) since she was three years old. We've always encouraged her and given her books about the theater, actors, acting, etc. Naturally, it all soon led to the Barrymores, and she fell in love with the whole family. After reading Gene Fowler's *Good Night, Sweet Prince,* she wrote to librarians here and abroad to get all possible information and books about them. She discovered so much—especially about John—that isn't usually known. Her aim is to be as great an actor as he was.

"One night we attended a play starring John Carradine. She was excited because she knew he had known Barrymore and he, too, had had great aspirations of nearing Barrymore's greatness. She remarked afterwards how much Carradine had reminded her of Barrymore that night. It almost seemed as if Barrymore was there too. We arrived home late; and as she had no school the next day, I allowed her to stay up until about 1:30.

"The next morning I arose and worked quietly so she could sleep. I was on the top floor in the room next to hers when I heard a loud whooshing noise from the ground floor. I sat a few minutes puzzling about this and decided it must be a pile of newspapers that had fallen. Then I realized there was no pile of newspapers down there, so I went down to the middle floor and was somehow made to turn into the kitchen to check the time. It was 10:27.

"When I reached the lower floor, the door to the basement, which is to the left of the stairs, was wide open. I stepped off the stairs and closed it carefully and heard it latch. My cat was standing on the arm of the sofa facing this door, and she was terrified. She was all puffed up, her back was arched, her eyes black and enormous, and she was growling steadily.

"I was going over to soothe her when I noticed what had made the noise. Charlene draws and paints and at the far end of this room she has an easel on which are about thirty of her drawings. One of these is a profile of John Barrymore. These sheets are always attached by two large steel clamps to the easel so they won't fall off. But the clamps were empty and the sheets were all scattered upside down over the floor. I bent over to pick them up and I had about twenty sheets back on the easel when I picked up the one of Barrymore; and when I placed that on the easel, the basement door that I had just closed and latched slammed shut with a bang.

"There was no draft in the room—no windows or doors open —and I definitely latched the door securely. It sounded as if the door had been wide open and thrown shut. This door could never close by itself. It needs force to make it latch. My cat was spitting and all puffed and arched again, staring at the basement door and backing stiffly away. She was almost out of control, and I had to let her outside. Feeling weak, I sat down in a chair, noticed the book, *Good Night, Sweet Prince,* lying beside me on the table. I picked it up, and it fell from my hands onto my lap, opening to pp. 462–463. On these pages I read as if in a trance that Carradine had been with Barrymore the night he was fatally stricken. And, Barrymore had died at 10:20.

"I wanted to tell Charlene but couldn't seem to get strength to get her, and then I heard a muffled clunk from her room. A minute later I heard her moving about. She came downstairs and just stared at me, saying how strange I looked. She still looked asleep. She said that a noise right beside her bed had awakened her, and she had looked down, and right below her head was a small metal object. She showed it to me. It was a drapery weight. We went to her room and checked her draperies. In the corner of the drapery next to her bed, right at her head, the weight was gone. These were new draperies, and I had inspected the sewing carefully before hanging them. The corner of this drapery next to her bed from where the weight had fallen was still knotted at each end, but the thread was split in the center thus allowing the weight to fall. This was new nylon thread that just doesn't split. All the other weights were in the other corners except this one. I told her all that had happened to me. She grew more excited and happy every minute. Then she told me that before she went to bed she had written a note to John Barrymore and left it lying on her record player.

"In the note she had written how he had inspired her in her drawing and poetry and how she was going to work hard to carry on in the theater. She also wrote that she had felt that he was on stage that night, and if he had been, or if he saw or knew she had written this note, to leave some sort of sign so that she'd know. She suggested that maybe he could move her note to a different position or turn it upside down. She thanked him for all the inspiration he had given her.

"So! Could all that happened have been his answer to this note of hers?"

However such mysteries may be explained, the fact remains that when PK seems to be related to human situations, the nature of the situation is not revealed by the occurrence. As message bearers, PK effects are the worst. Being so ineffective, they practically advertise the fact that they were not built for this job. The evidence suggests that, like hallucinations, these effects too have a secondary origin, which quite possibly also is in connection with the origin of intuitions.

Each of the four ESP constructs, and that of PK too, thus gives glimpses of its origin. Their various imperfections, decoded, tell something about the origin of and development of the constructs themselves. But it is a picture of variations resulting from both big and little causes; from the strongest to the weakest of emotions, the most powerful to the slightest of motives, and those very often tied up with personality, and the endless differences in the personality structure of people.

Obviously, some personalities do, some do not, permit complete intuitions into consciousness. Some construct dream imagery of one kind, some of another. Some permit changes from reality for the greatest, some for the least, of reasons. With hallucinations and PK too, it is obvious that personality factors are restrictive, but in the present state of limited understanding of what those factors may be, not predictably so for no one now knows what it takes to make a personality that can have ESP hallucinations, or can affect reality by PK.

Thus it is that the complexity of personality structure complicates the understanding of ESP. The extreme delicacy of the unconscious processes involved and the variations of personality together act like a weather vane veering with the slightest wind that blows. Yet the changes are not really erratic, but as one can glimpse are governed by their underlying causes which are as lawful as the rest of nature.

The detective job on the forms of ESP ends here. As in most such efforts it was limited by the available clues. But by putting the clues together, a fairly consistent kind of process can be envisioned in the development of each of the forms; consistent particularly in regard to the first three, intuitions and the two dream forms. It is less so in regard to hallucinations and PK. In these, the evidence certainly is still incomplete, and while it is not too early to do some supposing, it is too early to forget that the resulting suppositions are too fragile to sustain full weight.

All of this chapter, from the discussion about intuitions to that about PK, is a sketch of the possible, even probable, path of ESP information into consciousness, as *experiences* suggest it. But what about experiments? Experimental situations are so much more restricted than those of life that one may well wonder if they will show any effects analogous to these in cases. On the other hand, one can ask if these glimpsed processes in cases give any revealing hints for experiments. In the following chapter, the laboratory evidence will be assessed, and similarities observed.

CHAPTER 12

The Psi Process in the Laboratory

ESP in the laboratory is the same ESP as in spontaneous cases. But like the barefoot boy in boots, it does not look or feel the same. No longer free and unrestricted, now it is cramped and stylized. But for a reason.

Spontaneous occurrences, whether involving ESP or any other of nature's processes, do not automatically prove and explain themselves. They must be studied and analyzed. They must be subjected to controls, tested, checked, and rechecked according to the requirements of scientific method. And in the last analysis, the requirements of scientific method are simply those of making sure, not guessing, at interpretations.

The differences between ESP in life and in the laboratory go back to spontaneity. In life, material is admitted according to unconscious preferences and timed according to the nameless realities of the situations that exist below the conscious level. It is admitted because it is of interest or concern to the individual. His higher conscious levels know nothing of all this until finally by the chosen form—whether intuition, dream, or hallucinatory or PK sign—it comes, as a message, to his attention. However, even though its origin and path to consciousness is thus hidden, it may carry with it characteristics that betray its origin. Those characteristics, as it happens, are usually imperfections in the routine business of message bearing.

In Chapter 11, some of the kinds of imperfections were analyzed, and their probable causes were considered. This was done by taking the meaning of the real situation—the meaning that ideally should have been transmitted—as a standard of comparison for the message the person actually received. By contrasting the real message with an ideal one, an evaluation of the degree and kind of imperfection of the experience could be made. In this way it was possible to trace out in some detail what seems to be a reasonably representative outline of the basic process as it goes on in each of the four forms of ESP, and also of PK, when that seems to function as a fifth way psi may manifest itself.

The story was one of five different routes that ESP messages can take, each beginning in the same place, the deep unconscious, and ending at another place, the conscious attention. When all five routes were considered, both their similarities and their differences helped to reinforce the interpretation of each individual one. In a way and to an extent they were found to hang together and make sense, because one could see in them psychological factors operating that are in essence just the same as those that have already been recognized in nonparapsychological areas of psychology. The effects of memory, of expectation, of hopes, fears, anxieties, all are there, as well as the complexities of motivations, of ego involvement, and the rest. In its total, it turns out to be, as could have been expected, a very "human" process.

In ESP in the laboratory, the process looks quite different. Of course it is a human one too, but now it shows unexpected and puzzling angles. However, one must remember that this situation is a new and different—an unfamiliar—one. Real-life situations even in all their superficial diversity have occurred again and again in human experience, but laboratory test conditions are a new aspect. Human reactions to these new conditions consequently are new too and call for special study and analysis. If they require a lot of that, and if it is difficult to understand them, it is at least in part a mark of the uniqueness of the situation which puts spontaneous ESP into the confinement of the laboratory.

The uniqueness begins in an ESP test when the subject must, in effect, send an order down from consciousness, "Admit this target, and do it now. Process it at once. I need to know what it is at once." This, of course, is something new. In spontaneous situations the initial unconscious activation has no conscious impetus.

In a test, surprisingly enough, the order may be obeyed, for some tests are successful, in that the results show that ESP did occur. In them the order is obeyed, even though "this target" in a typical test is just a symbol, and not an event with living meaning, and even though now there is no choice of route.

With the conditions of origin so different, so unspontaneous, it is small wonder that the result in the laboratory test is as unlike that of a spontaneous experience as water in a city tap from water in a mountain stream. In this laboratory situation no five routes with differences and similarities that reinforce each other are possibilities. Here, only the intuitive form is a practical possibility to take the message, i.e., the name of the target symbol, into consciousness.

This intuitive form is the one which in spontaneous experiences meets its most obvious difficulty or obstruction at the threshold of consciousness, where it often shatters like a snowball hitting a target. Fragments of idea, emotion, action, and conviction fall apart, some on one side, some on the other of the barrier. But once one picks them up, the pieces can be fitted back together, reconstructed sufficiently so that something of their character and the circumstance that divided them can be deciphered.

It is not so easy in the laboratory. The ESP process may be the same essentially, but now it is constrained to act quite differently, or at least the way it acts in this new situation appears to be quite other than it seemed before. The pieces one finds in the laboratory do not so easily explain themselves. For one thing, the meaning of the message here is unitary. It is just an indivisible target, a symbol, without meaning of its own. And so it cannot fragment, nor leave traces like the real-life cases do. It must either hit or miss; either cross the barrier, or fail to cross. No halfway business here. And yet here too, telltale signs are given, for over the years of laboratory research numerous puzzling "side effects" have been encountered. These are the result of the restricted conditions necessary for controlled experimental method. Interpreted correctly, they should give an added angle of observation on the nature of the psi process.

Looking back, one can see that from the start of the experimental work on ESP, hints as to the kind of process it is were being given. Imperfections in the results of the experiments were telling something about it from the start, but it took time for the accumulation of evidence to make those effects recognizable for what they were. It took time for the dust of nonessentials to settle so that major outlines would be visible. It is still too early for all of them to be completely clear. However, each new answer yielded by the research gave increased understanding even though new questions constantly arose. There is a psi process, yes. The tests soon proved that. But a question was implicit even in the very classroom test in which Linzmayer was discovered and in all succeeding ones. Yes, there are special persons who "have ESP." But why is it limited? Why are they different from the rest? What is it about them that permits ESP to function and prohibits it in the others? This, of course, was the knotty problem of individual differences in personality raising its head at the very start.

Another question was implicit too, in that early test. As soon as Linzmayer's correct guesses had proven to be a statistically significant number, this question could well have been asked, though if it had been, no one then would have had time to pause to answer it. At that stage more evidence of ESP was necessary; more high scores from more new subjects, in order to "make a case" for a skeptical outside world. That world, of course, would say, "Yes, but those scores are only the result of some kind of sensory leakage. The conditions were not tight enough." As a consequence the early reports of all this, published in 1934, are so entirely devoted to descriptions of the conditions in an attempt to show that sensory leakage was impossible, that small hint is given that anyone then could stop to think even for a minute, about the questions these successful experiments raised.

The implicit question that was raised, even by Linzmayer's initial three hits in five, when "chance" was one in ten, was this: Why did he miss the other two? What was happening then? And on succeeding days when his scores, however significant statistically their average may have been, fluctuated apparently unsystematically higher one time, lower another, what was happening? Unnoticed then—at least unemphasized in the necessary preoccupation with the main objective of rolling up ever more impressive odds against chance—was the effect of slight variations of mood, attention, motivation, and all the list of personal day-to-day fluctuations that even today can still defeat an experimental project. Not all of the temporary influences that can affect ESP are known for sure even now, and those that are known cannot always be controlled. But in the early days, interfering circumstances could only be suspected and the fluctuating, temporary ones were baffling just because they changed so constantly.

Then another effect began to be noticed. The misses from call to call were not the only sign of the kind of process it was that showed, from Linzmayer on down the line of subjects. Sometimes, in spite of the fact that Linzmayer's average scores were too high for "chance," he would make a solid block of misses; one long enough so that it would have seemed that chance alone should have produced at least a few correct calls.

Linzmayer himself thought that at those times his "mental attitude was not right." Remembering this as a possible tip, the experimenter began to watch for a chance to test it.

It was at the end of the school year that an opportunity came. It was Linzmayer's last scheduled testing session, for he was leaving on vacation in the morning. He still had his packing to do, and was eager to be off. His final run of the session which had started out well enough showed only four hits out of twenty-five. It was plain the situation had "run down." It was just the time the experimenter had been waiting for. He decided to keep the boy, press him to do one more "very important experiment."[1]

And so, "heartlessly," as J. B. Rhine later confessed, he pressed the student to continue. The more Linzmayer protested that he was not doing well—he wanted to stop; he had to go; he still needed to pack and time was short—the more his tormenter persisted.

"Come on now! You can't leave this experiment half done. Just a few more runs. You can raise these scores. Try harder!" And so on and on until five hundred more calls had been made. And when they had, the score which by chance alone should have been one hundred hits, was only eighty-one, a *negative* deviation of nineteen.

In five hundred calls, when "chance" is five, nineteen below the mean is not merely low. For Linzmayer, who usually averaged

[1] Rhine, J. B. *Extra-sensory Perception*. Boston: Bruce Humphries, 1934, p. 83.

well above, it was strikingly low; so unusual for him that its suggestive value was probably almost as great as if it had been statistically significant. It was enough to set the experimenter thinking. Yes, it probably is possible to miss, not just by chance. Chance would give a general average of five. But this would be different from simply "no ESP." This would be *missing* by ESP. But how? And what would cause it?

These early questions—Why do only certain individuals "have ESP"? Why do their scores fluctuate from day to day and from run to run? What happens when scores go significantly negative, and how can such "psi missing" be controlled and prevented?—are not the only ones experimenters have raised over years of research. But these are probably the most basic, and when these are fully answered, many of the lesser ones will automatically be answered, too.

The first of these three questions, however, has long since been answered. Why do some people have ESP and others not? It was not answered by direct research, however, because it was not a proper question. It raised a pseudoproblem which research related to it soon wiped out.

Improper questions, of course, arise in any science, not especially in parapsychology. In any area of research a problem may loom up and confront the investigator, an obvious roadblock to progress as it seems. And then, a little later, the problem simply is not there. It was not solved. It just disappeared. The reason was that it turned out not to be a proper question, like the one in biology which long baffled investigators: "Why does spontaneous generation occur faster in a warm room than in a cold one?"

In the ESP research, the question why some people do, some do not have ESP, was one of these. The implication behind the question is that some kind of permanent, stable personality characteristic so differentiates individuals, that just as some have blue eyes for a lifetime, others never, some have ESP, and others never. This was not a proper question. It is fairly clear now that although stable personality characteristics exist which tend to influence the expressing of ESP, it is not, as it at first appeared, an all-or-none proposition.

It was not clear at first, however, and in the early years of research it did seem that only certain persons were endowed with ESP and that naturally they had to be singled out and experimented with individually. If they were not treated individually in a class like that from which Linzmayer was chosen, the low scores of those who had no ESP would cancel the high scores of those who did. This meant that ESP testing must be done with individuals, not in classes, even though no experimenter working this way could turn out as much research per unit time, as with a group. Like a one-chair dentist, he could do only so much per session.

Gradually the situation changed, however, as the understanding of the nature of ESP deepened. It is true, classroom tests in the early years were usually in vain. The results of high and low scorers did cancel each other. But sometimes fluctuations in the scoring of individuals in classes seemed to point to hidden meanings. They suggested that ESP might be operating even though the totals did not show it. But if so, it could not be proven unless some way could be found to separate the sheep and goats. And that is just what happened, eventually, when a basis for distinguishing psi hitters and psi missers was discovered. But the idea of ESP as an all-or-none occurrence faded slowly out, as it became obvious that the ability to express ESP is one of degree, not one of kind. True, there were "good" subjects, and "bad" subjects, but the differences in scoring which led to the original question, were soon shown not to be permanent characteristics, for daily fluctuations showed times when bad ones were good and good ones were bad.

Before long another observation was made that indicated that scoring was affected by external conditions, regardless of whether a good or bad subject was involved. Almost from the start of experimental testing it seemed to experimenters that their subjects tended to score better at the beginning of the runs than later.[2] As soon as a fair number of records of runs had been made, they were scored *crossways* to see if the hits did come mainly in the early calls of the runs.

[2] Rhine, J. B., and J. G. Pratt. *Parapsychology, Frontier Science of the Mind.* Springfield: Charles C. Thomas, 1957, p. 48.

This crossways scoring could be done easily because practically from the beginning records of tests had been kept on record sheets standardized for the purpose. These ten vertical columns had spaces for twenty-five card calls. On such a sheet, chance alone would be $5 \times 10 = 50$, so that an excess or deficit could readily be computed.

Now the accumulated pages of completed record sheets were tallied *across* the page, in the first check for what came to be called "position effects." On these, tallies on ESP records long antedated those on the PK data already mentioned.

The tallies showed that the experimenters' suspicions had a basis. More hits did occur in the upper part of the record sheets than elsewhere. The numbers of hits in each place, from one to twenty-five, showed a pronounced decline from the top almost to the bottom with a small increase in the final five calls. It was a somewhat uneven U-curve. It was a clearcut kind of testimony showing that subjects in general were affected by an influence as extraneous as the position of calls in the run.

Of course U-curves are nothing new in psychology and are almost to be expected in tasks when repetition without a break is involved. Changes in motivation, in attention, alertness, etc., occur, so that efficiency is almost certain to decrease as the task progresses, and perhaps to increase again, a bit, as the subject realizes that the end is in sight. The ESP test was such a task, and here the familiar effect was showing, too. It was one of the first demonstrable evidences that psychology's stepchild (some said, illegitimate), parapsychology, had traces of the parental blood.

The U-curve found in ESP scoring *was* a significant finding for two reasons. The first was that it reinforced the proof for ESP, which at the time was the supreme need for experimenter and the wider audience alike. If in addition to significant above-chance scoring, the hits occurred according to a lawful pattern, then the evidence for the reality of ESP was that much stronger. The deeper meaning of the U-curve was that it showed that the ESP process can be affected by psychological influences; and further, that these influences can be slight—like the effect of the position of a call in a run—and probably temporary, and are not stable personality characteristics.

At about the same time the U-curve and other position effects were being studied, another series of experiments began which eventually and quite unexpectedly showed definitely that ESP is susceptible to temporary influences. It is a long story, for it involves work that for nearly a decade absorbed most of the attention of two researchers.

These two were both young assistants at the laboratory, and their research articulated in an unexpected way, although it did not begin as a collaboration, nor did it aim at the point in question. That certainly was not one they could have had in mind at the time. In fact the full meaning of it on the point of temporary influences did not show until nearly a whole decade had passed. But the broad perspective of hindsight eventually showed it clearly.

The story begins with one of Rhine's young undergraduate students who had been among the dozen or so good subjects discovered soon after Linzmayer and Pearce. His name was Charles E. Stuart, and he had served both as subject and as student assistant in some of the early experimental research. He stayed on at Duke and got his undergraduate degree, and also his Ph.D., and then became an assistant in the newly established Parapsychology Laboratory.

Among a number of projects Stuart was interested in was one that looked like a throwback to an earlier day. But he instituted it because he thought he saw a way to tell quickly when a good hit was made by ESP without the many trials necessary for statistical significance in card-calling tests—with which in the late 1930s nearly all experimental work was done. It will be recalled that in earlier days, like the time of the Creery sisters, drawings tests had been popular, and that in these an experimenter made a drawing and the subject tried to match it. Sometimes he succeeded, more often he did not. And sometimes he made a partial hit. But no evaluation was possible, other than that of common sense, which of course in the scientific age is not sufficient. But now Stuart thought he saw a way by which such tests could be evaluated, and, if hits or partial hits occurred, he thought they could be identified even if only a few guesses had been made.

The actual method he devised is not important here. As it turned out, the direction of parapsychological investigation decreed that it was not to be important in the years ahead, but at the time it looked as if it might be a valuable technique. Stuart's work using this method is not in the direct line of interest here either, but it was a strong preoccupation of his over a number of years. Beginning in 1942, he published five papers about it in the *Journal of Parapsychology,* the last one, in 1947. His declining health and untimely death from heart disease in 1948 left one more unfinished paper, which his colleagues at the laboratory completed and published posthumously.[3]

Typical of pioneer research on a problem more difficult and complex than he or anyone else then realized, none of these projects of Stuart's yielded significant over-all results. But in each, for one reason or another, he had introduced a variation in conditions, and in each instance he got significant results under one or another of the varying conditions. These significant aspects of the different experiments were unexpected and puzzling. The total effort in fact, while it yielded a number of leads for future experiments which he himself was destined not to make, was characterized largely by the uneven and unexpected results it showed.

Such an outcome in a pioneer field, although giving much food for thought, is not very satisfying to the researcher at the time. Something of this feeling is reflected in the final paragraph of Stuart's last completed report. At first, he says, the method seemed to hold promise of isolating hits specifically so that reliable results could be easily secured with a few subjects only. But on the contrary, the results of these drawings tests turned out to be no better than those done with cards.

But there is a brighter side to it all, and before his death Stuart knew something of it. His work, when it was cut short, was not wholly an adventure in futility, for it yielded stepping stones for later workers.

This other side of his work involves another major effort, that of his colleague, Miss Betty Humphrey, and it too has its expected

[3] Stuart, C. E. An ESP test with drawings. *Journal of Parapsychology,* 6 (1942) 20–43.

and its unexpected side. Hers too represents nearly a decade's work by herself and other experimenters, for the research naturally ramified and interlocked. The work of no experimenter in the tiny laboratory cosmos really stands alone, any more than does that of any researcher in the large cosmos of life.

Miss Humphrey came to the laboratory upon her graduation from Earlham College, Indiana, and eventually earned her doctorate at Duke. At Earlham, she had already done research on the relation of ESP and intelligence, and found a slight positive correlation.[4] In other words, she found that the subjects with the highest I.Q. also scored slightly higher in their ESP tests than the others. However, her subjects were all Earlham College students, and so the spread of intelligence ratings was not very great. The result therefore did not actually permit the interpretation that high intelligence and success in ESP are necessarily related. Occasional mentally defective individuals have shown considerable evidence of ESP. It seems probable that the more intelligent students simply conformed to the conditions of the test better than the rest. However that may be, the project at least shows Humphrey's early interest in correlates of ESP. When she came to Duke, her first work at the laboratory involved a study of ESP in relation to various personality measurements, as developed by psychologists. She wanted to see if those measurements would offer guidelines for distinguishing personality traits which might govern ESP. In a paper published in the *Journal of Parapsychology* in 1945, she reported the results of a study made with a test known as Bernreuter's Personality Inventory, and as she and all other parapsychologists from then on found out, study using a personality inventory was a first step into a quagmire.[5]

The fact, however, that these psychological tests in combination with ESP tests have proved to be more baffling than interpretable is not the fault of psychologists, nor of the parapsychologists either. It is the fault of *people*. They are too complicated. No test yet devised is adequate to divide people into any but the grossest

[4] Humphrey, Betty M. ESP and intelligence. *Journal of Parapsychology,* **9** (1945) 7–16.
[5] Humphrey, Betty M. An exploratory correlation study of personality measures and ESP scores. *Journal of Parapsychology,* **9** (1945) 116–123.

of general groups, although progress toward refinement has been made over recent years.

In the present case it turned out that of the many traits that the Bernreuter attempted to measure, a few did show some degree of correlation with the ESP scores of the subjects involved. For instance, the subjects who were characterized as stable, extroverted, dominant, and self-confident tended to score above the chance mean, or "positively." Those who showed instability, introversion, submissiveness, and self-consciousness tended to score below the mean, or "negatively." The degree of correlation was not statistically significant, but as the editor said in the abstract introducing the paper, "positive indications were given that in general are in line with such impressions as experimenters through the years have reported concerning the personality make-up of good subjects." It was plain even then, however, that it would not be simple to arrive at personality correlates of ESP as measured by ready-made psychological inventories.

Obviously rather discouraged with the attempt to use a personality measure like the Bernreuter, Humphrey next asked the question of the relation of the person to his ability to score in tests in a different way: if permanent personality traits can give only a partial answer, then can it be that the general behavior of good subjects is somehow different from that of the poor ones, and that different ways of behaving may be associated with the different levels of scoring?

At the time, the idea was current in psychological circles that people's movements reveal personality traits and that these reveal the inner personality. In the field of psychological testing, a measure of this utilizing free drawings had shortly before been devised by Dr. Paula Elkisch, who wished to distinguish well-adjusted from maladjusted children. She reported having done so successfully through a study of free drawings made by the children.[6]

Humphrey got the idea that this method might be useful in dividing high and low ESP scores. Calling it an "expansion-compression" separation, she attempted to divide the subjects into two groups according to the characteristics of the drawings they

[6] Elkisch. Children's drawings in a projective technique. *Psychological Monographs,* 58 (1945) 1–31.

made.[7] In her words, expansion was "the potential ability of making contact; compression stands for isolation." These groups were thus suggestive of extroversion and introversion, rated by the act of drawing however instead of by answers on a questionnaire.

For this method the drawings of Stuart's subjects offered ideal material, and so Stuart and Humphrey pooled their efforts. Working on Stuart's data, without knowing his subjects' ESP scores, Humphrey rated their drawings as to their expansive-compressive characteristics. The hope, of course, was that one group would include those with the higher ESP scores, the other, those with the lower. If so, then, even though the total scores had not shown evidence of ESP, the canceling effect would be removed, and the results would show the presence of ESP.

It happened that in some of Stuart's drawings tests, a clairvoyant method had been used, which meant that the subjects had tried to reproduce hidden drawings which no one had in mind at the time. In other tests, however, he had used a general or GESP method, in which the experimenter had looked at each drawing at the time the subjects were attempting to draw it. Whether or not these two methods are basically different, and not just psychologically so (and more and more it is coming to be suspected they are not, and that the subject can get the target directly in either case), at least the experimenters and subjects thought they were different. One way was clairvoyant, the other could have been telepathic or a combination of the two.

When Humphrey was working over the drawings made by Stuart's subjects, the results of the two types of projects were kept separate, and eventually all subjects whose ESP tests were clairvoyant were put in one group and all his GESP subjects in another. As it turned out this was an important distinction for an unexpected reason.

Humphrey first rated all the subjects who had been given clairvoyance tests. Of the ninety-six, she found that forty-one classified as expansive and fifty-five as compressive. And when the ESP scores of each group were compared, the difference between the

[7] Humphrey, Betty M. Success in ESP as related to form of response drawings. I. Clairvoyance experiments. *Journal of Parapsychology,* 10 (1946) 78–106.

totals was great enough to be mathematically significant. The expansives had tended to score positively, the compressives negatively. They had indeed canceled each other.

Now it was clear why Stuart had labored in vain to get significant evidence of ESP. His subjects, because of personal differences, had actually fallen into two groups which had fairly systematically scored in opposite directions. The evidence for ESP had thus been obscured.

The result, however, raised a question. Why should a difference like that between the subjects who made expansive and those who made compressive drawings be reflected in their ESP scores? The answer was not any clearer when the rest of Stuart's data, that in which the students had been given GESP tests, had been examined.[8]

Humphrey now scored the drawings of the subjects in these other tests. Again ESP scores of the expansive and compressive groups were correlated. Again they separated into two groups, one positive, one negative, and again the difference was significant. But this time the compressives had the high scores; the expansives the low ones. This was a complete reversal. If any idea of the reason for the difference of direction in the clairvoyant tests had been dawning, this result entirely negated it.

It was as baffling a result as it was a pronounced and inescapable one. Later, similar analyses on other tests amenable to them also showed the effect. It was possible to conjecture that expansives tend to score positively on clairvoyance tests, but to score negatively when a second person intervenes as in telepathy or GESP. The compressives, just the opposite. Perhaps the freer expansive personality is challenged by the clairvoyant condition, but bothered by the idea of another person's intruding between himself and the target in telepathylike situations. To reverse the idea, the compressive kind of person may feel supported, helped by the idea of a second individual in telepathy, unsure and baffled by the idea of a purely clairvoyant kind of contact. It might mean something like that, but did it really? Even though it was clear that the

[8] Humphrey, Betty M. Success in ESP as related to form of response drawings. II. GESP experiments. *Journal of Parapsychology,* **10** (1946) 181–196.

expansive-compressive dichotomy was showing a real difference in the direction of the ESP response of individuals, the question why it should do so was far from being answered. At the same time, however, it did throw considerable illumination on Stuart's work and the reason it had not fulfilled his early hope.

This was not the end of the story, however. The real reason for reviewing these experiments here is, as noted at the start, because they showed the effect of temporary, rather than stable personality characteristics, and it took yet another experiment to bring out this fact.

After Humphrey's work on Stuart's subjects she and another colleague, Mr. Burke Smith, who was then an instructor in a psychology class at Duke, performed an experiment to try to find the effect of class discussion about ESP on the actual ESP scores of the class.[9] They used the expansive-compressive difference to separate high and low scorers. The experiment was carried out on two successive days. The order of procedure was that first an opaque envelope enclosing a stimulus picture was put on the chalk rail at the front of the classroom, and the students were asked to draw anything that came to mind. These drawings were the basis of their expansive-compressive ratings for the day. Then two runs (of twenty-five trials) of clairvoyant ESP were given, and then a half-hour of explanation about, and discussion of, ESP followed.

The next day the session began with a half-hour continuation of the discussion, then another drawing procedure just like that of the day before. Following this, two more clairvoyance runs completed the experiment. The aim was to see how scoring levels would be affected by the discussion, but the fact that the same subjects made drawings twice was the feature of interest here, for it turned out that a number of the subjects changed their personality rating from one day to the next. Twelve of the expansives became compressive, and nineteen of the compressives became expansive. And the trend of ESP scoring following the personality rating.

Inadvertently thus, the fact was stumbled upon that tendencies

[9] Smith, Burke M., and Betty M. Humphrey. Some personality characteristics related to ESP performance. *Journal of Parapsychology,* **10** (1946) 269–309.

toward expansiveness or compressiveness, as expressed in these drawings were temporary, not stable personality characteristics. It would be interesting to know why some of these students changed in their expansive-compressive ratings as they did, but no attempt was made at the time to find out. Apparently something like the mood of the day, or at least a different psychological situation had developed which could affect the way of drawing and perhaps other physical responses as well, and also the reaction to a parapsychological technique. The ESP process was here shown to be affectable by a psychological state so temporary that it could change overnight.

At the time this result was discovered the technique of correlating ESP scores with the expansion-compression rating was appreciated mainly as a way of detecting the presence of ESP in groups of subjects whose attitudes might differ enough to cancel their ESP scores. The temporary mood aspect of it there seemed only a secondary one. But even so, as a technique of separating subjects, the use of the expansive-compressive dichotomy did not become widespread. For one thing, it was rather cumbersome to administer. It depended on the judging of each subject's drawing and the decision, not always easy, whether the drawing showed expansive or compressive characteristics. In order to make the decisions less subjective it was necessary to have two or more independent judges, each giving weighted judgments. And these were then averaged. All of this was time consuming and bothersome, so that in the long run it developed that few researchers besides Humphrey made use of the technique in any major way.

Beginning in 1942, and with the results published several years before Humphrey's expansion-compression work on Stuart's data, another worker at a different place made an attempt to separate high and low scores on a different principle. This was Mrs. Gertrude Schmeidler, who was then a psychology instructor at Radcliffe College and is now a professor at City College, New York. She began to make ESP tests partly, as she said, because she was still more than a little skeptical about the occurrence of ESP, even though she was unable to see in what respect the reports of it she had read were open to criticism. She decided to see if she herself could get evidence of it. In a preliminary test on several friends and acquaintances she noticed that those who expressed themselves favorably about the possibility of ESP, and seemed to be interested in the test, scored higher than those who did not believe ESP was possible, and who felt the test was nonsense and took it only to be obliging.

With this tip as to the possible effect of a subject's attitude on ESP, she began asking her subjects to state before they took the test whether they believed in it or not. It was rather natural to refer to those who expressed belief as "sheep," the disbelievers as "goats." She began testing subjects in these two groups.[10] She tried them first individually, and got encouraging though not spectacular results. Then she tried the tests in her classes. As a result, a definite, and eventually, as numbers piled up, highly significant difference between the average scores of sheep and goats was reached. On the average the sheep scored positively, the goats negatively. The trend was unmistakable.

This attitude test, unlike that of expansion-compression, was easy to administer. The subject practically did it himself. And the difference in scoring between sheep and goats, while seldom very great, was persistent enough that nearly every group tested gave indication of it. This is probably the reason that many other researchers working with many kinds of tests have used it since. In too many individual researches to enumerate, the sheep-goat differentiation has shown the divergent tendency of the two groups. The total scores of all the subjects may not show any ESP, but when the sheep and goats are separated, the sheep prove to have scored significantly above the mean, the goats significantly below; even if the two groups are not each independently significant, at least the difference between them proves to be too great to be a purely chance distribution, and thus the occurrence of ESP is shown in situations in which it would otherwise not have been detected.

The question this dichotomy raises is, Why does the person's attitude toward ESP affect his ESP scores? At first it seemed that a stable personality characteristic might be at the bottom of it. Certainly some people believe things more easily than others.

[10] Schmeidler, Gertrude Raffel, and R. A. McConnell. *ESP and Personality Patterns.* New Haven: Yale University Press, 1958.

Some can be said to be natural believers, others, inborn skeptics. Was the sheep-goat separation simply a reflection of this difference? Repeated use of the test finally gave a different answer. Here, too, the determining factor proves to be not so much that of a personality characteristic as one resulting from the specific mental attitude which belief or disbelief in ESP creates in the person who takes the test. It is obvious that those who believe in ESP approach an ESP test differently from those who do not. The difference of attitude may be a very subtle one, for in this matter of expressing impressions welling up from unconscious mental depths, very slight changes may have an effect. By observation, the attitude of one who believes in ESP is likely to include a greater degree of spontaneity than that of a disbeliever; the goats are likely to be more involved in their own mental processes, less "open" to the task, less receptive to delicate impressions.

But now the question is, What do differences between sheep and goats, or expansives and compressives tell about the ESP process? When these dichotomies were first observed, the experimenters were looking for a way to separate those who "had" ESP from those who did not have it. The question then would have been, Do sheep have more ESP than goats? If so, the *size* of the deviation above chance which a group displayed would be a measure of the amount of ESP they possessed. But this idea passed out quietly, along with the one that ESP is an all or none ability.

One reason it passed out was because of the nature of the scores in situations as in these tests involving sheep versus goats or expansive versus compressive. In most of these, although the one group scored above the mean, the other scored just about as much below. The low scores, in other words, were not simply at the chance level. If they had been that, it might have meant simply "no ESP." But scores below the mean raised the same question suggested by the earlier test with Linzmayer, when he scored only eighty-one while chance alone was one hundred. The question, Can a subject *miss* by ESP? now came up again, and soon the evidence was strong enough to prove that he can. From then on the problem of understanding the tendency to score negatively under some conditions became a major objective in parapsychology.

It is clear now that the result of personality differentiations, like Humphrey's and Schmeidler's, is to separate subjects, not according to the amount of ESP they have, but rather according to whether they will tend to hit the target by ESP or miss it by ESP. This effect, however, was not formalized as such in published words until 1952, when, in an article in the *Journal of Parapsychology* on "The Problem of Psi Missing," Rhine declared of such tests, "It is only in the broad use of the word that these can be called personality measures; but in any case they appear to be psychological states important to psi performance. Their importance evidently has to do, not with the operation of ESP, but with the question as to the side of the mean on which the deviation will be produced in the total scores; in other words, whether or not *psi missing* will operate instead of the normal *psi hitting*."[11]

In this article the old problem of psi missing was for the first time recognized clearly and evaluated. Over the years experimenters had been bothered by it, and often the successful repetition of many kinds of tests had been prevented when scoring would unexpectedly turn negative, for reasons too obscure to be identified. Now in this article the problem was dissected plainly, even though its implications were not widely appreciated even then.

Of course it had been recognized from the start that according to the hypothesis of chance, average results will neither fall significantly above nor significantly below the mean, and if significant deviations below the mean are secured they are just as strong indicators of nonchance factors as are those above. But just what below-chance scores meant *psychologically* had not been asked very loudly, until now. When that question had been asked, the easy answer had usually been that consciously or unconsciously the subjects must have been trying to miss; in other words, if not conscious, then unconscious negativism must be the explanation. Now, evaluating all the evidence that had accumulated over the years, the answer as far as it was possible to arrive at one, was not so simple.

[11] Rhine, J. B. The problem of psi missing. *Journal of Parapsychology,* **16** (1952) 115.

It might be reasonable to suppose that some very actively disbelieving goats of Schmeidler's differentiation, for instance, because of their negativism, might well exercise it on an unconscious level too, even though they consented to try the test. The same excuse, however, would not apply to Stuart's subjects. For instance, the subtle difference between a clairvoyance and a GESP test caused his expansive and compressive subjects to reverse their scoring trends. It is not conceivable that any unconscious negativism they may have had would have been reversed for a cause like this.

The tendency to score negatively, or the psi-missing factor, it turns out, is much too ubiquitous a response, and too many different situations cause it, for it to be the result of any one circumstance alone. Instead the present consensus would probably run like this: Psi hitting occurs when all conditions are favorable. When they are, presumably the person unconsciously assumes a given "set" or "stance." This set involves all the conditions, known or unknown, that permit an ESP intuition to get to consciousness. But when anything disturbs this set, and does so in an orderly and sustained way, then psi missing must occur. As in marksmanship, let us say, when the aim has been correctly taken, any constant wind that comes up, unless correction is made, will regularly divert the bullet from its target. It cannot possibly make even a random hit. The result, in ESP, is psi missing, and if prolonged, it can become statistically significant, just as psi hitting does. Short fluctuations of hitting and missing, however, would leave the total score at chance, and be indistinguishable from "no ESP." Psi missing, then, is a more or less prolonged and consistent tendency to score below the mean, caused by a persistent unfavorable condition. Such a condition of course could be created by many different influences including negativism.

In spontaneous cases it was clear that in the processing of information into consciousness, many different psychological factors could influence the result and prevent a complete and perfect message from getting through. To differing degrees the factors were emotional and motivational. And they all, apparently, fluctuated with the differences in persons and the structure of individual personalities.

The evidence of barriers at the level of consciousness suggested that the difficulty of crossing was greater in some personalities than others. The evidence, however, involved only the crossing of barriers not surmounted without leaving a trace of difficulty in crossing. If in other cases the obstacles had been prohibitive, then those persons to whom it happened simply became part of the population which reports no psi experiences. The direct evidence from cases, then, can only be partial and in the nature of the situation cannot show psi missing. It can only testify to effects that show, not to those that do not. Even so, indirectly the evidence from cases has a bearing on the topic of psi missing in the laboratory, for it can give a suggestion as to the reason for it.

This suggestion goes back to the fact that in experiments the intuitive form is practically always the one which the subject must use for his ESP responses. But this is the form that in life situations produces many incomplete messages, as discussed in Chapter 11, in connection with the development of the intuitive form. The incompleteness of these intuitive experiences seemed to be the result of difficulty or blockage at the threshold of consciousness. This blockage sometimes caused one part of the message, sometimes another to be repressed.

In experiments, presumably the same tendency would exist. But in them the message is only a symbol on a card and not a topic that can be broken up into fragments of idea, emotion, or action. If the proper response was blocked here, it would mean that that particular symbol would be repressed. Still, the person consciously set to guess a symbol would fill in with one of the others, and never know the difference. The result would have to be a negative score. If the blockage continued, the absence of hits would pile up and eventually the result would be significantly negative. This would be psi missing, and it would be caused by blockage.

In all experiences, blockage seemed to have many causes, but most of them were more or less emotional. In experiments, effects arising from emotional factors are probably minimized, but on the other hand, those connected with motivation are more likely at a maximum. The proper "stance" for psi hitting in tests must certainly include a strong urge and effort to succeed. But could it be too strong? As in so many other processes besides psi, strong effort, if it leads to tension, may be self-defeating. Too little effort, and the item may not even be admitted, the result a purely random guess, too much and the extra tension may cause psi missing instead of hitting—or if not too much tension, then distraction of almost any kind, a bit of impatience or discomfort or annoyance for almost any reason.

With this in mind, one can return to Humphrey's subjects when they were making Stuart's clairvoyant drawings: interested, intrigued, extroverted, they undertake the test with enthusiasm. An intuitive message is sent up, it crosses the barrier, the drawing is a hit. The same kind of subject, when given a GESP task, however, still approaching the task in the same mood of interest and enthusiasm, must now stop to think of the person looking at the drawing, rather than directly of the drawing itself. This is a sufficient annoyance to divert or block the aim, so that the resultant drawing is something other than the target. It must therefore be a miss.

Such an explanation makes a degree of sense, for results like these of Humphrey and Stuart and many others since show that items which affect the scoring can be as slight as that of the position of a call in a sequence; effects which of course go back to subtle changes in attention, to fluctuations in motivation. The job of recognizing an entire series of cards in a deck of twenty-five means controlling all the correct conditions of attention and motivation for the duration. That, on anyone's count, is a nearly impossible piece of thought control. It's a good question whether it ever can be done very often or by very many people, although progress toward it will no doubt increase with understanding. And at least some degree of this has been achieved from the line of experimentation just reviewed, for now it is recognized that a subject will be more likely to succeed if interest, enthusiasm, and spontaneity are at a maximum level, and that psi missing will set in with the first touch of boredom, frustration, or discomfort.

Long before the psi-missing tendency had been delineated, experimenters, of course, were looking for effective "surefire" ways of eliciting ESP from subjects. One of the first methods hopefully tried in the early research at Duke University was that of hypnosis. The suggestion that subjects under hypnosis might express

ESP much easier or more freely than in the ordinary state of mind was natural because in the early history of hypnotism instances of apparent thought transference and of clairvoyance had occurred, as for instance in Professor Richet's work, mentioned earlier. In fact, the early association of hypnosis and extrasensory effects was so close that for a time they were scarcely distinguished. Even when research began at Duke, the idea that results would be enhanced by hypnosis was still strong enough that over a thousand trials were made using thirty different hypnotized subjects.[12] But the results, though encouraging as suggesting that ESP had occurred, were not appreciably better than those produced by subjects without hypnosis. The method was comparatively slow and cumbersome, and was therefore abandoned.

As a matter of fact, the hypnotic state is far from being a well defined or completely understood one. It may vary sufficiently from one subject to another and as induced by one hypnotist and another to be something of an unknown quantity in itself. With ESP also an unknown, it seemed unprofitable to continue to combine two unknowns. In the years since the early work at Duke, further work on the topic has been done, but the results have failed to show that the hypnotic state necessarily enhances the expressing of ESP. At least as it has been administered, it has not provided the open sesame to the unconscious that might have been expected.

Another general approach which also has failed thus far to produce magical results in "releasing" ESP is that involving the use of drugs. Early in the work at Duke, the effect of unusual physiological conditions was questioned and in some instances special tests were made to see what the effect would be. For instance, tests were made while subjects were sleepy, ill, fatigued. The general effect was always a lowering of the scores the same subjects tended to get under the reverse conditions. It began to be suspected from these and other reasons that the expressing of ESP depends upon the higher functions of the nervous system.

To test this some of the best subjects, including Linzmayer and Pearce, were tested before and after taking doses of the dissocia-

---

[12] Rhine, J. B. *Extra-sensory Perception*. Boston: Bruce Humphries, 1934, p. 47.

tive drug, sodium amytal.[13] As a result, their scores dropped markedly, but rose again when caffeine was administered. The effect of alcohol was also tested with somewhat conflicting results, but results that varied apparently according to the subject and his physiological response. In general the drug results suggested that ESP succeeds best when the person is in a psychological state such that his mind can function at its best.

In recent years the popular attention given to the hallucinogenic drugs, especially LSD and psilocybin, has raised the question of drugs and ESP afresh, partly because reports have been current, like that about "the sacred mushroom," that those under its influence have increased "psychic powers." As a matter of fact, however, formal, well-controlled ESP tests are difficult to administer to subjects under the influence of these drugs, and in no case yet reported has any evidence been given that the drug improved ESP ability. In a few instances it is said a person under the influence of the drug had a spontaneous psi experience, but these were individuals who had also reported them without the drug.

On the whole then, little if any encouragement has been given the idea that unusual physiological or psychological states can increase the expressing of ESP. Whatever may be the secret, if such there be, which will unlock the unconscious, none of these avenues seems to have it, at least as present indications go. This may mean only that as yet no experimenter has been successful in causing the material to be admitted in the first place, for most of the results have been at chance, rather than either positive or negative, so that one cannot even say that psi missing occurred.

Only recently have attempts begun to find physiological correlates to ESP. The supposition behind these experiments is that although ESP is unconscious, its occurrence nonetheless may affect the person physiologically, and if so the effect should be measurable. Accordingly experiments to try to correlate ESP results with changes in brain waves, in blood volume, etc., have been started. So far, encouraging but preliminary and unconfirmed results have been reported. It is not impossible, that when physiological techniques have been refined and subjects discovered

13 *Ibid.*, chap. 11.

who can demonstrate ESP under the necessarily rather distracting conditions, some correlation will be found—at least a correlation with the physiological conditions and the conditions that are most conducive to ESP, if nothing more. But on this, only future research can testify.

The most promising lead discovered thus far for the control of psi missing is one called the differential effect. It is based on a tendency subjects have shown when confronted by two tasks simultaneously or close together, to score differently on them; i.e., higher than chance on the one, lower on the other.

Although the differential effect has recently been demonstrated at the Parapsychology Laboratory by the work of several investigators and particularly by Dr. K. Ramakrishna Rao, it can be seen scattered here and there in the work of earlier experimenters, when their projects were so set up that it could occur. This generally meant when their projects involved the comparison of two conditions in the same experiment. Even though the full significance of the differential scoring which resulted may not have been recognized at the time, it was the accumulation of evidence of it, and the general increase in understanding of psi missing which led to the recent developments.

An experiment at the Parapsychology Laboratory carried out in 1940 is a good example of older work which showed the differential effect. This was a project carried out by a graduate student, now a college dean, Mr. Jack Bevan.[14] He undertook to compare the responses of subjects when they were in light and when they were in darkness. The test consequently was set up so each of his subjects worked alone in a small, windowless dark room and by means of a click on a telegraph system set up for the purpose, signaled "ready" to the experimenter, who was in another room outside. Although the test was arranged to bear on several questions besides that of light and darkness, that one only is of concern here. With the arrangement as indicated, the subject himself controlled the light, alternating one run of tests in light, and one in the dark. The experimenter was outside handling the cards without knowing which runs were in the light, which in the dark.

[14] Bevan, J. M. ESP tests in light and darkness. *Journal of Parapsychology*, **11** (1947) 76–89.

In darkness, in which surely most subjects would feel a degree of discomfort and strangeness as they worked alone in the cheerless confine of a darkroom, one might well expect no ESP to be registered. If a cheerful, pleasant mood is a requirement for successful ESP tests, this does not promote it even though, with the light on, the situation might be sufficiently relieved to allow ESP to function.

In Bevan's experiment, only half of this expectation was realized. The subjects in the light showed psi hitting. But in the dark, instead of not scoring at all, they showed psi missing, and to almost the same extent as the hitting. The difference between the high level and the low was mathematically significant, and this, of course, meant that about the same amount of ESP was displayed in the one as in the other. At the time there was no way to explain why the scores in darkness were not simply at chance, since it was easily recognizable that the condition was unfavorable.

It was from results like these of Bevan's, and from those like Humphrey's on Stuart's data, and like Rhine's in precognition with children versus adult subjects, and numerous others, too, that the way to avoid the cancelling effect of psi missing began to be clear.

Although the situations in the various experiments were not alike, still in each, psi hitting and psi missing had occurred, and something in each situation made it possible to detect the two divergent trends. For instance, in Stuart's case it was only found later because of the expansion-compression analysis made by Humphrey; in Rhine's case because a pilot study had suggested that children and adults would score differently in precognition tests; in Bevan's because his test happened to be so set up that the results under the two conditions could be considered separately.

Naturally since most of the experiments that showed this psi hitting versus psi missing tendency fairly clearly had been carried out at the Parapsychology Laboratory, workers there were especially alert to the occurrence of psi missing and to the possibility of segregating the section of the test in which it would be most likely to take place. They therefore began to try to plan experiments in such a way that they would have a legitimate basis (in the statistical sense) for separating the results of one group from those of the contrasting one.

Thus in 1962 an experiment was carried out which, although its objective was not directly on the psi hitting, psi missing dichotomy, still was planned to take advantage of differences in scoring direction. This experimenter was Mr. Michael Sanders, a graduate student from England who spent a year at the Parapsychology Laboratory,[15] and the objective was to find an easily applicable method of making quick and effective precognition tests. The aspect of interest here was one he introduced to add a novel feature for the subjects, Duke University coeds, with whom he had already made several experiments. In it, he asked them to alternate runs in which they wrote down their responses with runs in which they called them aloud for the experimenter to record. He asked each subject to note ahead of time whether she preferred writing or calling.

Sanders' results showed the subjects tending to hit their preferred targets, but on the nonpreferred they scored much below chance. The difference meant that ESP (of the precognitive type) was operating in both situations but the direction of the scoring, i.e., whether positive or negative, depended on the conditions.

Just before Sanders made his experiment, Dr. K. Ramakrishna Rao also started a test, which led to direct experimentation on the differential effect.[16] In the first of a series of tests he had his subjects prepare card decks of their own by using blank cards and writing or drawing on them symbols of their own selection. These "choice" decks were then used alternately with regular ESP decks, the subjects knowing which kind they were using.

The results showed the familiar pattern, psi hitting on one kind, psi missing on the other. Here the hitting, as expected, was on the "choice" cards, obviously the ones the subjects preferred. The unpreferred were not at chance, but instead about as far below as the preferred were above. Quite naturally this looked as if the subjects were scoring better on the cards they preferred because of

[15] Sanders, Michael S. A comparison of verbal and written responses in a precognition experiment. *Journal of Parapsychology*, **26** (1962) 23–34.

[16] Rao, Ramakrishna K. The preferential effect in ESP. *Journal of Parapsychology*, **26** (1962) 252–259.

their preference. In fact, Rao's assumption on the point was strong enough that he called the result, a "preferential effect."

His next test was a further attempt to demonstrate the same effect under conditions in which the subjects would show their preference by ESP only, so he arranged to make their choice an unconscious one.[17] This time the two kinds of cards, "choice" and ESP, were mixed together so that the subjects did not know until the checkup which kind was involved in any individual call.

Again the results yielded hitting on one kind, missing on the other, and the difference between the two was highly significant. But for some reason, this time the ESP cards were high, the others, low. This was a reversal. The cards which had appeared to be preferred were not preferred in this test. Now the scores on them were negative. But the scores on the nonpreferred were positive, so the divergence persisted, and showed differential scoring, even though it could not strictly be called preferential any more. Apparently the fact of conscious preference did not necessarily mean unconscious preference, too.

The idea that a reversal might occur which was not related to conscious preference dictated the test that followed.[18] Observing that the differential effect seemed to be most marked in the first runs of a series, Rao now made an experiment in which he had each subject complete four runs instead of only two as they had done before, to see if the difference would fall off significantly; or, in other words, whether the differential effect would decrease as the runs continued. It did. In fact, it did more; the differential trend reversed. When the direction of difference in the first runs was compared to that in the fourth runs, the changeover was highly significant. Whichever kind of card had been identified correctly too often to have been due to coincidence alone, in the first run, was missed too consistently for chance in the last one. So here was a reversal right within the session, instead of between

[17] Rao, Ramakrishna K. Studies in the preferential effect. I. Target preference with types of target unknown. *Journal of Parapsychology*, **27** (1963) 23–32.

[18] Rao, Ramakrishna K. Studies in the preferential effect. III. The reversal effect in psi preference. *Journal of Parapsychology*, **27** (1963) 242–251.

experiments. At last the differential effect was showing its true nature. Like so many processes in the unconscious, when dragged up for conscious inspection it did not show the logic which the judgments of consciousness would lead one to expect. And yet, it had a meaning.

In conscious choice, one expects to find a reason for a preference, and experiments like Bevan's, Sanders', and Rao's first tests seemed to show one and it appeared to be based on preference. But when the choice had to be made on an entirely unconscious level, the rules of conscious logic broke down. The result was *difference,* but not one made for any obvious logical reason. This of course is not to say that in such cases no reason exists. It is only to say that the reasons are obscure, and not to be explained by the logic of conscious life.

Two-task tests had been introduced in the first place because they seemed to constitute a good method of making comparisons under the same conditions. But now it can be seen that the unconscious does not look at it that way. Instead of doing each one on its merits, one of the two is apparently fixed on, and this is the one in which the hits occur. But when "set" to hit under these conditions, the opposite condition of the second task *must* produce psi missing.

This much is now clear, and perhaps not so illogical after one considers the nature of the psi process and the difficulties of the transfer of meaning from the unconscious into consciousness.

At the same time, no rule has yet been found to account for the choice in the unconscious of the kind of target that will be hit. If, as in Rao's experiment in which he used four runs per session instead of only two, a reversal occurred between the first and last run, then the position of the runs would appear to have caused it; a situation that emphasizes the fact that in psi hitting or missing the weather-vane analogy is a good one. About as far as one can go now, therefore, in trying to explain the differential effect and the fact that it can reverse without an obvious reason is to say that apparently the necessary "set" for ESP, whether it be psi hitting or psi missing, is delicate and brittle, disturbed by the slightest shift in any of the many influences which can play on and affect the human mind. Just as to get a perfect photograph, all the proper camera adjustments must be made, so here the set must be perfect before ESP can operate. Only this "camera" involved in ESP was handed the experimenters "blind." They got no instructions from the shop as to how it operates. The rules are only being found out slowly, as it were by trial and error—the trial and error of controlled experiments. Presumably when enough of these have been made, the basic lawfulness even of reversals will be disclosed.

By that time too, one of the current superstitions of parapsychological researchers will be explained. This is the superstition that if an experimenter discusses the results of a promising experiment, one "almost significant, only needs a few more runs to finish. . . ," the results from there on will reverse, and positive trends turn negative or negative ones positive. It has happened so often that the superstition at least has a basis in fact. With information given by the studies on reversals, these experimenter reversals, too, are not without a possible explanation. Certainly any experimenter who realizes his experiment is *almost* significant is affected by the idea. His tension builds up, his anxieties arise. In effect, he is a different person than he was when he began. As such his "nonverbal" communication to his subjects, if not his verbal ones, can affect them even if their own appreciation of the situation did not do so. This change, it now appears, could well be enough to cause reversal, at least with more sensitive types of experimenters.

The fact that subjects are affected by experimenters is no secret.[19] The records show that as experimenters, individuals vary in their effectiveness, just as do teachers or persons in other fields who must handle and manipulate people. Some experimenters are successful quite consistently, others who try may just as regularly fail. By now it is quite clear that testing for ESP is an art as well as science, because it involves creating a proper "atmosphere" so that the delicate process of ESP can operate.

From all this emerges the reason why the differential effect can be used as a tool for controlling psi missing. In the experiments of Bevan, of Sanders, and of Rao, the total results were at the chance level. They did not show that ESP had occurred for the hitting and

[19] Rhine, J. B., and J. G. Pratt. *Parapsychology, Frontier Science of the Mind*. Springfield: Charles C. Thomas, 1957, chap. 7.

missing cancelled each other, as they had in Stuart's long-ago experiments. But now, with an understanding of the differential effect, the experiment can be so set up that the hitting and missing tendencies can rightfully be separated and appraised on their merits. In this way psi missing can be handled. It is not eliminated, but controlled.

Of course, the experimenter still has to guard against situations that could cause reversal, but at least he knows now that he is dealing with phenomena which follow lawful principles, whether he has yet discovered them or not. They are not just haphazard effects that must always remain unpredictable, but they result from principles of unconscious mental action, which may not be rational by the criteria of conscious logic, but which nonetheless have a rationale of their own. ("Rationale" is hardly the precise word here, but the language, geared to conscious mental processes only, supplies no better one.)

Something of the stylized process of ESP in the laboratory is revealed by these effects; psi missing, differential selection of targets, reversals. They appear only in the laboratory, not in life experiences. No hint of them was given in the imperfect intuitive cases discussed in Chapter 11. Upon reflection, however, one can see it has to be this way, because actually a stage of the psi process is represented in the imperfections that show up in the laboratory, different from that which causes incompleteness in life experiences.

In the experiences from life situations, the stage of the process most clearly illuminated is the final one, when the impression from the unconscious meets the difficulty inherent in the change to consciousness. But in the laboratory, difficulty at this stage cannot be registered. If it is great enough, it produces a total miss, and that does not enlighten the investigator.

In the laboratory, the main sign of obstructions that registers is that of psi missing which appears to be caused by all unfavorable situations, from internal emotional complications to uncomfortable external conditions. But these come in at a stage earlier in the process than that of crossing into consciousness. Thus it is that life and laboratory each gives separate testimony about the "intuitive process," for each one reflects a separate and different segment of it.

The tendency for unconscious mental action to take a negative turn upon occasion was discoverable in parapsychological research because the preferred technique in it happened to be one by which the tendency could be revealed. In other words, the negative trend (psi missing) was detectable because in a series of trials like an ESP run it was possible to make fewer, as well as more, hits than would be expected by chance. This situation, which as statisticians would say involves a "two-tailed test," is different from those which have been necessary in the study of tests on other psychological processes; for instance, sense perception, learning, memory. In all of these, the phenomenon appears or it does not. Scores in tests used in such areas could begin at the chance level and go higher, but they could not go lower and show the process in reverse.

However, no one would presume to think that this negative tendency never operates except in ESP. Rather, it must be an inherent one, ready to go into operation at any time. One often hears of negative psychological processes. Probably the idea of accident-proneness comes first to mind. But no techniques in studies of any such kind have been developed by which to measure operations below the mean and so to show psi missing in psychological as well as in parapsychological processes.

From this comparison of ESP in life and in the laboratory it is possible to see the same kind of process in the background. In each it is a delicate mental one which fluctuates with every change, internal or external. In each, one sees it filtered through the maze of personality structure reacting to the objective world. In both it shows itself as a lawful phenomenon amenable to scientific method, and one that more and more makes sense as that method is brought to bear upon it.

A breakthrough in the handling of psi missing, too late for discussion here, was made in the summer of 1966 by the introduction of a statistical measure, the test of variance. Although this is not a new statistical device, it had not been used before in evaluating series of run scores. As reported in the *Journal of Parapsychology*,

Volume 30, 1966, a number of investigators have been able by this method to detect the presence of ESP even in series of test results that yielded no extra-chance deviation. In principle, this test measures the "up and down" tendency of the scores and so turns the "down" psi-missing score into a value just as it does the "up" psi-hitting score. Thus, without separating the two, as in the differential method, the value of each can be measured against the up and down tendencies of random (chance) series, and any extra-chance value detected.

This new method seems to have removed the chief technological obstacle to the progress of the research and at the same time makes possible further understanding of the unconscious processes involved. Its use promises to open a new vista of observation on that mental mystery, the human mind, in one of its most baffling unconscious reaches, the psi process.

CHAPTER 13

Questions Raised by Psi

ONE after the other, the preceding chapters have followed the course of the psi process from the deep unconscious into conscious levels. By assembling the evidence it was possible to reconstruct the pathway, so that now the background of an ESP experience need no longer seem a total mystery. Instead it can be considered to be a normal, though somewhat obscure, mental process, which needs only to be sufficiently studied to be understood. Something of an answer has been given to the initial question, What is ESP?

However, as in much of the psi research itself one answer only generates other questions, so, too, in the presentation of the psi process in general, the establishment of psi raises numerous questions, some of which are not in the direct line of evidence, but which nevertheless are basic to it. Most of them are still unanswered, for they are more difficult than the answers from which they grew. Some of them make up the deepest challenge of parapsychology.

The least answerable of all these questions at the present time comes up at the very inception of the psi process. At the very portal where mind and outer reality are in contact the great question of parapsychology arises. The question is, of course, How can this contact be? How can the psyche know the outside world directly, without the evidence of the senses? It is not a question belonging to parapsychology alone, however. It is everybody's question. But only in parapsychology is it being taken seriously now, and at least being asked. Elsewhere it can still be dodged for a while longer, until the full import of psi is more widely realized.

The question seems more impossible than it should, perhaps, because it appears to stand alone, with no supporting mysteries to relieve it. But in fact it is not alone. Even the manner in which the psyche can know the outside world by way of sense preception has no adequate explanation. The relation of the objective and the psychological world is still a profound mystery. It well may be that this question in reference to sense perception is no easier for psychology than the parapsychological one. It stands out less sharply, however, since so many generations of thinkers have encased it in the garments of familiarity that it no longer seems to be an undisguised challenge to an explanation of the universe.

The parapsychological question is still stark with unfamiliarity. Its answer as far as one can see now must lie in a fundamental rethinking about the structure of the universe; a rethinking that will take account of all the questions raised by the phenomena that show the direct contact of mind and matter.

The next question to ask is easier. Why has the fact that mind and matter do make contact directly been obscured for so long? The fact that they do make contact, as data of parapsychology show, is clear. The idea that the only avenue to the mind lies through the senses is outmoded; the psi process exists. Like the hidden figure in a childhood puzzle, which once spied among the obscuring foliage stands out, never to be missed again, so here, once the evidence for the reality of psi is faced, it too is inescapable. Whether in experiences or experiments, this is so, for they complement and support each other just as true life and laboratory phenomena in all fields do. But why was the discovery so long in coming; why is it still so slow in being recognized? As in the puzzle, once the meaning is seen, the reason why it was so long obscure becomes self-evident. This reason lies in the very nature of psi itself, a process almost designed as it might seem to be concealed. To begin with, it has no introspective identity or substance. In action, it is not the slow-motion affair which the stage-by-stage presentation in these pages might suggest. It may be slowed up at times, by barriers too strong to be overcome immediately, but never, either in life or laboratory, is it a deliberate process of reasoning, fitting, considering. Usually, whatever sign of it emerges into consciousness flashes from start to finish without a break, just as do many other of the mind's processes. And so when it comes in life situations it appears as a *fait accompli*—like a miracle. In the laboratory, it may be experienced as a mathematical value only. In this case too it is so unobtrusive, so hidden, as to baffle introspection.

At first psi was a mathematical value only in the laboratory; then the realization grew that it is a process that goes on quite unconsciously, and that this is the reason its operation is not open to introspection. This was a discovery in its day, a day not as far removed as now from the dawn of the concept that part of mental action is unconscious. That concept came late in the history of psychology, and even now it is a vague, disputed, and amorphous one. In spite of Freud, who first centered popular attention on it more than half a century ago, the area of mental action below the conscious level is still a largely uncharted one, whose function and content await a comprehensive and authoritative exploration. Small wonder then that an *unconscious* process like ESP was overlooked and unrecognized for so long. And since even the phenomena showing it were obscure and did not proclaim their origin, small wonder an assumption developed (the assumption that mind can make contact with matter only via sensory channels) in which, of course, no room remained for it. Instead the assumption grew until it was taken for established knowledge.

When the range of accessibility of the material of ESP is contemplated, another question automatically comes up. The answers of parapsychology show that this range is practically unlimited. It covers thoughts, things, and events still in the future. Theoretically at least, this is a range unlimited in the extended world.

At the same time, no man's ESP is perfect or complete, but, as the record shows, very far from it. In telepathy at its best, the individual in a life situation may get an item, a fragment, but rarely if ever the connected whole of another person's thought. Reports to the contrary come from mental hospitals, or easily *convinced* persons outside of them, who are ignorant of the need of careful checking. In neither has the claim been supported. In the laboratory, "pure" telepathy scores average a few hits over "chance" per run, but even at best, no extended perfect sequences of hits.

Clairvoyance, in life, brings knowledge of hidden items. A prospector may dream correctly of hidden veins of ore. But, after all, few persons have found their gold this way. In the laboratory a few rare cases of perfect scores in runs of twenty-five ESP trials are on record, but rarely more, and rarely this. In general, here as in telepathy—and also as in their combination, the GESP method in which thought and thing are both involved—a few points over "chance" is about the yield.

Precognitive experiences are probably nearly as common as acorns under oak trees. But what are they concerned with? Bits and snatches from an individual's daily life. Whether it be a looming crisis, or a casual roadside view, they are not connected, comprehensive wholes or major sections of an individual's life, although occasionally a person claims he has had revealed to him broad areas of his future life and its activities. Such claims are rare and doubtful, however, and even at their very best, if they ever do occur without contamination from faults of judgment or conjecture, they would still be far from perfect expressions of precognitive ability.

One thread of similarity runs through all of the experiences that can more safely be taken to involve precognition; they are all *personalized* items. On this account the sweeping prognostications of great public events sometimes made seem not to fit the picture. In the first place, they lack the "intimate" quality of regular ESP topics, which is a first reason for doubt as to their ESP nature. But second and most important, they cannot be judged to be actually the product of precognitive ESP, even to the tentative degree which experiences involving small personal topics can. The factors for such judgment are lacking. Informed guessing and likely supposition cannot be ruled out, and vagueness of wording makes specific interpretation impossible.

Sometimes prognosticators on this grand level think that by depositing their utterance at some center like the Parapsychology Laboratory, they will establish its validity if the event comes to pass. They do not understand that validity cannot be established this way, but that it depends on the elimination of counter explanations. No matter in what strong box the "prophecy" was deposited, it still cannot be evaluated. And so in spite of great claims like these, the fact still is that even though evidence of precognition comes from the laboratory, the general level of effectiveness it reaches is about the same as that of clairvoyance and telepathy.

In all of the impressions one can get about the efficiency of psi, the laboratory and life agree. The record shows that ESP messages, in comparison to total knowledge, are not grand insights into the secrets of the universe, but fragments from the lives of individuals. It is a seeming paradox, then, that the availability of material is unlimited, and that nevertheless, the reach of ESP in individual life actually is relatively infinitesimal.

The record on this, however, is not by any means a neutral one. It shows quite definitely, both in life and laboratory, that much, if not all, of the fragmentation and imperfection of ESP goes back to the limitations imposed by personality, rather than to restrictions on initial availability. In Chapter 11, the fact comes out the clearest. In the background of that chapter are literally hundreds of imperfect cases, and in each of them without exception the imperfection could most reasonably be laid to psychological causes; to difficulties in transmission of the message from unconscious to conscious levels, rather than to basic limitations in the availability of the material. The point perhaps would be a bit more difficult to make from the laboratory results alone. But even there, as Chapter 12 indicates, the difficulty in getting perfect scores appears to be personal and psychological. It seems to be a case of difficulty in mustering sufficient motivation so that the material will be admitted. The new material *can* be admitted; it is not unavailable. But motivation must be aroused in order for it to be accepted, then processed and projected into consciousness.

Along this line, the cases in Chapter 7 also have a bearing. In that chapter it was quite clear that the selection of the material of ESP experiences follows broadly the lines of personal interest, interest ranging from the most intense a human being can have, down to the slightest. Nevertheless, the personal element shows through it all. It shows particularly in the experiencing person's strong preoccupation with items of his own experience. And here, what they are not tells just as much as what they are.

In general his ESP experiences concerning himself are not about his more impersonal interests. He does not get the answers to his deeper intellectual questions. A few students may dream the answers to examination questions, an occasional individual knows which library or book to turn to, but few big intellectual problems are solved this way, nor are political questions or those about great world events. A few experiences may seem to foretell an election outcome, or who will be the one appointed to the vacancy, but no broad insights are found in this realm either, unproven claims to the contrary notwithstanding. Even business and professional matters seem mainly on the personal, not the truly professional level. Occasionally a doctor makes an "inspired" diagnosis, or a nurse appears uncalled when a patient sorely needs her, or a worker in an office or a factory "lives" beforehand some significant, or more likely insignificant, scene. But seldom are any of the larger professional problems solved this way. Seldom too are dreams and hunches about the outcome of bets and races, even though initially correct, likely to be so if many times repeated. The feeling "I will win this time," may sometimes be a true one, but repetition gives cause apparently for spurious hunches, non-ESP dreams, to confuse the situation.

In all these areas alike, the material that does not get through when surveyed from a remote, impersonal viewpoint tends to make that which does seem insignificant. It shows the material of ESP not only limited mainly to the personal, but to aspects of the personal that are primarily emotional rather than primarily intellectual. It is perhaps, in most general terms, mainly the more primitive, elemental human interests that find expression in ESP. This fact too tends to support the idea that the limitations of ESP, i.e., all the topics that do not appear, all the mistakes and incompletenesses of the messages, go back to personal factors rather than to inherent limitations on the availability of material.

The discussion in Chapter 5 about the frequent lack of conviction that the ESP message was true has some bearing on the same point. The lack of conviction could mean that the item was admitted as of doubtful status in the first place because it was not completely available. But as discussion there showed secondary influences could be found which could have eroded initial conviction, and sometimes it was obvious that they had. So that there too, it seemed more likely that the limitation had a secondary origin which was a personal one.

The considerations from Chapters 5, 6, 7, 10, and 11, then, all point the same way. They may not prove the point with finality but they do strongly suggest that the material of ESP is not limited by inherent unavailability but by the person, the individual himself, through whose psychological structure it must be filtered into consciousness.

If this suggestion is taken seriously, the human potential to which it points is practically boundless. The more the intricacies of unconscious mental action are investigated and their secrets understood, the more the control of them should be possible. Then what of the hidden potential scope of man? It could be that then one could wish to find some inherent limit to it, if only to protect the race from the responsibility of omniscience.

Along with such questions and considerations as these, and closely linked to the first and most basic one of all—How is it that mind and matter can meet?—are the twin questions about space and time. How can the psyche ignore these barriers and make direct contact with the distant, and the future? In sense perception, space and time are not ignored. Or not as much. Space is minimized. Distances must be short, or sense perception cannot operate. And time must be instantaneous. Sense perception has no past or future, only the present.

With a mind habituated by sense perception to perceiving in the present and in its own vicinity, it seems that the habit carries over. ESP experiences bringing in information of distant scenes or future times picture them practically always in the imagery of the here and now. For the eyes and ears, the future is out of bounds, and in ESP the same limitations are acted out, even though they do not limit.

If a census on distance in ESP experiences could be taken, it well might show a greater frequency of long-distance cases, since great separation might tend to stimulate rather than discourage the operation of ESP. The sense of separation between emotionally linked persons, not the actual miles themselves, may be a spur to this nonverbal kind of communication. The frequency of experiences showing what the absent one is doing is suggestive.

The future, of course, makes a different psychological impact on human beings than the distant. It can be said with some truth that distance sharpens a sense of separation, but time, at least in its longer reaches, dims it.

And yet in spite of this, the person's vista down the future—his own future, that is—is surprising in its reach. He is ever intrigued, it seems, by items, many of them trivial in his own more distant future. And then—what seems the most unaccountable of all —he even goes ahead occasionally, and meets a stranger or knows an item about one for no concrete personal reason whatsoever. The only link may be that at some *future* time he will read a news item about the stranger.

This is going precognition one better. The precognitive impression is not only an experience to be fulfilled later, but even the reason for having it is a future one. The experience occurs either for that most slender and improbable of reasons, that later he will know of the event, or else for no reason at all.

The latter possibility cannot be excluded. It carries with it a greater implication than at first appears. It could mean that ESP can occur without any personal reason, present *or* future, and that material supplied by ESP may be filtering into the unconscious at any time without a trace. If items of material can get to conscious levels without a reason, and without a need even for recognition (which in itself could be a reason of sorts), then the function of the psyche at the initial point of judgment would be somewhat different from the one herein pictured. It would mean that it is not what enters that is discriminated and chosen, but what it is that will be processed. Even if everything *could* enter, still it is clear that inhibitions of some kind do keep down the total conscious output to relatively inconspicuous levels, because, after all, evidence of ESP is relatively inconspicuous, since its occurrence can even be debated and denied at this present late date in history.

This line of thought obviously throws up another paradox. It is easy to see and say that many an ESP experience goes unrecognized. But lack of need for recognition could imply unguarded entry of material into the unconscious. The only way to avoid this contradiction is to suppose that each experience has a reason, whether that reason is ever recognized or not; that the psyche is on the job and knows its business. That is about as far as one can get today. Whatever the specific selective principle may be, at

least the material of ESP is not like that of sense perception, limited
to the close confines of time and space.

Undoubtedly, because the phenomena of parapsychology escaped the limits of time and space as well as because they were
not mediated by the senses, they were so often and for so long
judged as questionable and aberrant. Now it is clear that it is not
the phenomena that are questionable, rather the theory that the
universe is such that phenomena like these cannot occur is incorrect. The phenomena are still exceptional, even anomalous today,
but not aberrant because now their lawful nature is obvious. And
so a truly major adjustment of fact and theory is called for. New
viewpoints are necessary, and they do not depend on discoveries
in the objective world alone, but even more on changes that can
come about only in the slow swing of habitual patterns of thought.

In our contemporary world, the pendulum swings *against* ac-
ceptance of evidence for psi. A reversal will take time, of course,
for as everyone knows, radical changes only occur with difficulty,
and especially when, as in this case, almost total rethinking is
called for. No minor patching up will suffice in this repair job, for
this rethinking involves accommodation for clairvoyance and precognition. According to existing theory these pose threats to the
very concept of causality. Either to evade those threats, or to
accept them and find alternatives, necessitates a fundamental
readjustment.

CHAPTER 14

The Promise

THE ESP process has revealed itself, or enough of itself, in the studies of parapsychology so far made, that a consistent outline of it can now be seen. Naturally, because parapsychology as a science is very young, knowledge about this process is still far from being complete. No doubt it will be a long time before many of the puzzles it presents can be fully solved. Even so, there is little question that the outline of its progress as traced from the deep unconscious into consciousness is a true one. Probably only details, however important they may be, will be filled in later and relatively minor adjustments made in the routing up from unconscious levels already visible.

The point is that all of the intricacies of the route, although partly still undiscovered, now are discernibly *discoverable*. They are the intricacies of psychological processes, and however obscure and difficult, are lawful and at least theoretically possible to know. Science is never completely baffled before complexity. Only slowed down.

In untangling the complexities of the human personality, psychologists are making slow but certain headway. The level of common knowledge about people and their mental processes is higher now than even that of the wisest a few generations back not to mention those of still earlier times. Even though "schools," viewpoints, emphases, and interpretations may change, and do and will, the total adds up to progress, so that the complex of human personality is better understood today than it has ever been before.

In to all of this, the area covered by parapsychology, or rather that covered by the studies of parapsychology, could very well fit. It is just another psychological area. The forms—dream, intuition, hallucinatory experience—were psychological constructs long before parapsychologists noticed that they are also parapsychological vehicles. The fluctuations of motivation that affect the results of tests in parapsychology are no different from those involved in other psychological processes. It may be that some of the parapsychological test situations are such that they become more subtle indicators of certain psychological realities than is generally true of equivalent psychological tests themselves. If so, the difference is of degree, not kind. The emotional influences too, noticeable particularly in ESP experiences in life situations, are the same emotional elements that play in all of life's experiences. So it is also with the spread of interest in the world's affairs as shown in the range of topics of spontaneous ESP experiences. After all, it seems no different from the range of interests of human beings as displayed in life's sum total. None of these aspects is any different in or out of parapsychology.

The only difference is that the parapsychological phenomena *do not fit into* some of the current ideas of the universe, and this is the fact which most of all has kept them from being recognized and examined along with other psychological phenomena from the beginning of psychology as a science until now.

The aspect in which they do not fit, the difference they show— and it is total—is that the content of these is information *new* to the person. It is not the direct product of sense experience, or of stored remnants of earlier sense experience.

Although the forms in which the new information comes into consciousness are psychological, the *types* of information brought are not. Psychology knows no clairvoyance, telepathy, or precognition, no ESP, because the senses are blind to these just as they are to light vibrations above and below the optical range, and sound vibrations beyond the range of auditory sensitivity, and to X-ray or atomic structure. The senses are blind to all of these, and curiously, perhaps, ESP does not compliment them and extend their range into micro and macro areas of objective waves and vibrations of any kind.

Instead it is totally different. It ignores the entire range of objective methods of knowledge getting at the same time that it gets objective knowledge beyond the sensory barriers. Its barrier appears to be the person himself, and not the space-time world in which he lives. His limits are within himself, his psychology the force which limits and inhibits his parapsychology.

But not entirely. Sufficient material is secured by ESP to make the point that the current theory of knowledge getting is too small. The human being has a potential that goes beyond it. What all that potential may be, no one can yet know. All of that is the promise of the future. The thing the psi discovery does right now is make the promise. If the human being is not entirely limited by the bounds of time and space, he is not limited by the bounds of computers, of *mechanisms*.

This is knowledge desperately needed now when new scientific discoveries are almost daily showing that more and more of the attributes of human beings are traceable to chemical and physical reactions, whether it be the structure of the cells of the body or the fluctuations of the emotions. It is human to jump to conclusions, and to reason that if so much of man is mechanistic, the total must be, also. It is human, but not good science, for in good science, conclusions do not precede the evidence. And now come the findings of parapsychology to show that like the yeast within the loaf, there is leaven in this lump, too.

Parapsychological abilities may someday be put to work, and if they are, the result can benefit mankind very greatly. But whether or not they ever are, the very fact that they exist opens a big window for man's outlook. It tells him he need not consider himself relegated to the confines of mechanism. He will remain not the computer, but the man who made it, with values and aspirations his machines can never know.

This much the still incomplete discoveries of parapsychology show about man and his "destiny in the scheme of things." The fact that the psi process proves to be a real and lawful one guarantees the promise. It justifies the scientific method as applied to the age-old question, What is man with respect to the solid world of sense and mechanics? It enlivens the labor of discoveries still ahead, because the goal, to find out man's full potential and his destiny, is the greatest man can have.

Index

ABOUT THE AUTHOR

LOUISA E. RHINE'S previous book, *Hidden Channels of the Mind*, was published in 1961 by William Sloane Associates. She has also written numerous articles on the subject of ESP. She is the wife of J. B. Rhine, former head of the Duke University Parapsychology Laboratory in Durham, North Carolina, and now director of the Institute for Parapsychology sponsored by the Foundation for Research on the Nature of Man. Mrs. Rhine has been her husband's associate in both institutions, and is coeditor of the *Journal of Parapsychology*. She was a student at the College of Wooster, in Ohio, and received her B.S., M.S., and Ph.D. degrees from the University of Chicago. She and her husband now live in Hillsboro, North Carolina.